Imperial Refugee:
Olivia Manning's Fictions of War

IMPERIAL REFUGEE

Olivia Manning's Fictions of War

Eve Patten

CORK UNIVERSITY PRESS

First published in 2011 by
Cork University Press
Youngline Industrial Estate
Pouladuff Road, Togher
Cork, Ireland

This publication has received support from the Heritage Council under the 2009 Publication Grant Scheme.

British Library Cataloguing in Publication Data
A CIP catalogue record for this book is available from the British Library.

ISBN 978-1-85918-4820

Typesetting by Red Barn Publishing, Skeagh, Skibbereen, Co. Cork
Printed in Malta by Gutenberg Press

www.corkuniversitypress.com

Contents

For Kevin, Milo, Esme and Juno, with love.

Acknowledgements

This study engaged me over a number of years, and I am indebted to many people for their help in bringing it to completion. My thanks are due, first and foremost, to Olivia Manning's close friend and literary executor Francis King, a most considerate correspondent whose death occurred as this book went to press, and also to the late Neville Braybrooke, who supported the project in its earliest days. Several individuals read chapters in draft form and offered valuable observations, including Roy Foster, Gerald Dawe, Nicholas Allen and Mark Rawlinson. I must also thank Gerry Harrison for his time and generosity with sources, and Vesna Goldsworthy, whose own research opened many doors for me. Conversations with Derek Mahon, John Fairleigh, Heather Ingman, Eunan O'Halpin, Bill McCormack, John Scattergood, Jeremy Treglown, Ian MacNiven and Lavinia Greacen helped keep me on track, as did those happy hours spent with Richard Pine, Emilie Pine, Ronan Kelly, Anthony Hirst, James Gifford and my associates at the Durrell School of Corfu. Victoria Orr-Ewing, Carol Taaffe, Edwina Keown, Simon Workman and Niamh Dowdall assisted with references; Jean Levy, Poul Pedersen and Siobhan Savage sent copies of obscure material; Caroline Walsh at the *Irish Times* gave me space to develop ideas. I'm grateful for so many things (in this book and beyond it) to my Romanian colleagues at the universities of Bucharest, Cluj-Napoca and Timişoara, particularly Mihaela Irimia, Liliana Pop and Pia Brinzeau, and to my trusted colleagues in the School of English at Trinity College Dublin. Special thanks must go to the librarians at the McFarlin Collection in the University of Tulsa, the Harry Ransom Research Center at the University of Texas, the British Library, London, and to the treasured staff of Trinity College Library, Dublin. I should like to thank David Higham Associates for access to Olivia Manning's unpublished writings and for permission to quote from her fiction and correspondence. For textual quotations and excerpts, I must also acknowledge her publishers at Heinemann, Penguin and Mandarin Paperbacks (an imprint of Reed Consumer Books Ltd). My sincere gratitude goes to Jonathan Williams, who read the typescript with his customary expertise, and to my patient editor Maria O'Donovan at Cork University Press. Finally, warmest thanks to my husband Kevin Smith, tireless proofreader and companion on this long journey.

Abbreviations

BT Balkan Trilogy (London: Mandarin, 1990)
LT Levant Trilogy (Harmondsworth: Penguin, 1985)

Introduction

Olivia Manning's reputation as a difficult personality often threatens to obscure her reputation as a writer. Few twentieth-century novelists can have inspired such consistent dislike. The publisher Dan Davin, for example, who was devoted to Manning's gregarious husband Reggie Smith, complained of her as a shrewish woman whose aim was 'to be as unpleasant to as many people as possible', while the legendary denizen of Fitzrovia, Julian Maclaren-Ross, recalled among his Stag's Head drinking circle 'the taciturn, undemonstrative and physically unattractive Olivia Manning who, from the vantage point of her bar-stool regarded the others with an expression of amusement, mingled with contempt'. Fellow writer Inez Holden christened her 'whiney' Manning; Anthony Powell, her otherwise generous editor at *Punch*, admitted her to be 'the world's worst grumbler', and her publishers at Heinemann were forced to conclude that she was 'never an easy artist to handle'. Even Kay Dick, her lifelong friend and correspondent, depicted Manning in her 1984 novel *The Shelf* as the spiteful gossip Sophie, who, with her 'wry fragility, delicate hands and penetrating voice . . . often reminded me of a goshawk about to bite'.[1]

Can this reputation be challenged? Manning herself readily acknowledged her tendency towards maliciousness 'at least in the past', as she put it when interviewed by Dick in the early 1970s.[2] *Olivia Manning: A Life*, the biography assembled over several years by her friends Neville and June Braybrooke and completed after their deaths by the novelist Francis King, makes a valiant attempt at her rehabilitation, but from it nevertheless emerges a woman with a seemingly natural bent towards animosity, a peevishness exacerbated by what she took to be critical and public neglect of her writing. Undoubtedly this was a major source of her discontent, and letters to friends during her life constantly register her grievances against the numerous rivals, editors and reviewers seemingly determined, as she saw it, to keep her from the upper reaches of a literary hierarchy.[3] This was not simply vanity: her bitterness stemmed from a genuine sense of distress at how her work repeatedly failed to make its mark. 'I feel I have been a disappointment', she wrote to her publishers at Heinemann after poor sales threatened their investment in a novelist they had initially regarded as a major talent.[4] The recognition she did achieve, meanwhile, often tended towards the kind of damnation with faint praise suggested by Pamela Hansford Johnson's response to Manning's 1951 novel *School for Love:* 'among the best ten novels written by women in the past twenty-five years'.[5] Disconsolate, Manning seemed at one stage to hope for little more than the qualified glory hinted at in her introduction to a 1968 edition of Jane Austen's *Northanger Abbey*: 'Not all writers of genius take the public by storm. Dickens wanted, indeed, needed, immediate and unlimited fame; Stendhal wanted and correctly anticipated recognition only after his death. Jane Austen in her lifetime was successful without being a sensation.'[6]

The reputation is not to be challenged then. Rather Manning's bitterness needs, like the author, careful handling as a starting-point to recover her place as a pre-eminent novelist of British wartime experience. It was, after all, her embittered personality that sustained her scepticism towards what she regarded as the cultural bombast and vacuous political idealism carried by an inter-war generation of ideologues into the theatre of the Second World War. Manning's natural spite gives much of her writing its defining character as an aggressive riposte to the society and events around her, enhancing her fiction dealing with the wartime era and boosting, too, her literary criticism deriving from the same period. Significantly, the tenor of her critical voice was developed not in the London book pages of the 1960s but in the maelstrom of the war in the Middle East, when her shrewishness – looking in her younger years more like bravado – gave a sharp but welcome edge to the prolific review work she undertook during the 1940s for the *Palestine Post.* Here, for example, her private campaign against Penguin's *New Writing* shows her spirited contempt for what she regarded as the incestuous dross emanating from a navel-gazing literary London. 'It is depressingly certain that practically every number of this periodical', she wrote of a 1945 issue, 'will contain one of Mr Lehmann's inconsiderable poems and one of his ponderous prefaces and possibly pieces by other members of the Lehmann family, and a string of familiar rather than outstanding names'; in the same volume she grumbled that 'Rosamond Lehmann's "Wonderful Holidays" still go on – there is no reason, of course, why anything that must be so easy to write should ever stop.'[7] Throughout this decade, her epigrammatic and dismissive critiques (George Barker is 'rather a prodigious poet', Rex Warner 'a competent novelist of no great importance', Stephen Spender 'appears to continue writing from habit') would doubtless make her few friends, nor were her brash judgements always sound, but her distinctively caustic voice (toned down a little in later years for contributions to the *Spectator* and *Punch*) was sharpened on the jeering sidelines of metropolitan literary circles.[8]

Relocating this voice within the broader international context of the Second World War – the cradle of her major fiction – and within the political evolution of 1930s optimism into what she views in her fiction as its jaded aftermath, its segue into post-imperial *and* post-communist retreat, allows Manning's bitterness to be read as a rumbling critique of British naivety and ego. The journey which took her as a new bride from London in 1939, first to Bucharest, then Athens, Cairo and eventually Jerusalem, became the basis for an extraordinary individual encounter with history. Caught between the competing ambitions of the Allied and Axis powers and experiencing in each location the tensions peculiar to the British expatriate community, she absorbed the raw material of what would later become the basis of an extended post-war narrative of reproach. Throughout the works discussed here, the two novels set in wartime Palestine, *Artist Among the Missing* (1949) and *School for Love* (1951), the semi-autobiographical sequence fictions of the *Balkan* and *Levant Trilogies*, which appeared throughout the 1960s and 1970s, and, finally, her last single novel, *The Rain Forest* (1974), Manning's prevailing theme is the vanity of a diplomatic, military and imperial project which catastrophically failed to understand its European and Middle Eastern subjects.

As such, she can be located in two important novelistic contexts of the period. The first is the corpus of fiction generated during the war years in immediate response to the conflict, much of it produced by women writers whose work has now been positively re-evaluated through the concept of the 'middlebrow', such as Phyllis Bottome, Elizabeth Taylor, Edith Pargeter and Sylvia Townsend Warner.[9] More canonical figures appear in an adjacent frame, including Elizabeth Bowen and Storm Jameson, both of whom may be regarded as influences on Manning, along with her acknowledged mentor, Ivy Compton-Burnett. A second context is provided by like-minded chroniclers of British diplomatic eclipse and imperial decline in the post-war period, including Graham Greene ('a notoriously weak and rather mean-spirited character', according to Manning), Malcolm Lowry, whose *Under the Volcano* she read enthusiastically after its 1947 publication, and – more pertinently – various fellow practitioners of the post-war novel sequence.[10] Evelyn Waugh's *Sword of Honour* trilogy, with its definitive rendering of British military folly in Greece and the Middle East, offers close parallels for Manning's trilogies; so too do Edith Pargeter's *The Eighth Champion of Christendom* trilogy, Anthony Burgess's *The Malayan Trilogy*, Anthony Powell's *Dance to the Music of Time* sequence, Paul Scott's *The Raj Quartet*, and the *Empire Trilogy* (as it became known), composed by Anglo-Irish author J.G. Farrell, to whom, after his premature death in 1979, Manning dedicated her own novel *The Sum of Things*.[11] Like many of these contemporaries, Manning struggled with the difficulties of post-imperial epic fiction – its inbuilt belatedness, its necessarily panoramic scope, its tendency to wander from historicity into elegy – but the ways in which she grappled with these problems shed light on the serial form in the post-war period, and her place in this coterie deserves more attention than she has yet been given by critics and the reading public alike.

Beyond literary affiliations, Manning's life calls into question the relevance of her personal and family background to her perspective in the fiction. How, for instance, did her links to Ireland by way of her mother and maternal grandfather, both from Ulster, help set the terms of her intermittent self-appointment to a political and national periphery? The nature of her claims on Irish identity must be unravelled with care. Historian Roy Foster, who knew her, claims that 'in later life [she] took to describing herself as "Anglo-Irish", which was pushing it a bit', but what exactly did Manning herself mean by the term? The evidence of her 1950 travel book on Ireland, *The Dreaming Shore*, suggests her outright rejection of the aristocratic class usually designated by the label: here, her digressive tirade against the tweed-clad gentry met *en route*, 'that pathetic class of Anglo-Irish', as she called them, would in turn raise objections from the mild-mannered Louis MacNeice.[12] And perhaps 'Anglo-Irish', the affiliation adopted in various ways by several of her acquaintances, from Elizabeth Bowen to Iris Murdoch, was itself a distancing device, a useful distraction from her highly contradictory, intangible and recalcitrant roots (or *partial* roots at least) in a complex *Northern* Irish backwater lying outside the comfortable boundaries of both Irishness and Englishness.

If this fissured family background nuances Manning's writing, so too does the fact that she was female, and frequently at odds with the predominantly masculine company in which she found herself during the war years. There are many questions to be raised concerning the difference of perspective this facilitated. Jenny Hartley is one of several critics to suggest that women's wartime fiction can be read as a fiction of 'affirmation', typically charting the war as an interim of relative freedom for its female protagonists before the closure either of peacetime or marriage. Many women writers saw their work as intrinsic to the war effort in its collective emphasis on responsibility, both historical and political. Such an emphasis, Hartley contends – highly visible in the writings of Virginia Woolf, Elizabeth Bowen, Storm Jameson, Rebecca West and others – must challenge those accounts of a primarily male output of wartime prose, characterised by an inwards retreat to a private realm, rendered by two influential commentators on this period, Adam Piette and Robert Hewison.[13] A similar focus on women's war writing as resisting a masculine 'norm' is presented by the critics Kristine Miller and Gill Plain, who attend to the discrepancies of gender which disrupted the concept of a 'People's War' and led, in a literary context, to a body of fiction by women which tracked consistently what Plain has termed women's 'double alienation' in wartime from both national and patriarchal incentives.[14]

Situating Manning within feminist responses to women's wartime or war-related writing is clearly necessary in any engagement with her work, and existing criticism has already begun to suggest theoretical lines of enquiry. Jenny Hartley's discussion of the trilogies, for example, looks briefly to spatial readings of Manning's female odyssey, characterised by 'temporary halts round the edges of war', as a means of distinguishing a female perspective on the epic narrative. The critic Phyllis Lassner has provided a further model in grouping Manning alongside Ethel Mannin, Elspeth Huxley and Rumer Godden as hybrid postcolonial critics of imperial demise, a reading that is rightly attentive to Manning's individual and political sense of displacement.[15] However, further feminist engagements are needed, both on the nature of Manning's actual experience of the war as a woman and a wife, and on the particular slant with which she translated her history into the wry vision of her fictional counterpart in the trilogies, Harriet Pringle. To what extent do Harriet's persistent attempts to rupture a peculiarly British hangover of 1930s male camaraderie find a parallel in Manning's simultaneous challenges to the exhausted frameworks of epic romance in the *Balkan Trilogy*? How does the development of twinned male and female protagonists, set against a backdrop of neurotic sexuality in the *Levant Trilogy*, build towards a self-conscious reversal of a masculine hierarchy in the imposition of a female view of the battleground?

In Manning's fictionalised treatment of her own wartime experiences the persuasions of both national and female identity come into play, but linking these – and a major focus, therefore, of this study – is the recurrent theme of displacement. Indeed, beyond the novels discussed here, Manning's writing in general plays constantly on motifs of individual erraticism, peripheralisation and misaffiliation, highlighted for example in the alienation of Hugo Fletcher, returned from wartime Egypt to the cold climate of a southern English coastal town in *A Different Face* (1953), or in the desperate insecurity of Anglo-Irish socialite Petta Bellot in Manning's Bowenesque novel of bohemian London, *The Doves of Venus* (1955). In Manning's 1935 short story 'Portrait of a Hungarian Doctor', a young Ulster-born woman shares with a displaced Eastern European her feelings of existing as 'a kind of mongrel', belonging nowhere, sentiments echoing the author's own predicaments of nationality but heralding the broader concerns of a generation disturbed by conflict, transience and loss of place.[16] Like many of her contemporaries (and particularly Elizabeth Bowen), Manning saw that the active disturbances of war mapped a physical instability on to an underlying psychic unease. Her creative sensibility developed from personal insecurities of belonging into a fully fledged aesthetic of deracination, compounded by her own biographical war narrative and evolved through structures of travel, transit, flight and exile.

More important – and central to this account of her – is the fact that she was able to draw out her individual position in broader political terms. Like any autobiographical novelist, Manning builds on a creative tension between 'real' and textually enacted experience. It is essential to recognise that her textual counterpart, Harriet Pringle, is no simple Doppelgänger for the author but rather a systematic construct, a projection of thematic concerns stranded through a structured chronology. The point may seem self-evident but deserves attention in order to illuminate the full political reach of Manning's writing. The theorist Leigh Gilmore has described the process through which women's autobiographical writing spins out a 'poetics of identity', allowing authors to 'experiment with reconstructing the various discourses – of representation, of ideology – in which their subjectivity has been formed'.[17] In Manning's case, the project of the two trilogies is a subtle but discernible version of such experimentation, the novels providing a context for the alignment of the subject – Harriet Pringle – with other peripheral configurations of identity caught in the flux of European and Middle Eastern wartime reconstruction.

Specifically, in this respect, Manning's novels explore the figure of the wartime refugee. Her fiction implicitly connects her own compromised sense of nationality, her transient life experience, the instability of her marriage and her frequent exclusion from events on the grounds of her sex to the desperate predicament of the war's itinerants and enforced exiles. After 1939 the disintegrating political landscapes of Europe and the Middle East became a theatre of displacement, amplifying and grotesquely parodying in some cases Manning's personal insecurities of belonging. Her willingness to acknowledge not only the aesthetic potential of dislocation (developed through her affiliation with professional literary expatriate Lawrence Durrell and the *Personal Landscape* poets in Egypt) but also the plight of the actual *déracinés* of war – the hosts of refugees flooding south-eastwards across a European mainland in flight from the Nazi regime – gives her writing a thematic coherence and the rudiments of an ethical position. If her vision was far from sentimental, it was none the less pertinent and, as we shall see, despite its awkwardness her fictional negotiation of Jewish dispossession adds to the moral weight of her material in the context of post-war attempts at territorial settlement.

In this respect Manning may be seen to embody what I have termed an 'imperial refugee-ship', her writing providing a meeting-point for the remnants of British imperial sensibility on the one hand, and a post-war discourse of anxious displacement on the other. In her study of women writers of the Second World War, the critic Gill Plain determines, as fundamental to our understanding of the period, the fate of the refugee, who, 'in letting go of the framework of reality, experiences the full weight of repressed experience, and is brought face to face with the unbearable "reality" of war'.[18] Dislocated by circumstances from the relative securities of a domestic centre, Olivia Manning was thrown briefly into a life which paralleled this trajectory. She was not a refugee but her detachment from home – a *series* of homes – made her sensitive to the claims of countries and individuals in traumatic states of flux during the war. With this in mind, I want to read her novels not only historically but also spatially, revisiting their respective settings of wartime Romania, Greece, Egypt and Palestine in order to understand their author's priorities in her fictional treatments of territory, identity and displacement. How, exactly, did she encounter these countries in the most turbulent era of the twentieth century, and through what kind of creative transitions did she come to depict them in her fiction?

To recover fully Olivia Manning's presence within the landscape of post-war British fiction, we need to understand, finally, how the slow evolution of her major work – her two wartime trilogies – relates to the particular pressures placed on the novelist of wartime. The necessarily long gestation of Manning's writing was predicted, indeed, by her fellow writer Elizabeth Bowen, who, reviewing the author's short-story collection *Growing Up* in 1948, suggested that the book's publishers had been wise to list the author's wartime service roles (including her brief work stints in Greece, Cairo and Jerusalem) by way of explanation for a relatively small creative output since 'that unrewarding year' of 1939. 'In many cases, I don't think the biographical notes which publishers are so kind as to supply have a very direct bearing on the author's work', Bowen wrote. 'In the case of Miss Manning, however, I feel the above facts to be relevant. They explain, for one thing, why we have not had from this obviously born writer a greater body of work; also, I think we find in them the genesis of the best part of her present performance. Those very circumstances which, for years, withheld Miss Manning from continuous writing, provided her with an almost masculine outfit in the way of experience.'[19] The review – characteristically perceptive – reads Manning perfectly, Bowen sensing astutely how the chronology of post-war fiction would develop, and recognising, too, that Olivia Manning's absorption of uncommon events, the 'masculine outfit' of war at close quarters, would provide not for any short-term creative flourish but for considered fiction of broader narrative scope and density, drawn out over a lifetime. In this context my intention is to re-engage as far as possible with this writer's experiences and connections, and this book is essentially, therefore, a literary biography, shaped by the parameters of the Second World War. My aim is to relate Manning's life, and the lives of her numerous expatriate and literary associates in that period, to the body of writing that she produced after the cataclysm of 1939 and throughout the four decades that followed in its shadow.

CHAPTER ONE

A life in writing

Olivia Manning belonged to a British literary generation which held tenaciously to its diverse Irish connections in the wartime years, but, as with Cyril Connolly or Lawrence Durrell, her claims on Irishness were intermittent and often distinctly pragmatic. In her youth she was given to periodic outbursts of romantic nationalism: manuscripts of poems written while still at school and shown in later life to the poet George Fraser were awash, he noted, with Irish revolutionary pieces, while in her Irish travelogue, *The Dreaming Shore*, she quotes at length Irish patriot Roger Casement's speech on the 'indomitable persistency' of the Irish nation (though partly, one suspects, in an effort to animate the book's rather dull sequence of history, legend and landscape).[1] With similar headiness she applauded, in an early review of Mary Lavin's short stories, the Irish writer's departure from Celtic whimsy as 'an indication that the Irish are losing the self-consciousness of a subject people and are getting on their feet as a nation'. Such gestures may appear heartfelt enough but disguise a more conflicted view of Ireland's political evolution. More to the point, perhaps, Manning was alert to the idea that 'Irishness', by the mid-century, had become something of a literary liability, an outmoded cultural name-tag: '[I]t is now believed that owing to the Irish Revival which took place some years ago', she observed wryly, in 1945, 'everyone got so bored with the Irish that no one will read an Irish novel or short story.'[2]

Manning's Irish background was solid enough, nevertheless, to influence her personality and political outlook and therefore it offers a suitable starting-point for tracking her emergence as a writer. Born on the southern English coast, in Portsmouth in 1908, she spent three years in Ireland during the First World War while her father – then an officer in the British Royal Navy – served on a patrol vessel in the English Channel. Sojourns with her mother's cousins in Galway and Clare in the west of Ireland would later provide incidental material for the wild mountainous Irish landscape depicted in her curious 1934 tale of a dysfunctional Irish convent, 'A Scantling of Foxes', and for her portraits of a fading Irish Protestant small gentry class in several stories from her 1948 collection, *Growing Up*.[3] Her mother was from Ulster, from the town of Bangor, County Down, where Manning's maternal grandfather had settled on his return from America to become the proprietor of a well-known local public house, the Old Inn at Home. It was with Bangor that Manning kept her strongest ties, and in future years this reserved seaside town, with its peculiar and heady cultural mix of Presbyterianism, freemasonry, loyalism and political alienation, would become the shadowy elsewhere to her sense of Englishness.[4]

Though she frequently acknowledged her Ulster links, Manning affected to be disenchanted with the place in later life. Her grim visits to her mother's wealthy relations in Bangor were described to Kay Dick in 1954 ('It is simply golf, sport and canasta all day'), and when her husband Reggie Smith was appointed to a post at the University of Ulster in 1972, she wrote without enthusiasm of having to go and find him somewhere to live in 'the ghastly north'.[5] In some of her earliest writing, however, Manning makes use of Bangor – and Ulster in general – for key thematic purposes, drawing on her childhood memories of place to undermine both securities of belonging and, at the same time, any romantic instincts towards Irish nationalism. Her representation of a fractured *Northern* Irish experience, depicted in several of her early fictions, gestures towards the national disenchantments of later work. In her rather remarkable short story 'A Visit', for example, the setting of the Belfast linen factories grounds the misery of an emotionally strained, petty bourgeois family in the dourness and constriction of the northern city's industrial landscape, as a kind of Irish anti-romance: 'the black river crawling under the drizzle of rain; the wet cobbles; the dirty pavements; the stale fishy smell from the docks; the women with their hating, starved faces beneath their shawls; the cold...'[6] More expansively, in her 1937 historical novel of Irish independence, *The Wind Changes*, a sequence in which the protagonist Elizabeth Dearborn recalls her childhood in the grey northern seaside town of Carrickmoy (a thinly disguised version of Bangor) undermines the Anglo-Irish antagonisms of the main narrative and diminishes the romance plot into a dejected review of misplaced loyalties and bogus affiliations.[7]

If Ulster initiated a strain of scepticism in Manning's conception of nationhood, it also seems to have contributed an element to her prickly personality. In 'Portrait of a Hungarian Doctor', she tackled the contradictions of Northern Irish identity in a conversation staged between a European émigré and a young Ulster woman, the latter bent on trying to explain the curious positioning and personality of her stock, with its lack of love for England outdone only by its antipathy to the Irish South. In the North '[T]hey hate one another, but themselves most of all . . . they are bitter, sharp-tongued, malicious and vindictive, and envy you the very air they breathe.'[8] This viewpoint was certainly reinforced by her maternal lineage, and Manning's accounts of her Presbyterian, teetotal mother as a sharp and unforgiving woman tend to align the dourness of place with a sourness of personality shared with her daughter. Reggie Smith would remark after his wife's death on her maternal inheritance of a 'very Ulster' sensibility. 'She never let a grievance pass. She might forgive, rarely, but she'd never forget . . . She had all the Ulster guts and vivacity and . . . just a loathing of bull-shit and cant.'[9] Her mother's marriage to a drinker and philanderer significantly older than herself seems only to have exacerbated her cantankerous tendencies, particularly after the couple settled to raise their family in Portsmouth. 'Mother simply loathed being in Portsmouth to begin with', Manning later recalled. 'She hated all father's friends. He was a gentle, generous person, with a large circle of friends, and before he married her what money he had was more or less spent on his circle of friends. She must have resented this, and they obviously didn't like her – she was very outspoken.' The family's descent into genteel poverty as they eked out an existence on her father's pension did further damage to relations, as did Manning's perception that her 'hysterically anxious' mother began to ignore her once-favoured daughter after the birth of a younger sibling, her brother Oliver.[10]

It is impossible to miss in Manning's description of her parents' marriage ironic echoes of her own relationship with her husband Reggie Smith, and again of the grievances which develop between the withdrawn Harriet Pringle and her overly sociable husband Guy in the trilogies. But a more useful speculation has to do with the way in which the marital misfit represented by her parents offered a template of sorts for her understanding of the inherent fractures of empire. Her father – already fifty when she was born – clearly embodied for Manning the imperial confidence of a bygone era: in an article published in 1975, she wrote of him as a staunch Tory royalist and a figure who 'belonged to history'. His rise in life from First Class Boy, bound for the West Indies on the *Impregnable*, to a high-ranking position in the officer-class of the British navy became, for his daughter, a classic nineteenth-century seafaring romance; his accounts of participating in the Boxer rebellion in China at the turn of the century or the Urabi revolt in Alexandria in 1879 were in the same vein, adventure tales drawn from the age of an unquestioned Victorian imperial supremacy. 'Those were the great days of Empire', she wrote, 'and no proper naval man had any ridiculous ideas about the rights of lesser breeds'.[11] The undermining of this quasi-historical figure by another kind of history, embodied in his difficult, unhappy and deracinated Ulster wife, represented a version of imperial relations riddled with contradiction and disaffection, dragged from days of glory into petty constitutional wrangling.

The Ulster-born Louis MacNeice wrote frequently of his sense of divided allegiance, of a nationality compromised between Irish attachments and an England which, though it became his home, would always be foreign. Manning similarly lamented her fissured background in the familiar terms of her cross-cultural compatriots. 'It is awful being half and half', she remarked in a 1969 interview. 'I'm really confused about what I am, never really feeling that I belong in either place'.[12] Perhaps she exaggerated this tension; her difficulties had less to do with being half-Irish, in many ways, than with not being Irish *enough* to play convincingly on the consolations of difference. Still, these connections ultimately provided her with a usefully heightened self-consciousness, the same self-consciousness that in turn sustains Harriet Pringle's pervasive insecurities and sceptical perspectives. 'The quest after permanence by Olivia Manning's young heroine is accentuated by wartime conditions', the critic Robert Morris rightly observes, but 'as with the author herself . . . is, in the end, one imagines, a response conditioned by her cultural recalcitrance, a certain kind of upbringing.'[13]

Whatever other elements she took from her family background, Manning was sufficiently close to her maternal lineage when she began writing to adopt her mother's maiden name of Morrow as her pen-name. For her first name she took Jacob (from her favourite novel of adolescent years, Virginia Woolf's *Jacob's Room*), and in this guise she published three serialised thrillers during 1929, proving herself competent enough in *The Black Scarab*, *Rose of Rubies* and *Here's Murder* to take on a popular commercial genre.[14] By now she had left Portsmouth behind for London, where, struggling to make ends meet as an art student in a Chelsea bed-sit, she supported herself with a series of lowly jobs. This period of her life was later reclaimed for *The Doves of Venus* (1955), one of her most successful novels, which, in its descriptions of newly liberated and single young women adrift in post-war London, pre-empted writers such as Margaret Drabble and Lynne Reid-Banks in suggesting a female take on the 'angry young man' genre that characterised the decade. The novel drew heavily on Manning's own experience of sporadic unemployment in the capital. 'Before the war', she later recalled, 'the struggle to hold down a job, to maintain independence, a room of one's own, a life of one's own, devoured the youth and energy of thousands of young women . . . There were too many of them. They were still only partly emancipated.' Like Viola in *Artist Among the Missing* (1949), who recalls from the comparative luxuries of wartime Cairo the competitive struggle to survive as a woman in an overcrowded 1930s London, Manning's feminist sensibility was pragmatic and consequential, but no less pertinent for all that.[15]

Furthermore, life in the city had its rewards, particularly in the access she gained to other writers; this was a fertile period for her in making long-term friends and contacts. In addition to her first publisher Hamish Miles, with whom she soon embarked on an affair, she became acquainted with the writer William Gerhardi, already established by his 1925 novel *The Polyglots* as the doyen of modern European picaresque. Manning developed something of an infatuation with the writer, who would later (and rather ill-advisedly) place an extravagant review on her behalf in the *Times Literary Supplement* following the publication of her 1953 novel *A Different Face*: 'a devastating, an overwhelming social indictment, the novel might have been called "England, My England"', he enthused of the book. In the same piece, *Artist Among the Missing* was acclaimed for its 'brimming over of sheer pain' and Manning saluted as a most promising new writer of 'genius' and 'mystic intuition'. That the review ran in all its grandiloquence under the tight editorship of Anthony Powell was surprising; that it provoked at least one letter of outrage (from the poetry translator Arthur Waley) against its 'petulance and irrelevance' was perhaps not.[16] But Manning must have been grateful. She would remain faithful to Gerhardi long after the early flush of his own success faded, rewarding him with the dedication of *The Doves of Venus*, name-checking him frequently in reviews and eventually launching a campaign to have the forgotten hero of letters awarded a literary honour.[17]

Perhaps the most important friendship made during this period, however, was with the poet and novelist Stevie Smith. The two women became close during the late 1930s and maintained a correspondence after Manning went abroad, but in later years their relationship would be tested to the limits by various perceived slights and grievances on both sides, leading to long periods of estrangement. Smith would feature – though adjusted physically – as the character of Nancy Claypole in *The Doves of Venus*, the 'tall, thin, bespectacled girl with a prudish appearance' who provides a sidekick to the novel's young protagonist Ellie Parsons.[18] The fraught relationship between the two writers is evident in several of Manning's letters to various other acquaintances during the 1950s, which refer frequently and disparagingly to her friend's eccentric behaviour as 'very Stevie', and in 1955 Manning took Smith's relatively well-disposed *Observer* review of *The Doves of Venus* to be malicious in its underlying meaning.[19] 'I really think this girl is going off her head', she wrote to another literary acquaintance in 1956 after a characteristic spat with Smith at a party.[20] Manning seems to have remained antagonistic towards her former friend and fellow author even after Smith's death in 1971, writing to Kay Dick that 'perhaps it is too soon for a full-length portrait. One must not speak ill of the *recently* dead. But what about later?'[21]

Beyond these tensions, however, Stevie Smith provided a key point of contact in London and was without doubt a very significant literary role model. By 1936 Smith had published her surrealist *Novel on Yellow Paper*, which Manning greatly admired, and she followed her prose début two years later with a yet more brilliant sequel, *Over the Frontier*. The publication of *The Holiday* in 1949 (to which *The Doves of Venus* certainly owes elements of plot) completed one of the most challenging (and, until recently, undervalued) fictional sequences to emerge from the Second World War period. While Smith's *avant-garde* and phantasmagoric portrait of a London secretary caught up in international espionage, in *Over the Frontier*, is stylistically far removed from Manning's heavily autobiographical wartime chronologies, both novelists shared a recognition of the troubled interface between public and domestic narratives in this period. If Smith was influential, it was not only in proving that a woman *could* write about war but also in illustrating how fiction might render the often contradictory impulses of the private consciousness (specifically, a *female* consciousness) in the face of political uncertainties, to allow for inconsistency of perspective with regard to the rise of fascism or the failure of socialism or – more significantly for Manning – the Jewish plight, in the quest for an authentic response to wartime ideological pressures.

It was in the company of Stevie Smith and another fresh acquaintance, the critic Walter Allen (at that time working alongside Manning as a script-reader for Metro-Goldwyn-Mayer), that Manning met her future husband in July 1939.[22] She had at that time, Allen recalled, 'a wit that was devastating and was as formidable a young woman as any in London', convincing enough prerequisites, it seems, for him to introduce her to his old Birmingham school friend, Reginald Donald Smith.[23] Smith had already been appointed to the British Council as a lecturer in English and was home on leave from his first posting, in the Romanian capital of Bucharest, when he met Olivia. They were married within a few weeks in mid-August, the wedding an occasion that had all the feel of pre-war expediency and panicked gaiety. Louis MacNeice, Reggie Smith's close friend and formerly his Classics lecturer at Birmingham University, served as one of the official witnesses. 'We were all too late for the registrar and filled in time before he returned, drinking in the bar of the Ritz. Reggie and his girl and Walter Allen and myself and Stevie Smith. None of us had been in the Ritz before and we all felt like Tamburlaine – "Hola, ye pampered jades!"'[24] If MacNeice was dismissively vague here about Manning's actual identity, Stevie Smith, who served as the other witness to the ceremony, would be equally and forcefully dismissive of Olivia's new husband, immortalising him in the original version of her 1942 poem 'Murder':

My hand brought Reggie Smith to this strait bed –
Well, fare his soul well, fear not I the dead.[25]

Smith's death-fantasy for Reggie is not surprising – he tended to arouse strong feelings of one kind or another. MacNeice was clearly enchanted by the younger man's vivid personality, recalling him as a welcome figure of verve and energy in a period of torpor. In *The Strings Are False* he describes meeting up with his friend again after his own return from America to an England now tense with expectations of war: 'The summer of 1939 was a steady delirium, the caterpillar wheels of enormous tractors rearing on every horizon. As individuals there was nothing we could do – just mark time or kill it. Reggie Smith came back on leave from Bucharest and stayed in my flat, refusing to sleep in a bed but using the sofa in the sitting room, scattering his clothes over the room. His irrepressible cheerfulness was just what I wanted.' Walter Allen, too, remarked on the sheer strength of Smith's personality at that time, recalling him as 'a man very much in his own right, who went his own way, didn't give a damn for anybody and was governed only by his principles and affections'.[26] Indeed those who met Reggie Smith were always swayed by his charm, his enthusiasm and *joie de vivre* and were almost always forgiving, like MacNeice, of his untidiness, actual and emotional.

But what did this personality, these 'animal spirits', as Louis MacNeice celebrated them, mean for his new wife?[27] Politically the marriage exposed Manning to a social background quite different from her own, and she would later adapt elements of Smith's impoverished working-class Birmingham roots as a basis for Guy Pringle's ideological constitution and convictions in the trilogies. But Smith was more than an individual presence: he represented the leftist element in inter-war British cultural life which Manning (and Harriet Pringle) would necessarily approach from a tangent. Like Guy, whose heroes were the men of the International Brigade and who recites to himself their marching songs, Smith belonged to a generation still romanticising the Spanish Civil War while hearing on its own streets the footsteps of the blackshirts.[28] His friendship in the 1930s with novelist and campaigner Mulk Raj Anand (the model for Raji in Stevie Smith's *The Holiday*) linked him meanwhile to initiatives towards Indian independence and a growing anti-imperial momentum in

England.[29] More important in terms of his international interests (and, as we shall see, problematic for Guy Pringle's status and safety within wartime Europe), his probable engagement with British movements for Jewish relief in Europe tied him to an accelerating international Zionism. Walter Allen reports that in 1939 Smith, on his initial return from his posting in Bucharest, was accompanied by a party of Romanian Jews whose purpose, he came to realise, was to scope out a safe haven in England. Meanwhile, numerous details in Manning's trilogies (for instance, that Guy Pringle's chequebook stubs detail payments made to London banks on behalf of local Jews fleeing to Britain) hint that such commitments continued through the early years of the war at least.[30]

Reggie Smith's political beliefs were passionate and firmly based in the groundswell of international socialism in the period. He had become a card-carrying member of the Birmingham University Communist Society in 1932 and remained politically rooted in a solid Birmingham school of left-wing writers and intellectuals, a group dominated in the period by Marxist Professor of Classics George Thomson.[31] Exactly how far his youthful convictions later stretched towards subversive international affiliations (including the promotion of communist ideas within Romania during the war) remains questionable, however. In 'Notes towards an Autobiography' prepared in the late 1980s, Smith states that he was recruited by Anthony Blunt in 1938, teasingly noting Blunt's uncertainty when faced with his dishevelled working-class profile: 'was I a bit of rough trade or a spy prospect?'[32] MI5 files from 1947 to 1953, based partly on the bugging of the Smiths' London telephone line over this period, identify him as a member of the British Communist Party and do their best to secure evidence that he was acting as a covert channel of influence within the BBC, where he worked after the war as a Radio Features producer. However, his political convictions were hardly unusual for the time and any effect he might have had was undoubtedly compromised by his boisterous personality: as one of his BBC colleagues noted to MI5 officers in 1952, 'some of us who know him . . . are uncertain whether he is more of an exhibitionist rather, than a true communist sympathiser'.[33] Francis King offers a similar view in undermining any sense of Smith as a dangerous KGB operative: 'Since his death and even before it, people have often told me, "He was a KGB agent, of course." Some of these people were in a position to know . . . But Reggie was so indiscreet

I find it awfully hard to believe that he was a spy – even though, admittedly, he was no more indiscreet than Guy Burgess.' It appears that Manning herself was also characteristically dismissive, observing archly to her husband: 'Darling, you only know four words of Russian and one of them is "Pravda".'[34]

Whatever the extent of his involvement in the Communist Party itself, the significance of Smith's communism in the context of Manning's war-related fiction is straightforward, in that he provided so definitively the biographical referent for Guy Pringle. Absorbed in the work of D.H. Lawrence (Smith had embarked on a PhD thesis on Lawrence's poetry before the war), Guy attempts to live the part of a Lawrentian protagonist, stirred from working-class solidarity to a public life of passionate and dynamic engagement amidst the bourgeoisie. The representative of a naive international socialism in a collapsing European hierarchy, Guy is the optimist among the ideological ruins. His romantic dreams of Russian salvation are systematically undermined, his political shortsightedness repeatedly signposted by his literal myopia in the novels. But overall his ideological predicament is treated sympathetically, indulged even by Harriet, and set apart from the extremism professed by his various communist fellow-travellers, such as the bear-like David Boyd in Romania (a figure closely based on the historian Hugh Seton-Watson) or the odious Marxist Ben Phipps, whom the Pringles encounter in Greece.

In 1939, Olivia Manning found herself married, therefore, to a man *and* a world-view. Over the ensuing decade this collision of marital and ideological politics would provide the dynamic matrix of terms from which the trilogies ultimately emerged. Given Reggie Smith's personality, his political baggage would always be inextricable from the personal connections forged by the union, and there can be little doubt that Manning herself, like Harriet, suffered as a result of his reckless sociability. Sexually too, it seems, Reggie was profligate. His Bucharest contemporary, Ivor Porter, reports that he continued to 'sleep around' in Romania even after his marriage, as if nothing had been changed by his hasty pre-war wedding.[35] This may well have been the case; however, the fact that Reggie's behaviour does not translate in any straightforward manner to that of Guy Pringle in the trilogies is a useful reminder of the complex editing of biographical details which they repeatedly involve. In her fiction Manning blurs the border between warm-heartedness and sexual flirtation when it comes to Guy's dealings with female characters – Sophie Oresanu in the *Balkan Trilogy*, Edwina Little in the *Levant Trilogy* – reducing his potential for actual adultery to a simple schoolboyish inexperience with the nature of predatory women. Perhaps for Manning this was a protective move, or perhaps simply a writing strategy, given the gradual narrative of the marriage's disintegration which the novels foreground. Hints remain, nevertheless, of the early marital strains suffered by the couple and of the distress this inevitably caused the author in the early years of the relationship at least.

Olivia and Reggie's marriage on the eve of their departure for Bucharest, where Reggie was due back at his British Council posting, was also the prelude to their wartime lives and the critical juncture at which biography and the two fictional trilogies begin to blend and overlap. The dovetailing of Manning's sequence narratives with real-life experience hinges from the outset on a set of personal, but also *political*, circumstances, the latter providing her novels with their pervasive ideological motifs. In the fictionalised version of her own life, Manning uses the negative force of Harriet Pringle's scepticism and alienation to challenge Guy's narrowness of vision and ideological gullibility. Though Harriet herself is labelled a 'bloody conservative' by the obstinate Marxist Ben Phipps, her politics are undefined; *her* political role is to highlight the weaknesses and obsolescence of Guy's principles in the changed climate of war.[36] She acts specifically, the critic Fiona Tomkinson suggests, as a rebuke to Guy's Utopian Socialism, configured in the fiction in terms of his recurrent failure to recognise his wife as a distinct individual; to distinguish individual rights from the *communal* interests symbolised by his irrepressible sociability: 'In Manning's novels, Guy is presented as jumping . . . quickly and heedlessly from the "I" to the "We", whilst Harriet's female voice functions as a cutting edge driven through that seamless transition between the "I am" and the "We are", rupturing the sense of agreement taken for granted.'[37]

The implied similarities between this fragile marriage and the disintegrating contracts of old Europe extend, in turn, the political reach of Manning's trilogies. Analysing the structure of the novels, Theodore Steinberg observes that the crisis points in the Pringles' marriage both highlight and intersect with key moments of national and imperial crisis, drawing domestic and public narratives into a coherent process of exchange: 'The war dominates the first trilogy, and national imperialism dominates the second, but personal imperialism, the attempt to impose one's power on others, runs through both.'[38] In this respect Manning's positioning of Harriet as the insecure young woman caught up in her husband's political and sexual slipstream, spun in the whirlwind of Guy's ambitions, offers a paradigm for the fractures and secessions of an ageing European imperial order: 'Unmarried, she had been a personality in her own right. Married, she saw herself coming in, if at all, somewhere in Guy's wake' (*BT*, p. 274). In Harriet, for all her stubbornness and recalcitrance, we begin to recognise the mirroring of estranged European peripheries, such as Romania and Greece; of liminal ethnic and racial identities, the Jews, the Polish refugees, the gypsies; of volatile societies in Palestine or Syria, poised for the reformation of the Middle East; of cultures only loosely bound now by the centrifugal forces of the British or Austro-Hungarian empires, tense and alienated from the systems of power. And in tandem with her geographical passage from west to east we can trace a parallel political progress from hesitant belief to disillusionment as Harriet comes to appreciate the nature of her predicament:

> She saw that in the beginning she had engaged herself to someone she did not know. There were times when he seemed to her so changed, she could not suppose he had any hold on her. Imagining all the threads broken between them, she thought she had only to walk away. Now she was not sure. At the idea of flight, she felt the tug of loyalties, emotions and dependencies. For each thread broken, another had been thrown out to claim her. If she tried to escape, she might find herself held by a complex, an imprisoning web, she did not even know was there. (*BT*, p. 880)

If the marriage does survive it is only on radically adjusted terms and expectations, as the concluding volume of the *Levant Trilogy* makes clear, in a fragile post-imperial compromise.

This reading of the trilogies is by no means straightforward and obviously the marital metaphor is far from conclusive: it is Guy Pringle who expresses, after all, 'no belief in empire' and who suffers as much as his wife from the displacements of its wartime realignments.[39] Harriet, meanwhile, is both uncertain and inconsistent in her response, leading

Phyllis Lassner to see her as a more tenuous representative of a complex 'imperial femininity', both inheriting and subverting the project of empire, an 'ambivalent interpolation' into its governing ideologies.[40] Harriet's is *not* the defiant voice of a counter-epic anti-imperialism; her instability in this respect prevents a core metaphor from fossilising into allegory. But at whatever symbolic level it resonates, the marriage in its infancy and instability did resonate against a Europe facing into war. It is this Europe (and subsequently a would-be European Egypt) which the wartime fiction revisits, working through the subsequent layering of historical processes and events – decolonisation, the Cold War, the Suez crisis – to reproduce with extraordinary legitimacy a climate of tension, chilling uncertainty and violence. Manning's strained marriage to Reggie Smith was in this way mapped through her fiction on to a geo-political landscape fractured by the growing dissent of suppressed ethnic and religious minorities, or the frustrations of those peripheral territories caught up in the bartering of the 'great powers' across Europe and the Middle East.

Intrinsic to this process, and central to this study, is Manning's encounter in her fiction with the figure of the refugee. Harriet Pringle's position as the subjected term within the binary of marriage, and as the feminine Other to the masculine plot of war, locates her in strategic parallel to the displaced persons of wartime. The critic Jeremy Treglown has picked out Manning's attention to the 'stream after stream of refugees' as one of the strengths of her historical grasp, a quintessential element in her fictional scope.[41] In the *Balkan Trilogy* her portrayal of the hordes of wartime refugees, from the Polish evacuees swarming into Bucharest to the ethnic Romanians fleeing Transylvania after its transfer to Hungary, or of the saturation of Athens as it absorbs yet another trainload of panicked Yugoslavians, builds towards the impression of Europe as a crowded, contested space, both claustrophobic and nightmarish. But this is more than Tolstoyan landscape painting; it is a condition Harriet Pringle will also endure in her own experience of displacement. Through this cautious parallel, Manning effects a subtle identification of her fiction's transient protagonist and its most peripheral characters. At the end of the second novel in the trilogy, *The Spoilt City*, when Harriet stands bereft on a Bulgarian airfield caught between war zones, she enters a new and deeper phase of insecurity: 'As Dobson pointed out, she could neither stay here nor return whence she had come. She knew now what it was like to be a stateless person without a home' (*BT*, p. 577). Her subsequent flight from Athens just hours ahead of the German arrival coincides with the chaotic departure of those Greeks who can also afford to leave the city, while her fraught passage on a rusting steamer across the Mediterranean to Alexandria (an experience Manning describes in vivid detail in several factual accounts) marks a similar point of collision. By the time the Pringles reach Cairo, they share in the condition of the destitute and dislocated, their demarcation as British diplomatic exiles blurred in the city's accelerated multi-racial and multi-ethnic chaos, illustrated by the exchange, early in the opening novel of the sequence, *The Danger Tree*, between Clifford and Harriet as they tour the pyramids:

> 'They say Wavell's made plans for the evacuation of Cairo but, plans or no plans, it'll be plain bloody murder. It's already started. Every foreigner in Cairo's piling into trains, going while the going's good. I don't mean the British of course. The real foreigners. The crowd that came here from Europe.'
>
> Harriet Pringle said, 'We came here from Europe.'
>
> 'I mean the foreign foreigners. Dagos.' (*LT*, p. 21)

Manning's response to the concept of the 'refugee' deserves cautious interrogation. She was admittedly less direct in her response to this issue than contemporaries such as Storm Jameson, Inez Holden and Phyllis Bottome, who highlighted in their writing the plight of the European refugee in order to expose a flailing liberal British internationalism. The critic Jennifer Birkett has shown how Jameson's novels in particular illustrate a political interventionism in this respect. Having worked throughout the 1930s, and under the auspices of the international writer's association P.E.N., with refugee writers throughout Europe, Jameson channelled into her futurist dystopia *In the Second Year* (1936) and her faux travelogue *Europe to Let* (1940), a series of critiques on Britain's failure to comprehend and address the moral darkness she identified at the heart of Europe.[42] Highly politicised, Jameson saw her writing as intrinsic to her role as a voice of conscience within a British society ignorant of its refugee neighbours and 'sleepwalking' towards an international catastrophe.

If Manning was less overt with regard to the same theme, she moved further, nevertheless, towards recognising the nature of a refugee experience than many other writers within her wartime literary set. Her treatment of deracination is clearly distinguishable from the aesthetic of exile developed by the *Personal Landscape* group in Egypt, and captured in Lawrence Durrell's exaltation of the 'refugee habit' ('We are the dispossessed, sharing / With gulls and flowers our lives of accident: / No time for love, no room for love . . .').[43] As we shall see, Manning's attempt to connect to this group was treated with some ribaldry by its leaders ('She is determined to be *dans la mouvement*', Durrell wrote witheringly to *Poetry London* editor Meary Tambimuttu), but the tangential nature of her relationship with the Cairo-based coterie of Robert Liddell, Robin Fedden, Bernard Spencer and Durrell himself highlights numerous discrepancies of interest.[44] Indeed, it serves to emphasise her markedly different use of the refugee experience, which, shadowed by her own insecurities of belonging and invested in representative figures such as the wandering society parasite Yakimov ('typical Englishman, you might say. Mother Irish' *BT*, p. 718), forces in her fiction a series of darker confrontations and encounters with a European abject.

It forces acknowledgement, too, of the darkest element of all within the wartime refugee experience: a Jewish Europe abandoned to its desperate fate. Several of her female contemporaries had turned to the novel as a platform for anti-fascist polemic. These included Storm Jameson, as noted earlier, Phyllis Bottome, whose celebrated novel of a Jewish woman medical student in Nazi Germany, *The Mortal Storm*, was published in 1937 (and turned into a major MGM film in 1940), and the Irish-born Jewish writer Betty Miller – one of Manning's circle of friends in the capital – whose fictional portrayal of anti-Jewish prejudice in London, *Farewell Leicester Square*, appeared in 1941.[45] As the war progressed, the issue of Jewish persecution and exile was covered prominently by numerous male writers similarly seeking to foreground themes of failed paternalism, Western European guilt or the dilemmas of public morality – one thinks here of Louis MacNeice's 1941 poem 'Refugees', for example, with its portrait of desolate 'disinterred' European Jews arriving in the United States on the *Queen Mary*, or, in Evelyn Waugh's *Unconditional Surrender* (1961), Guy Crouchback's ill-conceived attempts to assist a community of displaced Jews in Yugoslavia.[46]

Drawing attention to the situation of Europe's Jews was not the same, however, as interrogating the conflicted and often unpalatable attitudes expressed by Britain towards this constituency, a more introspective project taken on by a select few of the writers among Manning's contemporaries. In *Over the Frontier*, Stevie Smith's protagonist Pompey Casmilus is given to sporadic bouts of antisemitic feeling, both in London and in pre-war Europe, where she gives vent to an anguished confession of antipathy towards the Jews: 'I am in despair for the racial hatred that is running in me in a swift sudden current, in a swift tide of hatred, and Out out damned tooth, damned aching tooth, rotten to the root. Do we not always hate the persecuted?' Virginia Woolf's characters register more sympathetically the threat against Jews in 1939, during the course of their conversations in *Between the Acts* ('And what about the Jews? The refugees . . . the Jews . . . People like ourselves, beginning life again . . .'), but Woolf presents this as a token gesture of concern, a vague allusion couched between discussions of royal gossip and the problems of litter.[47] If Manning's fictional accounts of the war were to address the same subject, how exactly should she navigate both personal pressures (notably her husband's long-term commitment to the Zionist cause) and the weight of hindsight, writing in the shadow of the Final Solution? How were the trilogies to register an authentic note, to admit the inconsistency and uncertainty of a British wartime mentality with regard to the defence of Jewish communities and refugees within Europe?

Her approach to the problem reveals itself in the *Balkan Trilogy*, where Manning negotiates the question of Romanian antisemitism with caution, configuring it tangentially through the fate of the young Jewish deserter Sasha Drucker (whom the Pringles hide in their apartment) and of his father, the Jewish banker imprisoned and tried by Romania's wartime fascist regime. In these episodes, the symbolic conflation of woman (Harriet) and Jew (Sasha) is applauded by Phyllis Lassner, who identifies in this strategy a positive location of both as 'dependent but subversive Others' within the structure of the epic.[48] But elsewhere (and indeed, elsewhere within the same novel), Manning's treatment of the Jewish situation within Europe is more ambivalent, registering self-consciously a wartime mind-set resistant to (and even repelled by) a refugee claim to compassion and protection. Specifically through Harriet Pringle's muted but discernible uneasiness at the perceived vulgarity of the Jewish Drucker family, she indicates the evasiveness of a British response, a failure to confront the fundamental truths of Jewish persecution during the progress of the war.

The difficulties in tackling this topic are also evident in her cautious negotiation of the question of Palestine, where Manning settled with her husband for a period of three years in 1942. With its Middle Eastern settings, the *Levant Trilogy* inevitably touches on the internecine volatilities of the region as a backdrop to the desert campaign, but in fact the issue of Jewish immigration and settlement in Palestine is more thoroughly dealt with in the two individual novels Manning published much earlier in her writing life, soon after the end of the war itself. *Artist Among the Missing* (1949) and *School for Love* (1951) both emerged from the author's three-year sojourn in Jerusalem following Reggie Smith's appointment to the headship of the Palestine Broadcasting Service in the autumn of 1942: it is Mandate Palestine in wartime that provides the significant setting for half of the first and all of the second novel. During this period Manning was involved through her literary work with various largely pro-Jewish organisations. These included the English-language newspaper established in the 1930s by the Zionist editor and correspondent Gershon Agronsky, the *Palestine Post*, through which Manning would come into contact with various politically animated individuals (including the writer and Zionist Arthur Koestler) and the Jerusalem Forum, a movement founded during the war by the British broadcaster John Connell, ostensibly to promote closer cultural relationships between Arab and Jewish communities in Jerusalem.[49] In such a context, that of a British diplomatic culture already highly vexed by the issue of Palestine and torn (as *Artist Among the Missing* conveys so well) between what many regarded as an obsolescent British Arabism on one hand and an urgent commitment to Jewish wartime resettlement on the other, Manning developed a political astuteness often missed in readings of her later work.

If Ireland provided the cradle for Manning's insights into a faltering Empire and national misalignments, wartime Palestine would subsequently offer her a complex revisiting of these themes. Chronologically, Jerusalem was Manning's last wartime destination before she and Smith returned to London in 1945, and therefore her Palestine-set novels are discussed in the final chapter of this study, although of course their publication precedes that of the two trilogies. In its turn, my conclusion looks briefly to Cyprus, which Manning visited on a holiday with her husband in 1944. Although outside the linear itinerary of their wartime years, the Mediterranean island almost certainly provided her with elements of a model for Al-Bustan, the Indian Ocean island setting for *The Rain Forest*, her last published individual novel. The culture, politics and ecology embodied by Cyprus in the post-war decades provide a source for the escalating tensions of Al-Bustan, where, in one of Manning's most pessimistic stories, an estranged English couple witnesses at close hand the awkward, violent endgame of British imperial control.

Olivia Manning's biographical experience of the war comprises a major aspect of this study, but my interest also lies in *how* her novels were composed. Inevitably several questions emerge relating to her use of the serial form, or *roman-fleuve*, for the trilogies and to the prolonged length of time between the end of the war itself and her translation of it into fiction. Her use of autobiographical experience and of a large cast of real-life contacts and acquaintances from the period as a basis for various characters in her books also demands attention; so too does her disingenuousness as a creative artist who was highly responsive to the plasticity of lived history. 'The thing is, I haven't got a lot of imagination like Iris Murdoch', she once remarked. 'I write out of experience. I have no fantasy'.[50] Yet none of her work represents a straightforward transmission of fact into text. Her characteristic tropes and metaphors, her notable agility with dialogue and in particular her skills in figurative landscape and scenic imagery contribute to a complex engagement between material and form. Less obvious, but very revealing of the trepidation felt among post-war literary circles generally in Britain, is the question of her heightened self-consciousness as a writer attempting to recover the convoluted and often diverse experiences which marked the wartime period. Her writing during the later stages of the war and its immediate aftermath, including her many review articles of the 1940s and her letters throughout the 1950s and 1960s, are a useful gauge of the literary temperature of a generation adapting slowly and hesitantly to an altered cultural climate and aesthetic.

Unlike Stevie Smith, Manning never attempted to build on the modernist experimentalism of her early literary influences. She maintained her adolescent admiration for Virginia Woolf, in spite of her publisher's retort when Manning asked to be introduced to her idol ('Certainly not . . . she hates young women writers. She would cut you to pieces'), while her reviews of the early Woolf scholarship emerging after the writer's death in 1941 suggest a solid grasp of the Bloomsbury aesthetic: Woolf's novels 'are penetrated through and through with a sense of the strangeness of human life, as though there were some other life guessed at, more ordered and significant, of which men catch an occasional glimpse', she wrote in her assessment of Joan Bennett's 1945 study.[51] Joyce too is frequently name-checked, a Parisian hand-bound copy of *Ulysses*, given to her by Hamish Miles, being one of the precious volumes she took with her to Europe and the Middle East during the war.[52] And, predictably enough, D.H. Lawrence was another early literary hero, though her claim in later life that news of his death sent her weeping all the way to school seems to be, as Braybrooke notes, one of her frequent attempts at strategic 'age-management', given that in 1930 she was already in her early twenties.[53]

As far as Manning was concerned, the novel form itself had reached a finite point of evolution: 'it may be smaller or larger, darker or fairer, more or less comely, but cannot drastically change without a decrease in usefulness', she wrote.[54] Her own fiction avoided experimentalism and, indeed, through a series of literary references, the trilogies effectively internalise the sense of contradiction, heightened by the war, between what was increasingly viewed as modernist indulgence and the tougher commitment of realist forms to the conflict. Throughout the *Balkan Trilogy*, Guy Pringle's political naivety goes hand in hand with *his* worship of Lawrence: in the first novel, *The Great Fortune*, the contents of his bookshelf afford the snide Clarence Lawson a chance to offer Harriet a pertinent dismissal of the modernist achievement.

> '*Kangaroo*,' he read out scornfully. "These modern novelists! Why is it that not one of them is really good enough? This stuff, for instance . . .'
>
> 'I wouldn't call Lawrence a modern novelist.'
>
> 'You know what I mean.' Clarence flipped impatiently through the pages. 'All these dark gods, this phallic stuff, this – fascism! I can't stand it.' He threw down the book and stared accusingly at her.
>
> She took the book up. 'Supposing you skip the guff, as you call it! Supposing you read what is left, simply as writing.' She read

> aloud one of the passages Guy had marked. It was the description of the sunset over Manly Beach. 'The long green rollers of the Pacific', 'the star-white foam', 'the dusk-green sea glimmered over with smoky rose'.
>
> Clarence groaned through it, appalled at what was being imposed on him. 'I know!', he said in agony, when she stopped. 'All that colour stuff – it's just so many words strung together. Anyone could do it.' (*BT*, pp. 187–8)

If Harriet is unsettled by Clarence's critique of the writer in whom both she and her husband have so heavily invested, she is further troubled by his disparagement of Virginia Woolf ('I think *Orlando* almost the worst book of the century'), and in particular by what she regards as the surprising originality of his somewhat unpalatable remarks on Woolf's writing, 'so diffused, so feminine, so sticky . . . just like menstruation' (*BT*, p. 188). Harriet's confusion at his insight is telling. And Manning's efforts to include within the course of her narrative the grounds for her own stylistic conservatism – a defence of a documentary realism, which, for all its limitations, will never meet with such objections – is an important, if contrived, critical juncture, a recognition of modernism's latent weaknesses and probable irrelevance in a new political environment.

The passage above was not published until 1960 but it reflects the backlash against modernism which had accelerated during the course of the war and to which Manning contributed at the time. In a scathing 1945 review of Elizabeth Smart's *By Grand Central Station I Sat Down and Wept*, for example (in which she mooted a group dismissal of experimental writing as 'that sort of thing'), she described the book as a poor attempt at the stream-of-consciousness technique employed so well by Stevie Smith in *Novel on Yellow Paper*. 'Miss Smith's book was full of wit, wisdom and genuine poetry', she concluded, 'Miss Smart's is hysterical where it is not pretentious'.[55] Her enthusiasms were reserved instead during the 1940s for those writers who had best managed to situate a modernist residue in new ironic fictions of individual volatility and national malaise – Stevie Smith perhaps, but, definitively, Elizabeth Bowen, 'the foremost woman writer in England today', as Manning acclaimed her in a review of a reissued *To the North* in 1947.[56]

In the light of this stylistic self-positioning, one might usefully view

Manning's writing in the context of 'intermodernism', the term construed by the critic Kristin Bluemel to describe the phase of literary culture spanning the inter-war to immediate post-war years, and including writers such as Stevie Smith, George Orwell, Storm Jameson and Stella Gibbons. Intermodernist writers, with their close alliances to the middlebrow and their re-valorising of a contemporary realism that was, above all, socially responsible – if radical – were intrinsic to an adjustment of critical and ideological terms in modernism's wake. As Bluemel details it, 'while intermodernism might initially function as modernism's other in academic practice, it has the potential to be the concept of space that inserts itself between modernism and its many structuring oppositions, reshaping the ways we think about relations between elite and common, experimental and popular, urban and rural, masculine and feminine, abstract and realistic, colonial and colonized'.[57] This definition is suitably broad to encompass those writers such as Storm Jameson (in *Documents*) and Inez Holden (in *Night Shift*) who were experimenting with fictional convention in response to wartime pressures for an increasingly documentary realism, at the same time as accommodating other novelists who, while adhering largely to middlebrow genres such as romance, thriller and historical saga, were none the less ideologically and politically subversive with regard to a social and cultural revision of values in the period. Reading Manning as an intermodernist in the latter category begins to illuminate the ways in which her use of conventional realist genres may disguise a series of radical adjustments – in particular, adjustments to a masculine discourse of war – contained within the novels themselves.

As a novelist, Manning was also alert to pressures particular to the generation of writers who had lived through the war. In the first place, she recognised the need to demarcate the work of those geographically displaced by the conflict from the outpouring of travel literature penned by a 1930s coterie distinctly more cavalier in its treatment of Europe and beyond, and hailed by Paul Fussell in his account of inter-war literary travellers as the distinctive 'diaspora' of literary modernism.[58] Readers at home had been inspired by the foreign landscapes presented by writers such as Norman Douglas ('a writer of wit, selectivity and objectivity', according to Manning), but in the wake of the war a new category of writing began to emerge, based largely on military or diplomatic experience, and burdened, unlike its carefree predecessor, by a sense of responsibility for a collapsing Empire and a lost political innocence.[59] This loss was most visible, Manning felt, in the work of her contemporary Evelyn Waugh. Before the war he had been one of her literary fixtures (Felix Latimer is depicted reading Waugh's *Put Out More Flags* in her novel *School for Love*), but like many critics – and, indeed, Waugh himself – Manning sensed that the comic turn was out of touch with the realities of conflict and suffering. In particular, she identified Waugh's travel writing with a bygone and lamented age of indulgence, a point she forcibly expressed in her review of his *When the Going was Good* in 1947: 'It is hard to remember that during the *inter-bellic* period there was a time in the early thirties when a writer could actually travel for pleasure', she wrote. 'It passed very quickly, of course, and there then crowded upon anyone who put a foot outside his own country the need to be politically conscious if he hoped to interest the reading public.' With a timely allusion to Churchill's 'Sinews of Peace' speech, delivered the previous year, she suggested that matters had become even worse since the end of the war: now 'it is unthinkable that even the most aesthetically old-world of our writers could go abroad without trying to peep through some sort of iron curtain'.[60]

Getting the balance right was awkward nevertheless and Manning's late fiction, in particular, often bears the heavy imprint of local colour or travelogue diversion. But in confronting issues of historical and political responsibility in the novel she brought a distinctively post-war (and post-imperial) mentality to her task. Mixed critical responses to her own travel book on Ireland, *The Dreaming Shore*, would reinforce the complexity of writing about elsewhere and of combining the tourist gaze with the perspective of political witness in the post-war period. Indeed, as we shall see for Manning, idioms of representation tied up with the configuration of 'foreign' landscapes or with the use of 'painterly' perspectives were already inextricable, in the context of a late imperial Western European hegemony over territories farther east, from idioms of political power. In these respects the evolution of a responsible 'English novel abroad' tradition was by no means straightforward. Nor would Manning's efforts to this end be fully appreciated: Ivy Compton-Burnett would complain vociferously of how 'a great many novels nowadays are just travel books disguised . . . Olivia has just published one about Bulgaria [*sic*].'[61]

More difficult questions again emerged around the positioning of war-related fiction in a literary hierarchy. Having begun her career as a popular thriller writer, Manning might have moved quickly to capitalise on the taste for the kind of fast-paced action material several of her contemporaries produced in the wake of conflict. The engaging Geoffrey Household, for example, whose undercover stint for British Intelligence in Romania overlapped briefly with the Smiths' sojourn in Bucharest, had already risen to acclaim with *Rogue Male* (1939); he would go on to produce a series of similar thrillers over the ensuing decades. After the war, Patrick Leigh Fermor's exploits in Crete in 1944, and specifically the plot to kidnap the island's German commander General Heinrich Kreipe, were written up by William Stanley Moss for the 1952 thriller *Ill Met by Moonlight*; the Smiths' former Egypt acquaintance P.H. Newby produced his novel of a wartime deserter, *The Retreat*, the following year.[62] The immense popularity of Agatha Christie, meanwhile, who adapted her detective fiction to wartime scenarios of espionage and 'fifth columnism', proved the appetite for such material was undiminished on the home front. Manning was keen to avoid this trajectory and, indeed, she had already made characteristically acerbic predictions on the kind of literary climate which would emerge after the end of hostilities: 'There is little doubt that we shall have to wait until commercialism defeats itself before serious writers can again feel it is worth their while to compete'.[63]

But what kind of 'serious' writing, what kind of novel, had the capacity to register the huge geographical, political and emotional canvas which presented itself after 1939? On the domestic front, those who had remained at home carved fictions from the experience of the Blitz – Graham Greene in *The Ministry of Fear* (1943), Henry Green with *Caught* (1943) and Bowen in *The Heat of the Day* (1949). Or they mined a vast array of service-related experience, a category that drew many women into the popular literary market for the first time. Pamela Frankau's Auxiliary Territorial Service novel *The Willow Cabin* (1949), which the author wanted to be read by 'an enormous number of ex-ATS and dull educational girls and boys in technical schools and gravediggers in Bangor and unhappy married women in Belfast', was an unprecedented publishing success; novels of wartime factory life, such as Inez Holden's powerful documentary-fiction *Night-Shift* (1941) and Monica Dickens' *The Fancy* (1943), were also well received.[64] Indeed the prolifacy of women's writing in the period serves to challenge the prevailing assumption that most writers were distracted and even hamstrung by the war. The critic Victoria Stewart has shown convincingly that, in fact, the conflict not only served to focus attention and debate on the responsive role of the novel in the period but increased levels of creativity, a view that undermines the image set so definitively by Evelyn Waugh as he entered a *Work Suspended* mode, the writer self-consciously setting down his pen as the first air-raid sirens sounded.[65]

Nevertheless, the sense of a caesura was prevalent among many writers, and particularly those who, like Manning, had lived or served abroad and then returned, disconsolate, to an unfamiliar literary landscape. Discussing this sense of post-war creative lag, Jeremy Treglown complains that *Horizon*'s lament, in 1947, of how no 'new crop of novelists' had emerged to match the experimental glories of an earlier generation grievously overlooked the six hard years of war service many promising talents had endured in that period.[66] Manning herself wrote of the late 1940s as a time when prose writers, 'hampered by war', struggled to begin publishing again: many of them were no longer young, she later observed, and had difficulty finding their feet in 'the confusing civilian scene'.[67] Elsewhere she noted the same predicament, with poets faring even worse than their fellow novelists: 'The devastation of six years of war is still as clearly marked among our writers as our townscape', she wrote, in relation to the poets Keith Douglas and Alun Lewis, wartime casualties in Normandy and Burma respectively. Established pre-war writers such as Louis MacNeice and George Barker, she continued, 'are in achievement so far beyond the promise of the post-war men, that one wonders if the war has actually wiped out our younger generation of poets'.[68]

For Manning there was no stagnation as such: she *had* been writing fairly prolifically during and just after the war. The two novels of the 1940s and early 1950s, together with numerous wartime short stories, testify to her productivity in the period, as does *The Remarkable Expedition*, her 1947 book on Henry Stanley's Sudanese expedition to rescue the governor of the province of Equatoria, Emin Pasha, besieged by the Mahdi uprising of 1887. More to the point – and significant to questions of historical hindsight in her later work – she had completed substantial sections of material later developed in the trilogies. *Guests at a Marriage*, a 166-page typescript collected with her papers, is specifically the embryo of the first two volumes of the *Balkan Trilogy*, while other material of this period existing in draft or short-fiction form provided the seedbed for the *Levant* sequence.[69] Individual stories published during or immediately after the war are clearly foundations for distinct episodes in the novels. 'A Journey' (published in her 1948 collection *Growing Up*), a story based on a reporting assignment that Manning herself undertook in 1940 to see the Romanian town of Cluj as it fell to the Hungarians, evolves into Yakimov's visit to the same stricken region in *The Spoilt City*. Again from the 1948 collection, 'A Spot of Leave', Manning's heady, atmospheric tale of adulterous liaisons in the laconic setting of wartime Alexandria, contains scenic elements later reworked in *The Danger Tree*, while a short piece, 'Holy Fire', which she first offered to Kay Dick for the literary journal *The Windmill* in 1946, is the basis for the description of the Greek festival in Damascus which Harriet Pringle attends in *The Sum of Things*.[70]

Nevertheless, the fifteen-year gap between the end of the war and the publication of the first volume of the *Balkan Trilogy*, *The Great Fortune*, in 1960, hints that she also felt the disorienting effects of circumstances registered by many of her peers. The delay also reflects, on a more personal level perhaps, Manning's need for time to absorb and process events in her own life. Questioned later by Kay Dick about the twelve-year stretch between the publication of *The Wind Changes* in 1937 and the appearance of her next novel in 1949, she alluded to the emotional traumas of war (in particular the loss of her brother, killed in action in 1941) that had interrupted her progress, but she also spoke of her need for comparatively *more* time than other writers in order constantly to rewrite her material, to work towards what she called 'thinning things down'. In simple terms, the scale of the war and its disturbances, even for one individual, put extraordinary pressure on novelistic form. 'I don't think anything I've ever experienced has been wasted', Manning explained to Dick, but the price of such inclusiveness would be the extended duration of composition.[71]

More to the point, Manning's uncertainties highlight the strained dynamics of the relationship between Second World War history and the sequence novel. 'How long will the post-war last . . . shall we win the post-war, how does it go?' asks Celia in Stevie Smith's *The Holiday*, a plaintive question framing the several fictional sequences which, in concert, drew out the experience of war itself until it merged naturally into the teleology of prolonged imperial decline. Just as the most famous sequences of First

World War writing – Siegfried Sassoon's *Memoirs* or Ford Madox Ford's *Parade's End* tetralogy – took time to emerge over a decade after the Armistice itself, so did the multi-volume treatments of the 1939–45 conflict extend well beyond its chronological boundaries. Waugh's staggered output of the three linked novels *Men at Arms* (1952), *Officers and Gentlemen* (1955) and *Unconditional Surrender* (1961) eventually led to the publication of the *Sword of Honour* in trilogy form in 1965; the three wartime-set novels in Anthony Powell's *Dance to the Music of Time* sequence, *Valley of the Bones*, *Soldier's Art* and *The Military Philosophers*, were completed only between 1964 and 1968.[72] Durrell's *Avignon Quintet*, including the remarkable individual novel, *Constance*, with its prismatic account of occupied France, did not appear in that format until 1985 (though the *Alexandria Quartet* preceded it in 1962). Writing at length, in sequence format, brought its own difficulties therefore, with the inbuilt time-lag and inevitable political belatedness of such constructions raising questions as to their impact or pertinence.

The compositional timeframe of Manning's trilogies places her in the company of the writers above, and comparison with several of them helps validate her efforts, in many ways, to chronicle the war on such a scale. It supports at the same time the critical observation that, in writing, the conflict over-ran its chronological parameters: '[T]he social, cultural and psychological impact of the events of the war', Victoria Stewart reminds us, 'cannot be contained within the temporal span of 1939–45.'[73] But did Manning ever intend to write at this length, towards the six sequential novels that Anthony Burgess would later term a 'hexateuch'?[74] To Kay Dick she remarked that 'I really only meant to write the two Rumanian volumes', and Braybrooke confirms that her initial plan in 1956 was for a 'double-decker' work, the idea for a trilogy emerging only when she had completed the first volume.[75] More revealing of the gradual development of the project are her letters during this period to fellow novelist Jocelyn Brooke, whose own autobiographical sequence of novels – *The Military Orchid* (1948), *A Mine of Serpents* (1949) and *The Goose Cathedral* (1950) – was finally published together posthumously as the *Orchid Trilogy* in 1981. Manning developed a sympathetic and seemingly mutually beneficial relationship with Brooke. The two had first come into contact shortly after the war, when Manning remarked on the 'deserved success' of Brooke's *The Military Orchid* in a review of his 1949 publication *The Scapegoat*.

With its story of an orphan sent to live with a sinister and fascistic uncle, Brooke's novel bore uncomfortable similarities to her own *School for Love*, published two years later, yet, as Manning insisted, they had conceived the plots independently. Brooke responded to the praise and wrote to Manning suggesting that they keep in touch, initiating a close if sporadic correspondence which spanned the next fifteen years.[76]

In 1955 Manning wrote to Brooke: 'I have started on a long novel about one year in Rumania – 1939–40 – practically an historical novel.' Already she was anxious about the project, adding that 'I will probably be slanged for writing of something in which no one is any longer interested. Journalists can rush into print immediately after events. Novelists take too long, I'm afraid.' Later she posted him a copy of *The Great Fortune* and requested his 'absolutely honest opinion' of the work. 'It is the first part of a trilogy and probably suffers from the fact that it is a build up for the second part in which most of the action takes place.' A few months afterwards she wrote to Brooke again, expressing her gloom at the second part of the sequence, which seemed 'lifeless and wretched'; she was too tired to do much rewriting. When *The Spoilt City* was finally completed, she admitted to Brooke that she found it 'laboured, dull and too long'; and even at this stage the concept of a trilogy seemed insecure. 'I really think that *Great Fortune* and *Spoilt City* should have been one book, very much cut down, and perhaps one day, if anyone think it worth it, I'll set to work on them', she concluded. Brooke appeared to differ, reviewing the latter work favourably for *The Times*, and Manning, who kept a cutting of the review among her papers, must have been encouraged, battling through what she described as an 'exhausting time' with the third novel, *Friends and Heroes*, to complete the Balkan sequence. '[N]ow it is written', she surmised in May 1965, 'I think it is probably the best of the three'.[77]

The correspondence with Brooke reveals not only the faltering evolution of the first trilogy and the considerable workload it involved but also Manning's awareness of how her contemporaries were managing the sequence format. Brooke, in particular, had provided the rudiments of a template for her own enterprise. Characteristically, Manning was later rather harsh in her treatment of her ally. In an article for the *Times Literary Supplement*, written three years after Brooke's death in 1966, and drawing partly on his idiosyncratic modernist memoir *The Dog at Clambercrown* (1955), she described him as a largely unfulfilled writer and a demonised man who 'exhausted himself in battle with an imaginary enemy'.[78] But arguably it was Brooke's *Orchid* sequence which gave Manning some idea, first, of how the *roman-fleuve* might operate within a modern British literary climate, and, second, of how autobiographical matter might work as fiction; how fictional characters might be developed from real people and the weight of historical events contained within the boundaries of conventional narrative. For all their differences of style, the two had much in common, Brooke's Proustian nuances of time and personality lending structural models, at least, to Manning's more prosaic fictions of war.

The manner in which Manning's writing engages both the determining contexts of historical event and, at the same time, the machinery of autobiography will be examined at various stages throughout this account of her writing. By way of introduction, one might stress the pressure she felt towards a documentary responsibility in her treatment of history, a responsibility visible in the occasionally wearisome listing of international conferences, treaties and battles which characterises *The Spoilt City* in particular. On the other hand, her quest for historical authenticity in these terms should also be admired as a strength of the novels. Not surprisingly, perhaps, in tandem with her fictional venture she frequently 'wrote up' her experiences in historiographic form. In 1966, she was an invited contributor to Basil Liddell Hart's *History of the Second World War*, an encyclopaedic photo-journal published in weekly parts in cooperation with the Imperial War Museum. Individual issues contain Manning's autobiographical accounts of wartime events, including the Romanian *coup d'état* in 1940, the flight of British expatriates from Athens as it fell to the Germans the following year, and the episode of civilian panic, known as the 'Great Flap', in Cairo in 1942. These are clearly skeleton versions of what was almost certainly, given the publication dates, in parallel fictional development and, as such, the *History* contributions were probably a useful enabling exercise for the writer. More to the point, perhaps, the journal also supplied vast amounts of primary historical material from other writers covering the same contexts, and relevant to the future composition of the *Levant* sequence. Reggie Smith's friend Dan Davin submitted two pieces on the Battle of Crete, for example, while the Smiths' Jerusalem colleague John Connell, by this time author of a well-received biography of General Wavell, contributed detailed material on the Western Desert Campaign.[79]

The push for veracity and the legitimacy of the 'fictionalised history' crossover also meant a research burden on Manning which no doubt slowed down her progress. This was particularly marked in her treatment of conflict itself and her venture in the *Levant Trilogy*, through the character of Simon Boulderstone, into the male preserve of the battleground. Some of the resources on which she drew for this imaginative leap are worth noting. Along with obvious stalwarts of battle literature, including Stephen Crane's *The Red Badge of Courage* and Tolstoy's *War and Peace* (apparently she first read the latter after the battle of El Alamein), she collated a range of newspaper and journal material on Rommel, on individual battles of the desert campaign, on Alamein itself and the military chronology of the North African front.[80] These documentary elements combine with key literary writings from the period (to be further discussed in Chapter Four), including, for example, Keith Douglas's *Alamein to Zem Zem* (1946) and Davin's *For the Rest of Our Lives* (1947). Writing the visual and visceral landscape of war was never going to be easy, but Manning's attempt at it through the lens of a male counterpart to Harriet has a confidence gained through the sheer detail of her research: even Treglown, who elsewhere complains about Manning's tendency towards caricature and repetition, is persuaded by the 'impressive restraint and conviction' of her battle scenes.[81]

In the translation of history into novel there were practical difficulties too, with the use of real people as the basis for fictional characters. Manning was very much at one with her peers in this respect: Waugh cheerfully drew on his friends and associates for thinly disguised counterparts. So of course did Stevie Smith; less frequently, Elizabeth Bowen.[82] Manning's position in this regard was already circumscribed by autobiographical structures, and several characters in her books are drawn directly from the 'real life' individuals with whom she and her husband came into contact. In *The Great Fortune*, for example, Guy Pringle's friend David Boyd is obviously based on the Marxist historian Hugh Seton-Watson (serving in 1939/40 with the British Legation in Bucharest), the fictional diplomat Dobbie Dobson is a relatively straightforward take on real-life Foreign Office official Adam Watson, and the effete Colin Gracey, Guy's erstwhile superior in Athens, is recognisable as a version of Reggie Smith's British Council superior in Egypt, C.A.F. Dundas.[83] But in fact Manning's practice was more often, as her husband later explained it, to produce 'composite' characters from several individuals.[84] Inevitably this leads to speculation. In the *Levant Trilogy* the poet Bill Castlebar has affinities to the real-life poets Bernard Spencer and Lawrence Durrell, but is there also a possible element (particularly in his sudden early death) of Cairo-based poet and schoolmaster Keith Bullen? The infuriatingly self-centred Professor Lord Pinkrose, whom several readers have traced back to the Irish peer and literary scholar Lord Dunsany (Edward Plunkett), may well merge details of other high-ranking cultural diplomats Manning encountered in the period, including H.V. Routh, the 'very tactless and unpopular' holder *before* Dunsany of the Byron Chair in Athens and (briefly) wartime administrator of the British Institute in the Greek capital.[85] Prince Yakimov has attracted most interest from readers keen to identify his origins, with both the high-society designer and writer Derek Patmore and Soho *flâneur* Julian Maclaren-Ross claiming responsibility for his unconventional personality, although neither seems to be the single source for his character.[86] Meanwhile, one might speculate on the genesis of numerous other characters whose lives or personalities bear correspondences to individuals within the Smiths' expatriate circles. Is Alan Frewen in *Friends and Heroes* overlaid with aspects of philhellene travel writer Patrick Leigh Fermor? Did Manning's Cairo acquaintance Elizabeth Gwynne (later the cookery writer Elizabeth David) provide some of the inspiration for embassy darling Edwina Little, in the *Levant Trilogy*?[87]

The drift towards this kind of patchwork attribution process can be a distraction for readers of Manning's writing (and of wartime expatriate literary fiction in general). Real-life identifications usually add little, if anything, to a narrative that works independently of them. Manning herself was disparaging of fictions that tracked too closely their life sources. Reviewing her acquaintance Dan Davin's autobiographical fiction of the desert war, *For the Rest of Our Lives*, in 1947, she remarked dismissively that 'His novel reads like a conscientiously kept day-to-day diary'; the characters were 'crude, shadowy and seem to be seen, not with the dispassion of the artist, but in the light of an old grudge'.[88] At the same time (and particularly in this study, where the composition process itself is under scrutiny), the tracing of source characters from within Manning's expatriate community is frequently an important means of establishing the kind of political ideologies in circulation around the author – and therefore around Harriet – together with a sense of the values and incentives in transition within British cultural imperialism in the period.

Just as relevant to the question of Manning's fictional method, perhaps, is how the translation of fact into fiction exposed the risks in her use of autobiographical and actual sources. She narrowly avoided trouble with her 1951 novel *School for Love*, in which the unscrupulous and manipulative boarding-house landlady was taken to have been modelled on Clarissa Graves (sister of the poet Robert Graves), in whose house she had lodged at one stage in Jerusalem.[89] There were also serious legal difficulties in 1968 when Manning, attempting to change publishers, from Heinemann to Panther, discovered that *The Spoilt City* had become the subject of a libel challenge from within Romania. In the novel, she had made reference to the 1939 massacre of Romanian Prime Minister Armand Călinescu and his family. After Panther published the paperback edition of the novel, Călinescu's son, Barbu, contacted the publisher to point out that he and certain other relatives, having in fact survived the attack, might now be considered imposters in the light of Manning's narrative. Panther withdrew its support for the novel out of fear of incurring hefty libel penalties and Manning was obliged to offer public acknowledgement of her mistake.[90]

The trilogies perform at some distance from the *roman à clef* proper, but situations such as these highlight the tensions in their evolution. Manning's use of particular incidents also illustrates her technique as one of adaptation from events rather than straightforward inscription, yet here again her reliance on figures drawn from real life sometimes raised questions of etiquette, if not ethics. This was the case in her use (for the *Levant Trilogy*) of the actor Stephen Haggard as the basis for actor-turned-army-captain Aidan Sheridan (serving in Egypt under his own name of Aidan Pratt). By the time he arrived in the Middle East with the Department of Political Warfare, Haggard was already an established stage and screen star whose pre-war performances included a role in the 1939 film version of *Jamaica Inn*. Reggie Smith, who knew him well, took advantage of his talents for his Palestine Broadcasting Service productions of *Henry V* and *Hamlet*. As Aidan Sheridan, he becomes one of the most intriguing, resonant personalities in Manning's cast, his voice lending huge emotional capital to *The Battle Lost and Won*, in particular, through his account of surviving the torpedoing of a civilian evacuation ship. His embittered acknowledgement that, for all his theatrical distinctions, he will return from the front too old for decent acting roles renders him symbolic of an English youth and talent squandered by the war effort.[91] When the real Stephen Haggard committed suicide in 1943, the incident was covered up by military authorities, who informed his family simply that he had died in the line of duty. In *The Sum of Things*, however, not only does Harriet learn the details of how Aidan Sheridan has shot himself on a train, it is also implied that his distress is, in part at least, a result of his unrequited affections for Guy Pringle. Given the length of the intervening time, this might be considered harmless, but the context was still a sensitive one and Manning's development of the incident was regarded by several contemporaries as somewhat tasteless.[92]

If Manning avoided actual criticism on this occasion, she drew fire for a more dramatic translation of fact to fiction in the same trilogy through her use, specifically, of the family of well-known Cairo diplomat Walter Smart and his wife Amy. While accompanying his mother on a painting expedition into the desert, the Smarts' young son picked up a live grenade which then exploded in his face. Manning's invention of the scene of his desperately painful death in the arms of his distraught parents – a scene coincidentally witnessed in the novel by Harriet Pringle and Simon Boulderstone – provides what is undoubtedly one of the most disturbing moments in all her work. Critically, as discussed below in Chapter Four, the material is defensible on the grounds of its relevance to Manning's thematic developments, but several of her contemporaries found it none the less dubious. They were similarly perturbed by her transformation of the dead boy's mother (in real life Amy Nimr, a distinguished painter and sister-in-law of the highly respected moderate Arab nationalist writer George Antonius) into the footloose Angela Hooper, whose liaison with poet Bill Castlebar is Cairo's *scandale du jour* throughout the *Levant Trilogy*. Dan Davin was among those critical of Manning's treatment of the incident (though his view was perhaps compromised by his relationship with the dead boy's nanny); Lawrence Durrell, who had used Smart as the partial basis for the diplomat Mountolive in the *Alexandria Quartet*, also regarded it as inappropriate, and Patrick Leigh Fermor was reportedly outraged by Manning's blatant disregard for the family's sensitivities.[93]

Engagements with a real-life history could be fraught, therefore, but issues such as those noted above were predominantly legalistic rather than interpretative. They distract, at the same time, from a more problematic aspect of autobiography in its most literal sense – the writing of the self. Manning's task was not only one of adaptation, of drawing on her own life experience as the basis for Harriet Pringle's wartime journey, but of *insinuation*: the positioning of a female protagonist in a context conventionally loaded with expectations of masculine centrality. In his account of late modernism and national culture, *A Shrinking Island*, Jed Esty identifies in the wartime period and afterwards an emphatically masculine literary constellation embodying a pervasive sense of national decline: 'Most of the writers conventionally taken to represent English literature in the mid-century – Greene, Waugh, Orwell, Auden, Larkin – remain committed to a literature of existential male anti-heroism in a world of corrupt politics and culture.'[94] As a critical overview, this should no doubt be challenged from the perspective of several female novelists of the period, and with reference in particular to Phyllis Lassner's study of various women writers whose work engaged closely with the themes surrounding imperial dissolution.[95] But the characteristic end-of-empire novel, Greene's 'white men going to seed in outlandish places', held sway as the persuasive idea, one that Manning (in her youth an avid reader of Rider Haggard's *Zulu Trilogy*), fell in with in her portraits of post-imperial casualties, such as the febrile Geoffrey Lynd in *Artist Among the Missing* or the alienated Hugo Fletcher in *A Different Face*.[96] Even within the trilogies, vignettes of *masculine* mental disintegration in the face of wartime pressures – in *The Sum of Things*, for example, reporter and spy Jake Jackman goes insane and destroys the interior of Mrs Rutter's Gezira mansion; Simon Boulderstone's post-battle breakdown leads to a psychosomatic paralysis – are intelligible in terms of a distinctively masculine inflection of imperial disarray in fiction, embodied elsewhere in Greene's Scobie (in *The Heart of the Matter*), Geoffrey Firmin in Lowry's *Under the Volcano*, or again, Waugh's Guy Crouchback.[97]

This convention explains why, inevitably, some critics have continued to read the trilogies as Guy Pringle's story, and to focus on him as the protagonist of the narrative. Anthony Burgess, for example, describes him as 'one of the most fully created male leads of contemporary fiction . . . he is a kind of civilization in himself'.[98] On the other hand, it is by no means straightforward simply to treat Harriet Pringle as the protagonist as such.

In so many instances the peripheral or choric aspect of her position is what nuances the narrative and underlines its cutting ironies. Theodore Steinberg suggests that 'epic has often been viewed as a male genre, that is, a genre reflecting, monologically, the concerns of men, primarily in terms of military activity and conventional definitions of the heroic . . . Manning's approach overtly challenges that treatment'.[99] However, the nature of that challenge is sly and sometimes even a little pernicious, not forthright. Again Manning's comments on Jane Austen are telling, and her distinction of the author's irony as a means to expose 'the wretchedness that follows from self-absorption, complacency and unawareness of other people' a neat enough description of the role she creates for Harriet Pringle to play.[100]

The change of perspective implied by Manning's sustained positioning of Harriet as, in effect, a voice of scepticism from the sidelines also requires an adjustment to our understanding of autobiography itself. The trilogies reverse a conventional masculine version of this genre, in which personal convictions are sustained, even enhanced, in the face of ethical or political collapse, and they foreground instead a version of individuality which is permanently and resonantly insecure. Read in terms of her insecurity, Harriet offers a more subtle profile than Guy, with his clear bearings in Reggie Smith's political composition, as discussed above. Her lack of personal connection to a solid background (we learn simply that she is the child of divorced parents to whom she was an 'inconvenience', and brought up by an aunt who found her a 'nuisance') provides for her troubling presence in the lives of others.[101] Unlike Guy, Harriet carries *no* cultural and political baggage, and her insubstantiality in this respect renders her threatening and perverse. In Manning's hands, autobiography becomes what critic Laura Marcus terms a 'paranoid' form. In place of the subject's progress towards individual assertion and completion, there is at best only alienation and doubt; any identity that does emerge is relational, not self-contained.[102]

This perspective may help to align Manning with a female tradition of the serial novel obscured by the masculine end-of-empire sequences and pre-dating the war. One thinks obviously of Rebecca West's *Cousin Rosamond* trilogy, in progress between 1957 and 1985, or earlier, of Dorothy Richardson's groundbreaking *Pilgrimage* sequence, begun in 1915 and running to thirteen volumes. Closer still perhaps to Manning was

Storm Jameson, with whom she became acquainted during the years leading up to the war.[103] *Mirror in Darkness*, Jameson's autobiographical fictional sequence published during the 1930s, anticipates Manning's trilogies in many respects, notably in its careful dovetailing of the personal and political and in its use of a quintessential anti-romance format as a means of accessing broader ideological positions on class, sexuality and fascism. Though it moves beyond the scope of this study, Jameson's work might well be explored further as a model for Manning, particularly as regards its situation of the female body as a metaphoric site for political statement: the hysterectomy episode of the last volume in her series is a dynamic means of conveying an ethical stagnation in her political community, a symbolic strategy echoed by Manning in the use of miscarried pregnancies as a device in both *School for Love* and *The Rain Forest*.

There is potential, then, to adjust commentary grounded in the traditional shape of masculine epic and to explore how Manning's work develops focus on the position – politically, spatially and in the narrative – of the female subject. In future discussions, such readings might follow, for example, a distinct school of feminist criticism by attending to the representation of corporeality in her work. There are references throughout the trilogies to Harriet's physical presence, or, rather, *lack* of presence. In constant comparison to Guy's bulk and stamina, she is depicted in terms of her 'thinness', her frailty, her insubstantial physique. Her weight loss in the course of the Balkan episodes is sustained, and by the time the couple reach Athens, where food becomes worryingly scarce, she is visibly almost at starvation point, as a soldier remarks in the military canteen where she works.[104] In *The Battle Lost and Won* she is hospitalised for amoebic dysentery, her body ravaged further by anxiety and local conditions until she appears as no more 'than a puff of wind' to one observer.[105] Indeed, her progress towards physical diminishment suggestively anticipates her metaphorical 'disappearance' from the text in the final volume of the *Levant Trilogy*: believed to have drowned, she is removed altogether (though temporarily) as a physical entity from Guy's frame of vision, and from the masculine and military plot of the second sequence.

This sense of a Harriet who both shadows and *is* a shadow changes the tenor of the trilogy texts, forcing the reader to negotiate her *tangential* presence within them, her subject position as self-consciously adjacent to but often countering the masculine epic figure. An accidentally apposite response to her, in this respect, came from J.B. Priestley, who noted in a letter to Reggie Smith that, though he and his wife much admired Manning's creation of a wartime atmosphere in the *Balkan Trilogy*, they disapproved of the character of Harriet, 'who was not as a heroine should be'. Manning's response to the comment comes across as equally apposite. 'Poor Harriet! . . . I have been in despair and wonder if the only people who can tolerate her are those who have pictured her as me. To those who cannot overlay (and clarify) her by reference to me, is she merely a shadow?'[106] Yes, and pertinently so: Harriet functions as a signifier in this way of physical, emotional and even geographical dissipation, registering through her insubstantiality the successive political anxieties that shadow the fiction as a whole.

The present study is largely concerned, however, with recovering Manning's presence in the context of the Second World War and its novelistic legacies. In the chapters that follow, the relationship between her writing and her experience of place and history is explored in detail. Reading the sequence of her novels in the context of the war which inspired them, and taking account in the process of a political and ideological climate that changed beyond recognition over the intervening years, creates innumerable problems of reading. The nature of this material makes it difficult to avoid the pitfalls of determinism, anachronism, and even the tempting byways of biographical speculation. Accepting this, my hope is simply to illuminate the landscapes of Manning's wartime displacements, to assess what critical purpose, if any, her novels aimed to serve and to understand in turn how a fictional oeuvre of such sustained atmospheric integrity came to be written across a span of four long and difficult post-war decades.

Chapter Two

The Balkan Trilogy:

Romania and the far end of Europe

In the summer of 1940 the Athene Palace was the last cosmopolitan stage on which post-world-war Europe and the new-order Europe made a joint appearance. There was, of course, the Hotel Aviso in Lisbon, Portugal, but there the old society, harried and terrified, just waited around for the boats to America. There still was the Serbsky Kral in Belgrade, Jugoslavia, where the two orders mingled, but here the setting as well as the cast lacked glamour. In the Bregues in Geneva or the Dunapalato in Budapest, there was no play on at all. Only in the Athene Palace, a glamorous setting in the traditional style of European Grand Hotels, the cast of post-world-war Europe and the cast of the new order, all-star casts both, still had equal billing and the play itself was full of suspense.

R.G. Waldeck[1]

'At the first mention of going to Roumania, a great many persons, as did myself, would take down their atlas and open the map', wrote Sacheverell Sitwell at the beginning of his account of a four-week visit to the country in 1937. The efforts of locating this exotic destination 'at the far end of Europe' were more than worthwhile, he continued, delighting over a land rich in agriculture and food stocks, picturesque – if one overlooked a few seemingly inappropriate twentieth-century innovations – in its ancient landscapes and peasantry, and well ruled since his return to the throne some seven years earlier by a solid and amiable King Carol II. The travel writer's confidence in this obscure and romantic territory was ill-founded, however, and indeed in many respects already obsolete. The Romanian monarchy would shortly be revealed as one of the most corrupt in Europe, Romanian peasantry the most disaffected and oppressed. Sitwell's visit took place at a time of tense political transition in a country already fractured by ethnic and economic discrepancies and now threatened too by European conflict on its many vulnerable borders. In his introduction to Sitwell's account, the travel writer Patrick Leigh Fermor was obliged to adjust his predecessor's portrait considerably, pointing out its grievous misrecognition of reality. 'By 1938', he wrote, 'Romania was already clouding over with the threat of a war that nobody had their heart in; when it burst, the country was dragged into a chain of events that ended in half a century of tyranny from which it has only recently half emerged'.[2]

Olivia Manning arrived in Bucharest with Reggie Smith two weeks after her marriage, on 3 September 1939. The couple would leave again just over a year later in October 1940, as German troops and the Gestapo were bedding down in the city. Given this timeframe, the country to which she came as a new bride was far from stable. Historically bound up with the 'Balkan problem' (despite the persistent efforts of Romanians to detach themselves from the Slavic identity this connoted), Romania shared much of the insecurity of her neighbouring states and regions, a victim, like them, of the tendency of great powers to use this fraught post-Habsburg landscape as a political playground.[3] The country's modern difficulties lay deep in a convoluted European past. Romanian insecurity was not simply a product of wartime (when the country was officially designated as neutral) but of diverse social, political and ethnic neuroses accumulated over a long history of invasion, counter-invasion, geographical reconstitution and border realignment, all hampering its struggle to emerge from feudalism into a modern independent nation.

Manning's sensitivity to this volatile and evolutionary social landscape is evident throughout the first volume of her *Balkan Trilogy* and particularly in her portraits of the capital city, its centre swarming with 'minor government officials and poor clerks, a generation struggling out of the peasantry', its merchant laneways peopled by 'ringletted Orthodox Jews' and its outskirts teeming with 'peasants in their astrakhan caps' (*BT*, p. 17). Her descriptions also detail, famously, the bourgeois repositories of the city: the Athénée Palace hotel; the central boulevard Calea Victoriei with its elegant shops and cafés; the restaurants like Capşa's and luxury grocers like Dragomirs; even the fading elegance of the Cişmigiu gardens, where the Pringles stroll through the changing seasons. These represent the '*lux nebun*' – the insane luxury – of the capital's brief heyday at the heart of old imperial Europe. In Manning's rich though melancholy descriptions, suggests Vesna Goldsworthy, the city found its literary Canaletto. Contemporary reviewers took the trilogy's colourful depiction of the Romanian capital to be its most distinguishing feature, and a vivid treatment of the era, with Jocelyn Brooke in *The Times* suggesting that Manning (if forgiven her tendency to subordinate characters to landscape) should be praised for so accurately conveying 'the atmosphere of the squalid, corrupt and inevitably doomed city; the dust and the glare, the smells, the horrible beggars, the smart café life, the increasing nerviness and tension of that torrid summer of 1940'.[4]

Beyond its provision of local colour, however, Bucharest is also the backdrop to some of the most politically and historically precise material of Manning's entire wartime oeuvre. Specifically, she tracks the convoluted triangular struggle for power which took place immediately before and during the first year of war between King Carol (damned alongside his Jewish mistress, Elena Lupescu), the Transylvanian-based peasant party, led by Iuliu Maniu (and championed in the novels by communist activist David Boyd), and the fascist Legion of the Archangel Michael – better known through its political wing as the Iron Guard. The Guardists had risen to prominence in the pre-war years under the supposed visionary and rabidly antisemitic Romanian nationalist, Corneliu Z. Codreanu: in 1938, the king had Codreanu imprisoned on a false charge and secretly executed, reporting to his followers that their leader had been shot while trying to escape. In revenge, the Iron Guard assassinated Carol's prime minister, Armand Călinescu, in September of the following year (the shots are overheard by the newly arrived Harriet Pringle), and the country descended into a maelstrom of massacres, assassinations and political intrigue. On the wider horizon meanwhile, both the Soviet Union and Germany were advancing on an oil-rich territory which Britain and France, for all their promises and guarantees, would be unable to protect. After losing the region of Bessarabia and some of northern Bukovina to the Soviets in June 1940, Romania was reluctantly drawn into the Axis camp and, in August of that year, under an agreement drawn up by the German foreign minister von Ribbentrop, ordered to cede almost half of Transylvania to neighbouring Hungary. It is at the news of this cataclysmic loss – the loss of their emotional touchstone and their foothold in Western Europe – that Harriet Pringle sees Romanians weeping in the streets. In September, the Iron Guard finally forced the king to abdicate and the country, now under German control, came under the harsh rule of military dictator and pro-German nationalist Ion Antonescu.

Manning's attempts to harness the detail and sequence of this material in the first two novels of her *Balkan Trilogy* – *The Great Fortune* (1960) and *The Spoilt City* (1962) – convey her willingness to foreground the domestic convulsions of this troubled country over the course of the war's opening act. Her precise (and, on occasion, laboured) tracking of diplomatic manoeuvres, including the various international conferences and treaties which would eventually determine Romania's fate, indicate her heightened sense of the novel's responsibility to hard historical fact. Crucially in these novels, larger international themes are also engaged and broader questions raised about the concept of Europe in a *post-war* climate shadowed by guilt and uncertainty over appeasement, or the plight of Europe's Jewish population, or, again, the perceived betrayal to the Soviets by the West of the smaller nations (including Czechoslovakia and Yugoslavia). In writing superficially characterised by the standard templates of wartime travelogue but strategically employing, too, the discernible vampiric tropes of nineteenth-century Gothic, Manning confronts in her fiction the paranoid interplay of political hegemony between Western and Eastern Europe, between major state and developing nation, and between dominant culture and minority voice.

In particular, the opening volumes of the Balkan sequence display a sustained attention to two overarching pressures on Romanian society during the late 1930s. The first, obviously, relates to the fact of Soviet ambitions on the political horizon. The trilogy was finally composed in the early 1960s and against the backdrop of the Cold War, but Manning purposefully avoids the tug of hindsight in this respect. Her work plays out nevertheless as a subtext the issue of an imminent Soviet advance on Romania, combining this with the author's hallmark narrative excursions into the naivety of the British left and its communist romance, the indulgence marked out in both Guy Pringle and his ally David Boyd (the character closely based on one of the Smiths' contemporaries in Romania, Hugh Seton-Watson).[5] David and Guy 'resembled each other in outlook, both believing that a Marxist economy was the only remedy for the feudal mismanagement of Eastern Europe' (*BT*, p. 308), with Boyd insisting on the need for Britain to liaise with Maniu's peasant party in a rejection of the 'dictator king' and as a means of resisting at the same time the pull of the German leadership (*BT*, p. 375). In 1940, when the Russians retrieve the disputed northern region of Bessarabia and put to flight its grief-stricken nobles and landowners, Harriet Pringle raises the question of larger Soviet territorial ambitions, realising that, beneath the temporary fog of war, 'the Communists, with their ungodly Marxist creed, were more dreaded here than the Nazis' (*BT*, p. 292). At no stage does her credulous husband admit to such dangers, however, and only the world-weary hack Mortimer Tufton will acknowledge the implications of a long history of Soviet encroachment south into the country: '"The fact is", he concluded, "the friendship of Russia has been more disastrous to Rumania than the enmity of the rest of the world"'(*BT*, p. 298).

Secondly, Manning raises a parallel spectre – one even closer to the heart of Romanian society during the late 1930s – in the virulent fascism of the Iron Guard. Even before their successful coup forcing the abdication of King Carol II, and despite the inconsistency of their relationship to Antonescu and the German military mission to Romania, the Guardist faction rose to great heights of coercive power and even popularity within the country itself during the war (indeed, Harriet Pringle is not entirely surprised when her own landlord appears one morning dressed in the Guardist uniform). The fiction encompasses the historical reality of the Iron Guard but Manning also uses the movement to represent more broadly the trajectories of unbridled nationalism and ethnic idealism rampant in a small nation, spurred on by international manipulation or, worse, neglect. At the heart of this enterprise she locates the predicament of Jewish Romania, a subject highly sensitive in view of a history during the 1930s of pogroms and brutal purges, and the attempt of the wartime regime in the country to establish its own version of the Final Solution. Manning's Jews are not straightforward as victims, and her representation of Bucharest's Jewish society through the Druckers – the Jewish banking family briefly befriended by the Pringles – picks up a thread of ambivalence on this topic explored in her earlier Palestine-set novel,

School for Love (to be discussed in Chapter Five). Their depiction in the *Balkan Trilogy* is at once a critique of a Jewish non-conformity within an unsympathetic Europe *and* a recognition of their desperate vulnerability to the prejudice of the age. In the background, meanwhile, more ruthless and determined than the Nazis themselves, Romania's fascists emerge as the Jewish nemesis, a monstrous byproduct of European political deformity. The Iron Guard not only wanted a 'pure Romanian race', Manning later explained, but were determined to pursue this through policies based on the most extreme practices of ethnic and religious eradication. 'It had taken the Germans six years to root the Jews out of public life', she reported. 'The Guardists declared their intention of doing it in one.'[6]

If the *Balkan Trilogy* aspires to a high degree of political precision in its treatment of wartime events, it also draws back from purely journalistic recreation. The fictional vehicle of the Pringles' relationship is key in this respect. Critical and popular readings of the sequence simply as an account of a strained wartime marriage have failed to discern the compositional and conceptual strategy through which Manning maps an autobiographical narrative on to a political landscape so that each informs and, at a stretch, allegorises the other. In the growing uneasiness of the couple's marital relations, and in the patterned breaching of contract into which the Romanian context forces the Pringles, we recognise, together with Harriet, the marital partnership loosening and faltering in parallel with the disintegration of international agreements. Concepts of alliance, union, protection and then exclusion and betrayal shape the first year of the marriage as they shape, simultaneously, the early progress of the war in Europe. Distinct stages or moments in the Pringles' relationship are contrapuntal to the political events that also bind them. Just as the journey to Eastern Europe is a crossing from the familiar to the strange, so is their marriage a journey into alien territory. On the train to Bucharest, hearing Guy break into Romanian to speak to some fellow travellers, Harriet is suddenly aware of a gulf between them. 'Though she would have claimed to know about him everything there was to be known, she was now beginning to wonder if she really knew anything' (*BT*, p. 14).

Beyond this anatomy of marital strain, the two initial volumes of the trilogy also negotiate Harriet Pringle's persistent exclusion from the community so easily assembled by her extrovert husband. Doubtless this again extends from biographical reality. The diplomat Ivor Porter, who knew the Smiths in Bucharest ('him a little too woolly, Olivia a little too severe') recalled Manning's frequent anti-social attitude and reserve, although with hindsight he also acknowledged the difficulties of her isolation from the Romanian scene and, in all probability, her loneliness. Reggie Smith, Porter claims in his account, continued to have relationships with other women in Bucharest as if his marriage had never taken place: 'Cut off from her own country with war approaching, without friends or even the language to help her, she watched her young marriage breaking up, seemed incapable or unwilling to do anything about it, and hated the place where it was happening.'[7] Denis Hills, another contemporary appointed during the same period to the British Council, recalls Manning in similar terms: 'She was not very approachable – she had a sharp tongue and she was not finding it easy to accept Reggie's gregarious ways and the corrupt atmosphere of a Balkan city.'[8]

On the back of biographical circumstances, however, the fiction develops Harriet's exclusion towards an important thematic current, providing what critic Phyllis Lassner has read as a distinctly female narrative of war: '[A]s a result of being marginalized by her husband's play-acting, the forces of war, and the literary marriage plot, Harriet's point of view becomes increasingly depressed, reflecting not only her own position but the unremitting necessity of fighting a war whose sweep and horrors so often obscure its goals.' Against the broad and dynamic canvas of characters and plot, she is configured with what Lassner sees as an ironic refusal of agency, becoming almost a sleepwalker throughout the progress of the epic and a visibly redundant presence in a masculine orientation of events. Harriet, in short, 'is allowed no space in the theatre of world war in which to construct her identity of expression'.[9]

From this perspective, Harriet's marginality is a subtle critique of a dominant masculine war rhetoric, with Lassner's reading endorsing a pattern in which the protagonist of the epic is consistently positioned as liminal or peripheral to its key events. Despite her frequent attempts to stake her claim both to Guy and to her rightful place in a country veering towards disaster, Harriet's natural inclination is to side with those 'feminised' others on the fringe of circumstances – the abandoned and elderly English governesses stranded in Bucharest, for example, or the young Jewish deserter Sasha Drucker. In his political and social passions, meanwhile, Guy repeatedly ostracises her from the company he keeps; his frequent retreats to the left-wing intellectuals' meeting place, the café *Doi Trandafiri* (in English, the 'two roses') leave her standing – literally on one occasion – outside. The intensity of his friendship with David Boyd, meanwhile, the two men bound together in their political self-belief, further excludes her from an ideological communion in which she cannot invest, and from the seemingly endless impassioned debates they conduct with Klein, the Jewish economist:

> She sighed at the thought of so much talk. It was not, she told herself, that she was unappreciative, but the impersonal quickly tired her. She felt she was a little out of it, a little jealous.
>
> Perhaps sensing this, Klein turned smiling to her to include her. He said: 'So here we are all Left-side men, eh? And Doamna Preen-gel? She is, too, Left-side?'
>
> 'No,' said Harriet, 'I am fighting the solitary battle of the reactionary.' (*BT*, p. 177)

Harriet is politically sidelined and physically peripheralised – the latter predicament exacerbated when Guy stages his production of Shakespeare's *Troilus and Cressida*. The play itself, appositely chosen for its juxtaposition of a public theatre of war with the fraught world of private relationships, becomes a battle-campaign, with Guy as its general, marshalling and orchestrating the cast as if in tandem with the theatre of war beyond. His speech to the assembled cast and crew before the opening performance is a parody of military rhetoric, echoing Churchill's address after Dunkirk (mentioned by Manning a few pages earlier in the novel). Guy's tactless replacement of Harriet with the coquettish Romanian beauty Sophie Oresanu in the role of Cressida results in his wife being moved *physically* to the edge of the stage, overhearing rehearsals from a distance (and rather patronisingly charged with overseeing the costume design) but cut off from the central performance itself, which she will view in the end from within the audience.[10]

Such incidents manifest a concern with patterns of female exclusion running through both the Balkan and Levant sequences. Manning depicts a domestic and civilian landscape marked with the scars of female embattlement and the bruises of spatial claims for legitimacy. For all her apparent passivity, Harriet is constantly engaged in a struggle for room and space: during the incident at the Athénée Palace hotel, for example, when she sticks pins in the backsides of the assembled Guardist sympathisers who will not let the English party pass, or when her evening promenade through the streets of Bucharest becomes, Romanian fashion, an act of territorial warfare:

> The promenade was for her a trial of physical strength. Though leisurely, the Rumanians were ruthless in their determination to keep on the pavement. Only peasants or servants could be seen walking in the road. The men might, under pressure, yield an inch or two, but the women were as implacable as steam-rollers. Short and strong, they remained bland-faced while wielding buttocks and breasts as heavy as bladders of lard.
>
> The position most fiercely held was the inner pavement beside the shop windows. Guy, too temperate, and Harriet, too light-boned for the fray, were easily thrust out to the kerb, where Guy gripped Harriet's elbow to keep her from slipping into the gutter. She broke from him, saying: 'I'll walk in the road. I'm not a Rumanian. I can do what I like.' (*BT*, p. 27)

These manoeuvres both parody and critique the international climate. Harriet's individual campaign for position and status slowly gains ground, undermining the protocols established by an international cultural and political regime. Her ostensibly passive role is underwritten by her active presence as an interruption to a masculine narrative based on political and military strategy, even if this is simply achieved through an attitude of truculence, petulance and reserve. In the same vein she uncovers and sabotages Guy's planned participation in the ludicrous *Boy's Own*-style plot to blow up the Iron Gates and block the oil and trade routes down the Danube, a move that ultimately leads to the expulsion from the country of the unlikely British secret service agent Commander Sheppy.[11] For all her negativity, Harriet *does* produce a positive charge of sorts therefore, simply as a doubting thorn in the side of Guy's blithe leftism and in an Allied war narrative based on hopelessly outdated versions of what Europe in fact constituted. Her faltering marriage envelops an ironic critique of international military strategy and territorial ambition, and produces a deep scepticism with regard to both personal and international relationships.

When Harriet Pringle pauses to look down at a stream during a trip to the Predeal mountains, north of Bucharest, the diplomat Dobbie Dobson observes that, were she an eighteenth-century traveller, she would be standing on the boundary between the Austrian and Turkish empires (*BT*, p. 518). His flippant remark is a reminder of Romania's position as a newly formed nation caught between imperial aggressors, struggling to keep afloat in the strong wake of those empires even as their ambitious post-war replacements lined up on her borders. Romania, for all its would-be assertions of democratic emancipation in the early years of the century, merged in the imperial mind-set with its smaller neighbours, subjected to ideological, ethnic and political definitions persisting since the Ottoman occupation. 'Balkanism', the term conventionally given to this construct of imperial desires and anxieties projected onto the region, is elaborately defined by historian Maria Todorova in her 1997 study *Imagining the Balkans*; in tandem with Todorova's work, Vesna Goldsworthy has analysed, in *Inventing Ruritania* (1998), the recurrent stereotyping of the Balkans, including Romania, in Western literature and culture, from Byron and Bram Stoker to Lawrence Durrell and Rebecca West. While not all such representations are malign by any means, Goldsworthy suggests that, as a discourse, they none the less contribute to ingrained Western perspectives on a Central and Eastern European landscape. The parallels with Edward Said's thesis of Orientalism become self-evident in Goldsworthy's development (from its usage in Anthony Hope's 1894 *The Prisoner of Zenda*) of the concept of 'Ruritanianism' to reflect this systematic cultural categorisation of the Balkans by its Western neighbours – the travellers, explorers and writers who painted its regions across an exotic spectrum of barbarism, retardation, corruption and superstition.[12]

Various other commentators who have examined the concept of 'Balkanism' in Western culture from the Enlightenment to the communist collapse (a subject of renewed academic interest since 1989) confirm the surprising endurance of the discourse historically, bringing particular focus to its strategic redeployment during the Cold War and, again, in the current context of European enlargement.[13] Such studies have confirmed too, by tracing a long literary heritage of travelogue, memoir and both literary and popular fiction produced by Western Europeans, recognisable similarities to structures illuminated by postcolonial theorists; perceptions, in short, of Eastern Europe as an antithetical territory to a Western counterpart grounded in the values of Christianity and the Enlightenment, and set in contrast by the forces of barbarianism, superstition, and the unpredictability of both Orthodox and Islamic religious influences. But what has also emerged is a key point of deviation from the colonial model: that the Balkans are often perceived as a greater threat to European stability than Arab or Asian regions because of their location *inside* the boundaries of the European continent, and, indeed, because of the frequency with which their constituent groups may share in, rather than deviate from, characteristics of Western European religion, ethnicity and culture. For Goldsworthy, Balkan identity is conceived of as 'an ambivalent oscillation between "Europeanness" and "Oriental difference"', or, as Andrew Hammond puts it, seen 'less as the "alien other" . . . than as the "outsider within", an entity whose European location and marks of similarity to Western European culture produce a very particular form of anxiety'.[14]

How relevant are such arguments to Manning's fiction? Certainly, in a range of commentaries on the subject, the *Balkan Trilogy* has been cited frequently, and Manning criticised just as frequently, for upholding in full a hierarchical literary Balkanism. Extracting a series of the author's descriptive episodes from the Bucharest-set novels, Hammond argues that Manning sustains in her treatment of the Romanian social and political landscape a highly conventional reading of the country, emphasising its primitive Oriental decrepitude. Moreover, he suggests, the publication of this portrait gave it ideological purpose in a specific period: 'its publication during the 1960s not only helped to reinstall the traditionalist modes of Balkanism during the Cold War period, but also – with the ongoing popularity of the work – to maintain those modes in circulation right up until the end of the 1980s'.[15] Pia Brinzeau is among a number of Romanian critics to take a similar view: examining a tradition of travel writing and fiction about Romania, from Thomas Hope's *Anastasius or Memoirs of a Modern Greek* (1819) to Malcolm Bradbury's *Dr Criminale* (1992), she aligns Manning with Conrad and Forster as writers of imperial culture clash, suggesting that her trilogy represents the 'repellent' exoticism of the Balkans through Harriet Pringle's reactions on arriving in a country where 'she is unable to offload the debris of accumulated cultural imperialism'.[16]

More admiring of Manning's descriptive skills and, indeed, of her attentiveness to issues of marginality exposed within the country, Vesna Goldsworthy none the less includes her work alongside that of Evelyn Waugh and Lawrence Durrell on the same landscape, in showing 'the persistence and continuous attraction of certain types of Balkan imagery'.[17]

And indeed Manning's Bucharest novels *do* fit into a category of writing which portrays Central and Eastern Europe generally as a region of instability and unpredictability under a series of corrupt and primitive regimes. To see them as contextualised and even determined by the Cold War is an ambitious critical stretch, however: they reflect more readily a literary era existing before a generation of Cold War thriller writers had changed the contours of the novel of international relations. Despite its dates of publication, the *Balkan Trilogy* registers clearly the novelist traits of its original period of conception (and particularly its origins in the unfinished wartime novel composition *Guests at a Marriage*, the manuscript held with Manning's papers at the University of Texas).[18] Moreover, the work echoes the pragmatics of inter-war travelogue in its comparatively genteel narrative of geographical and diplomatic displacement; one might compare it, for example, to Evelyn Waugh's 1947 novella *Scott-King's Modern Europe*, with its invention of the Balkanesque country of 'Neutralia', largely inspired by his experience of Yugoslavia. The proximity of Manning's fiction to the travel writing of this earlier period is more than apparent too in the Romanian novels, where she clearly echoes images and phrases from Sitwell's *Roumanian Journey* (cited above) as elements of background material, and perhaps refers also to Derek Patmore's travelogue *Invitation to Roumania*, published in 1939.[19]

It is worth noting at the same time that Manning plays on an inter-war literature based on European rail travel, the dominant metaphor (and reality) of connection and disparity in the period, used famously in novels of the period such as Graham Greene's *Stamboul Train* (1932) and Agatha Christie's *Murder on the Orient Express* (1934), both set on the famous train of Christie's title. In particular, Greene's dramatic short thriller, with its conflation of Jew, murderer, revolutionary and chorus girl thrown into sudden cataclysmic proximity when their train stops just inside the Yugoslavian border, offers a particularly aggressive and, for some, even racist version of the Oriental reversal of order. Manning's use of the Simplon Orient Express as the stage on which to introduce not only her two main characters, Guy and Harriet, but also the White Russian freeloader Yakimov (together with the unnamed, ticketless German refugee who is ejected from the carriage) offers yet another nod to Greene in her writing, though of course it captures too her own experience of the train as a less than glamorous entity, reduced in wartime to 'a jumble of dirty carriages', as she describes it elsewhere.[20]

This standard narrative of arrival in the East also enables Manning to engage tropes of Gothic convention harking *further* back along a literary time-line to Bram Stoker, who famously exploited the associations of the region in *Dracula* (1897) and again in his less well-known tale of a mythical Eastern Europe, *The Lady of the Shroud* (1909), in which an English adventurer strays into the mythical but recognisably Balkan 'Land of the Blue Moutains'. In *Dracula*, Jonathan Harker's journey into Transylvania and his initial disturbing encounters with its strange lands and customs set a paradigmatic shape to the West–East encounter that subsequent writers doubtless found difficult to ignore.[21] Manning's opening sequence can be read as a self-conscious echoing of Stoker's classic tale. In *The Great Fortune*, the Orient Express is described making its way through the familiar and safe landscapes of France and Italy towards what Harriet perceives as 'the end of the known world' (*BT*, p. 11). Eventually, it crosses the flat Slovenian plain and comes to the Romanian frontier, where she looks out into the night to try to see the mountains and the pine woods. 'As she gazed out into the dark heart of the forest, she began to see moving lights. For an instant a grey dog-shape skirted the rail, then returned to darkness. The lights, she realized, were the eyes of beasts' (*BT*, p. 14). Later, in the darkness of Bucharest itself, her impressions of an animalistic and predatory country return, together with a sense that, here, civilisation is merely a veneer over an essential barbarity. Driving at night in a *trăsură* (a horse-drawn carriage) with her husband down the deserted main boulevard, Calea Victoriei, 'it seemed to her she could smell in the wind those not so distant regions of mountains and fir-forest where wolves and bears, driven by hunger, haunted the villages in the winter snow-light. And the wind was harsher than any wind she had ever known. She shivered, feeling isolated in a country that was to her not only foreign but alien' (*BT*, p. 123).

The early chapters of *The Great Fortune* in particular rely heavily on a conflation of the Gothic with the picturesque as a mode of vision.

Harriet's senses are assaulted from all sides by the alien and the barbaric. The detailed and at times almost set-piece travelogue descriptions of Bucharest's beggars and gypsies underline the abject difference of this country, as do the couple's strained smiles on breathing in the 'peasant stench' of the crowd in the picturesque city gardens of Cişmigiu. At Pavel's, the open-air restaurant where they dine on Harriet's first night in the city, the singer Florica gives herself over to an animal passion, her violent gypsy howl ending in 'an elemental screech' (*BT*, p. 38). Frequently, the exotic quality of the landscape merges with the Gothic shadows of an alien territory, as in the description of a carriage ride Harriet and Guy take through the night-time streets of Bucharest, when the street-lights show up 'a phantom horse, a skeleton in a battered hide' and the huge figure of the coachman, 'a vast cottage loaf in a velvet robe'. He is, Guy explains to Harriet, one of the notorious sights of the city: a Skopit, or a member of the Russian sect of eunuchs who mutilate themselves in a frenzied orgiastic ritual. 'She gazed at the vast velvet backside of the eunuch before her, then she gazed out at the dark reaches of the Muntenia plain, on which the city stood like a bride-cake on a plate. "A barbarous country," she said' (*BT*, p. 30).[22]

Yet to dismiss this novelistic approach on the grounds of its subscription to clichés of Balkanism or Ruritanianism misses the degree of descriptive and social responsibility evident in Manning's writing. It blurs, furthermore, the extent to which her engagement of various Stokeresque tropes was a deliberate means of raising contemporary anxieties about Eastern Europe's riven and repressed identities, and also the extent to which her writing responds politically to the implications of Romania's wartime realignments. Even before her Bucharest experience and certainly by the time of the trilogy's composition, she had access to various other accounts of the country's condition, quite different in focus to the imaginative and travel-based accounts noted above. Of particular importance in this respect was the primary (pre-war) authoritative source on the history of modern Romania, the Scottish historian Robert Seton-Watson, whose *History of the Roumanians* had been published in 1934. As a likely source for Manning, the tenor of this work is significant: Robert Seton-Watson (father of Reggie's friend Hugh Seton-Watson) had made several visits to Romania before the war and subsequently maintained links with the peasant leaders Iuliu Maniu and Alexander Vaida. He was regarded as an authority not only on the background to Romania's precarious route to nationhood but also as an advocate for a paternalist West to recognise the significance of minority cultures and ethno-regional diversity in the Balkans generally.[23] His 1934 historical study testifies to the genuine constitutional and ideological interests which countered, at least in the inter-war years, the continuing evolution of a more opportunist 'Ruritanian' discourse based on memoir, travelogue and fiction.

In this respect, one can see an ambiguity in the novel's treatment of the Bucharest landscape, and a split in Harriet's perspective as she attempts to distinguish between an immediate political and social reality and the stuff of Ruritanian legend. Even Manning's own ironic use of the term 'Ruritanian' in the fiction suggests a will to undermine its value; discussing the unlikelihood of the Jewish banker Drucker being given a fair trial, for example, it is the diplomat Dugdale who invokes the cliché of Romania's barbarism: '"Aren't we in Ruritania?" he said. "What do you expect?"' (*BT*, p. 156). The English teacher Clarence Lawson is also given to standard Western European prejudices on the country's disorder: '"If Rumania had been as long under the Austrians as she was under the Turks, she might be civilized by now"' (*BT*, p. 88); or elsewhere: '"This may be Ruritania, but it is no longer a joke"' (*BT*, p. 377). This is *not* Harriet's terminology, however. Increasingly she comes to challenge or resist the idiom in which the country is contained, refusing the collegiate perspectives of a diplomatic and expatriate corps with which she finds herself so frequently at odds.

The Bucharest-set novels also engage a vivid realism, intersecting with their episodes of Balkanist cliché. In 1961 Manning wrote in reply to Jocelyn Brooke's query regarding the extent to which elements of the work were taken 'from life': 'Yes, I think Bucharest was more or less as it appears in my book, although people like Derek Patmore adored it and give glowing pictures of life there as being compounded exclusively of princesses, pearls, wonderful parties, drink and rich food', she explained, continuing of Patmore's version, 'When I asked him why he never spoke of the beggars, he said, "Oh, one mustn't mention things like that. The Rumanians wouldn't like it."'[24] Harriet's progression as a character is evident in her gradual loss of faith in a Ruritanian romance and her struggle to detach the country's actual condition from its picturesque image, as in the passage below with its veiled criticism, we might assume, of Sitwell's 1937 portrait:

> Before she left England, she had read books written by travellers in Rumania who had given a picture of a rollicking, open-hearted, happy, healthy peasantry, full of music and generous hospitality. They were, it was true, mad about music. Music was their only outlet. They made themselves drunk on it. As for the rest, she had seen nothing of it. The peasants in this city were starved, frightened figures, scrawny with pellagra, wandering about in a search for work or making a half-hearted attempt to beg. (*BT*, p. 123)

The effect is an inconsistency of perspective, which switches from glimpses of exotic excess in 'this strange, half Oriental capital' (*BT*, p. 303) – the orgiastic revelry of the dissipated Romanian Phanariot aristocrats in the Athénée Palace, or the grotesque sensuality of Yakimov's landlady, who reclines half-naked on her couch eating Turkish delight (scenes closely echoing Derek Patmore's account of Bucharest) – to Harriet's focus on what is visible, rather than projected: the country's economic and social degradation. In this respect Manning's study of how the 'great fortune' of Romania was lost takes its lead in the end from Tolstoy rather than Stoker, her debt to the Russian novelist evident in the rich and lengthy descriptions of Harriet's encounter with the frozen deathly grip of Romania: Bucharest, when the snow finally stops falling, is revealed 'white as a ghost city agleam beneath a pewter sky':

> Beggars were now more plentiful than ever. Hundreds of destitute peasant families, their breadwinners conscripted, had been driven by winter into the capital, where, it was believed, a magical justice was dispensed. They would stand for hours in front of the palace, the law courts, the prefecture or any other large, likely-looking building. They dared not enter. When cold and hunger defeated them at last, they would wander off in groups to beg – women, children and ancient, creeping men. Lacking the persistence of professionals, they were easily discouraged. Many of them did no more than crouch crying in doorways. Some sought out the famous Cişmigiu, that stretched from its gates like a vast sheeted ballroom. Some slept there at night beneath the trees; others took themselves up to the Chaussée. Few of them survived long. Each

> morning a cart went round to collect the bodies dug from the snow. Many of these were found in bunches, frozen inseparable, so that they were thrown as they were found, together, into the communal grave. (*BT*, p. 166)

Manning can be defended then against charges of an exploitative 'Ruritanianism' and shown to be a sympathetic if not entirely forgiving witness to the country's plight. At the same time there are inflections of a Gothic mode which deserve further attention here in relation to Manning's treatment of the shifting identities of wartime Europe. The critics Andrew Smith and Jeff Wallace have identified the persistence of a Victorian Gothic mode within a modernist canon (and visible, they suggest, in T.S. Eliot, D.H. Lawrence, Elizabeth Bowen, Virginia Woolf and Djuna Barnes), which serves to register anxieties of the collective body caused by perceived threats to the human species, or to concepts of race, nation-state, and culture.[25] It makes critical sense to extend this useful structure of identification to a Second World War literature in which the marks of anxiety – particularly those connected by popular novels of the period to 'liminal' threats from infiltrators, fifth columnists and spies – are sustained and recurrent. In this context Manning's employment of Gothic elements in her configuration of wartime Romania suggests an entirely appropriate, rather than a simply sensationalist, harnessing of a distinct literary genre.

The portrayal of Eastern Europe as superficially, at least, a quintessentially Gothic location also aligns Harriet Pringle with literary heroines such as Charlotte Brontë's Lucy Snowe from *Villette* (1853), the English ingénue who, through her encounters abroad, exposes continental culture in terms of its menacing otherness, evident in any number of dimensions from its deviant Catholicism to its overt sexuality.[26] We see this enacted in Harriet's encounters with the city's beggars: on one particular occasion the scene converges on an act of sexualised physical violation, even rape, reminiscent of nineteenth-century Gothic grotesque. In one of the poorer streets of Bucharest, Strada Lipscani, where the gas-lit windows throw out a greenish glow, Harriet is assaulted by a nightmarish vision of the savage side of Europe:

> When she stopped at a meat stall to buy veal, she became conscious of a sickening smell of decay beside her. Turning, she

> saw an ancient female dwarf who was thrusting the stump of an arm up to her face. She searched hurriedly for a coin and could find nothing smaller than a hundred-*lei* note. She knew it was too much but handed it over. It led, as she feared, to trouble. The woman gave a shrill cry calling to her a troupe of children, who at once set upon Harriet, waving their deformities and begging with a professional and remorseless piteousness.
>
> She took the meat she had bought and tried to escape into the crowd. The children clung like lice. They caught hold of her arms, their faces screwed into the classical mask of misery while they whined and whimpered in chorus. (*BT*, p. 122)

Such scenes allow the country to stage the rupture and even reversal of rational, civil normality: this is a darkness at the heart of an enlightened European land mass. In patterning the novels so, Manning self-consciously renews the imagery and stereotype of her Ruritanianist predecessors as a means of illuminating the deep political, cultural and economic fissures running across Europe in wartime (and well into the decades that followed), with the Gothic idiom recruited to an updated and purposeful rendition of what Romania, in the scheme of European affairs, might serve to represent.[27]

To reinforce the point, the physical instability of this landscape is continually emphasised in the Bucharest novels. Romania is shown as a territory plagued by ongoing border insecurities: its already precarious nationhood still cannot be, in the twentieth century, properly and adequately defined. The constant threat of erupting minoritarian and ethnic conflict across the country as a whole combines with a physical landscape simultaneously subject to constant shifts, transitions and disturbance. Key to this is the process of architectural destruction and rebuilding remarked on intermittently by Harriet and Guy when they arrive in the centre of a city undergoing strategic redesign, with the gradual erasure of its old Austrian–Hungarian identity (the rococo houses and 'Biedermeier prettiness' [*BT*, p. 23] so much admired by Harriet) and the construction in its place of Carol's new royal square, immediately in front of the palace and just outside the Pringles' lodgings. As with everything related to the king – a monarch depicted in the novel as fraudulent in every respect, from his bogus attempts to speak Romanian to his 'contrived' grief over the loss of Romanian territories – there is no confidence in the new construction. Rather, the rebuilding of Bucharest suggests a political lacuna, the dissolution of architectural integrity into simulation, fragility, a lack of authenticity. The process is regarded by the English visitors as uncanny and unnerving. Early in the first novel, Harriet, looking out from her hotel balcony on the Calea Victoriei, observes her husband walking towards her shrouded in smoke dust rising from a new area of demolition:

> Where he had been a moment before, a wall came down. Its fall revealed the interior of a vast white room, fretted with baroque scrolls and set with a mirror that glimmered like a lake. Nearby could be seen the red wallpaper of a café – the famous Café Napoleon that had been the meeting-place of artists, musicians, poets and other natural non-conformists. Guy said that all this destruction had been planned simply to wipe out this one centre of revolt. (*BT*, p. 23)

This instability of place is reflected across the domestic arena and in tandem with the border conflicts over Bessarabia and Transylvania. Like the Pringles' new flat, a cheap construction built with the proceeds of blackmail in a notoriously flimsy apartment block, the country has come to lack stability and conviction. Its desperate fragility is confirmed by the earthquake described in the opening section of *The Spoilt City*, and which Harriet experiences on her balcony: 'She saw, or thought she saw, the cobbles before the church. In terror she put her hand out to hold to something, but it was as though the world had become detached in space. Everything moved with her and there was nothing on which to hold' (*BT*, p. 334).[28]

Beyond the instability of geography and architecture, the political landscape also lends itself to thematic extensions of the Gothic, specifically in Manning's treatment and depiction of the Iron Guard. Initially in the two Bucharest novels, the subject of Romania's fascist legion is veiled in rumour and speculation which emerges largely in relation to fears that Guardist legionnaires, having fled to Germany after the assassination of their leader Codreanu, are now returning, trained and armed by the Nazis, to infiltrate Romanian society. Manning evokes the paranoia surrounding the prospect of this surreptitious invasion on a number of levels, but with perceptible allusion to the kind of Romanian vampire legend drawn out by Stoker (and others such as the Irish writer Sheridan Le Fanu) in the 1890s. Just as Dracula's minions slowly infiltrated England, the Guardists now begin to emerge, discreetly, in the streets of the Romanian capital. At first their presence is restricted to the occasional sighting of a strange figure, different in some indiscernible way from those around him, yet able to blend with the crowds. One wet morning, Harriet Pringle observes such a figure sheltering under the trees outside the Athénée Palace, a silent yet menacing presence:

> The rain had stopped. The young leaves flashed their green against a sky of indigo. The cloud was breaking. A gleam touched the wet tarmac. The young man, although neither beggar nor peasant, remained by the wall with nothing to do apparently but stand there. He was dressed in the city grey much worn by the middle classes, but he was unlike any middle-class Rumanian Harriet had ever seen. He was hard and thin. His was a new sort of face in this town. (*BT*, p. 236)

As the Guardists begin to secure their presence, such sightings become more frequent and the public anxiety surrounding them intensifies to feverish levels. Eventually, having secured an amnesty with the king, they take centre stage in the government under their new leader Horia Sima, whom Harriet witnesses being greeted with fascist salutes as he arrives at the Athénée Palace: a small, lean man 'holding the salute dramatically for some moments, his head thrown back so all might see his hollow, bone-pale face and lank black hair' (*BT*, p. 168).

If there are echoes here of Stoker's Transylvanian count, these recur during the disquieting process through which the memory of the dead Guardist hero Codreanu is gradually revived and reanimated by his followers. Harriet reads the Guardist pamphlets telling the 'true' story of Codreanu's assassination with growing apprehension. The persuasive aura of this supposed visionary is reflected in their descriptions of a saintly man, inspired by the Archangel Michael to redeem Romania by forming the Iron Guard:

> He possessed a mysterious power which was felt by all who approached him. When he appeared, dressed in white, on his white horse, the peasants at once recognized him as the archangel's envoy on earth. His purpose was to unite all Rumanians in brotherhood, not only the living but the souls of the unborn and the dead . . . Codreanu was an immortal. Even now his spirit was moving through the land . . . regathering forces. (*BT*, p. 389)

The associations with an 'undead' element are extended as the situation disintegrates during the early autumn of 1940, and Harriet watches the macabre funeral ceremonies organised by the Guardists for their 'Martyrs', those assassinated in the clamp-down by the king: 'Raised in batches to which were given heroic names like the *Decemvirii* and the *Nicadorii*, the bodies were paraded in giant coffins all over the city and reburied with ceremonies that must be attended by anyone who hoped to maintain any sort of position in public life' (*BT*, p. 477).[29] Like the undead of Transylvanian legend, these names live on, invoked at all the Guardist meetings, appearing even on the editorial board of the Guardist propaganda pamphlets; it is no wonder, Guy Pringle remarks, that 'the Iron Guard is called the "legion of ghosts"'(*BT*, p. 459).

Manning takes various risks in presenting the fascist Guardist presence as Gothic, not least perhaps the risk of sensationalism at the expense of a more exacting political critique, but her strategy in developing this aspect of her historical fiction pays off in the successful creation of an atmosphere of deep suspicion, paranoia, anxiety and insecurity in the two Romanian novels. That the first year of the war in Europe was characterised by such sensibilities, by emotions constantly charged by alarmism and unsubstantiated reports, lends to the authenticity and primacy of her account and reinforces, if anything, its purchase at the same time on a more academic political chronology: 'Bucharest was a city where everything was kept secret and everything, sooner or later, known', Manning wrote later of her experience of the country.

> The people, vivacious, gossip-loving, always talking in cafés, now gave themselves up to a ferment of rumour and counter-rumour, accusation and counter-accusation. The English-speaking

> journalists who frequented the English bar at the Athénée Palace and sent their spies abroad were the first to learn that assassination was a key move in a plot intended to give Germany control over Rumania in the simplest way possible.[30]

Nor are Manning's Gothic metaphors limited to her treatment of the Guardists: this is, after all, a study of the vampiric in wartime across its various international guises with Romania as prime territory, prey to the 'devouring' instincts of both Hitler and Stalin. Germany is referred to as the country's 'voracious' ally (*BT*, p. 453): the Germans, like the Russians, are waiting to 'devour' the country (*BT*, p. 533). It might even be argued that her treatment of the 'well-meaning' Allies, the British Institute with its rapacious cultural evangelism, is shaded in similar colours. Inchcape's insistence on bringing out the odious Lord Pinkrose to lecture at a time of crisis smacks of an all-consuming cronyism and little-Englander greed. That the British engineers stationed in the Ploieşti region are in the country specifically to extract Romanian oil supplies for the Allies is further evidence of an external parasitism, a will to drain the country's precious domestic resources. In parallel terms Manning satirises the journalists who crowd into the English bar in the Athénée Palace, hungry for news of atrocity, depicting in particular the English foreign news reporter Galpin as a blood-sucking grotesque: 'As he drank, his yellow wrist, the wrist-bone like half an egg stuck out rawly from his wrinkled, shrunken, ash-dusty dark suit' (*BT*, p. 299).[31] Romania is rendered Gothic and abject by its own desperate position as victim, relentlessly haggled over and exploited. Nowhere is this better conveyed than in Manning's descriptive tableau of the casino in the faded aristocratic spa resort of Sinai (now Sinaia), where Harriet observes the monstrous figures at the gambling table:

> One man, whose shoulders were abnormally wide but who rose barely eighteen inches above the table, had a vast, formless face, like a milk jelly, glistening with ill-health. Beside him was an ancient, skeletal female, her mouth agape and askew, as though she had died without succour. One male head was abnormally large like a case of giantism. Here and there were faces, not aged and yet not young, having the immaterial look of arrested decay. (*BT*, p. 521)

Through such images, a pre-war version of the country – Sitwell's 1937 version perhaps – is adjusted to a wartime context, with Manning's updated Balkanism deliberately inflecting that of her literary predecessors in order to reinvest her narrative of a fracturing Eastern Europe with fear, trepidation and even elements of horror.

Her most significant use of the Gothic mode in the *Balkan Trilogy*, however, surrounds Manning's treatment of Romania's refugee population. In much of her previous writing, composed during and shortly after the war itself, she dwelt repeatedly on the figure of the refugee as a repository for the anguish and turbulence of Europe. Her wartime short stories, such as 'A Journey' (published in the 1948 collection *Growing Up*), in which a young female reporter is trapped on a train overcrowded with refugees fleeing the Transylvanian town of Cluj before its secession to Hungary, reflect her concern and even obsession with this theme.[32] One of her best short stories of this period, 'In a Winter Landscape', extends the Balkan vampire metaphor into the territory of the refugee in a subtle reading of European abjection. In the story, three English visitors – a married couple and a friend – travel from Bucharest to the mountains for a few days' skiing. *En route* from the slopes to their hotel, they are joined in their train carriage by a Polish soldier, a refugee from the chaos of the German invasion of his country. 'We had seen hundreds like him coming in lorries to Bucharest', the narrator explains. 'One could see them with the windscreens blotted out with mud, mattresses tied to the roofs, the people inside sprawling open-mouthed, their exhaustion overcoming for a while cold and hunger.' The Pole engages the English party in conversation but his attitude of 'sullen self-possession' is truculent and aggressive; he maintains 'the expression of an injured person who hopes his presence is causing you discomfort'. He has no money but accepts their payment of his ticket, a meal and a hotel room without any expression of thanks. They, in turn, begrudge him the responsibility they feel obliged to take for his welfare. When they share a dinner table the English characters fail to understand the Pole's attempts to tell stories of his home, and their awkwardness and lack of compassion are matched by his ingratitude and resentment. His shady presence on the edge of their lives disturbs their equanimity and contaminates their holiday.[33]

This highly atmospheric tale epitomises Manning's attempts to portray the refugee as a disturbance of the complacent British or Western psyche. Its title offers an ironic play on a European visual art tradition of a romantic sublime; here, the peasant picturesque is figuratively replaced by the spectre of social and geographical dispossession. Moreover, the story's setting in the frozen landscape of Europe's most central region provides the symbolic backdrop to what might be considered a wartime version of the vampire tale (indeed, the town in which the travellers decide to stay for a night, still dogged intermittently by the thankless Pole, is recognisable from the text as Sighişoara, the Saxon citadel known in Romanian legend as the birthplace of Vlad Dracul or Dracula). The overlap between Stoker's tale and Manning's is again subtle but discernible. As the characters walk through the ice-cold streets, the presence of the Pole as a graceless, dispossessed Other both caricatures and subverts their own claims to refugee status; when he finally disappears, they remain confused and disturbed, both by his aggression *and* by his need.

Manning's treatment of the European refugee remains, by and large, abstract. For the most part she keeps an uneasy distance from the displaced. In this manner she depicts, for example, the mass arrival of Polish exiles in the city as a perverse form of invasion, threatening and moving in the same instance. Arriving in Bucharest in their hundreds, the Poles seem like an army in defeat, dejected and exhausted as their mud-caked lorries and overloaded cars come to a halt in the city's central squares: 'The windscreens were cracked. The bonnets and wings were pockmarked. Inside the cars, the passengers – men, women and children – lay about, abandoned in sleep. The drivers nodded over their steering wheels' (*BT*, p. 20). She does engage more closely at times nevertheless with a refugee experience through the predicament of her central characters. In the Bucharest novels Harriet and Guy are positioned between the apparent securities of empire and privilege, on which they maintain a grip through the structures of the British Legation and Institute, and the trauma of dislocation. The geographical route they are forced to follow throughout the final *Balkan* volume and *Levant* sequence leads them increasingly further away from the securities of home and towards, instead, the uncertainty and alienation of the wartime refugee. Even in Bucharest they begin to encroach on a kind of refugee identity: Guy, for example, wears clothes that have been collected for distribution to the Polish refugees; Harriet wanders the city alone and without any sense of purpose or belonging; both will experience, at the abrupt end of their Romanian sojourn, a raid on their apartment and a scramble to safety beyond the country's borders. Their insecurity is extended and expanded through the character of Prince Yakimov, whose liminal existence shadows the protagonists in the *Balkan Trilogy*. Yakimov, with his convoluted ethnic origins – half Irish, half White Russian – enjoys the last remnants of the old Habsburg empire, partying with the Phanariot aristocrats in the Athénée Palace and spinning out to their bitter end the spoils of affluence and privilege, tokenised by his now shabby sable-lined coat and his car, the impounded Hispano-Suiza. Yet he is plunged repeatedly into the pitfalls of homelessness and itinerancy, exiled from his own history and from a disorientating present, a pathetic victim of old imperial Europe's collapse.

In contrast to her general allusions to a European refugee presence, however, Manning devotes specific attention to the situation of the Jewish population within Romania. In this respect, the Bucharest sequence retreads some of the ground covered in her Palestine-set novels (to be discussed in Chapter Five). The predicament of Europe's Jews is close to the heart of the *Balkan Trilogy* but Manning is characteristically cautious in her use of hindsight and seems determined to recuperate a contemporaneous wartime prejudice and shortsightedness even under the burden of post-war knowledge. In addition, she uses the Jewish-related material of the Balkan-set novels partially to mirror the theme of Harriet Pringle's exclusion and dissent from the expatriate community, Harriet's close identification with the young Jewish boy Sasha Drucker serving to mirror her own uncertain status and her point of connection therefore to the marginalised and excluded elements within a volatile Europe.

In confronting the subject of Romania's Jewish households and their fate under the Iron Guard, Manning was obliged to deal with a history of antisemitism deeply entrenched in the country's past, a long-term inheritance of prejudice and suppression which reached its height under the Antonescu dictatorship from 1941 to 1944. While much of this history remained obscure until the 1990s, it was clear certainly from post-war diagnosis of the Holocaust and its context that the country's wartime treatment of its Jewish population was cruel in the extreme. In *Eichmann in Jerusalem: A Report on the Banality of Evil*, first published in 1963, Hannah Arendt states that '[I]t is hardly an exaggeration to say that Rumania was the most anti-Semitic country in pre-war Europe.' Under the Iron Guard in Romania, Arendt continues, 'even the S.S. were taken aback, and occasionally frightened, by the horrors of old-fashioned, spontaneous pogroms on a gigantic scale', often intervening to save the Jews from the sheer butchery of their fascist compatriots. While Arendt's figures have been challenged in recent years, the nature of the Romanian holocaust remains gruesome. The worst of the antisemitic purges in the country and the mass deportation of Jews from the regions of Bessarabia and Bukovina to prison camps in the north at Transnistria did not begin until the summer of 1941, after Romania had joined the war on the Axis side, but their fate was becoming apparent earlier the previous year. In August 1940, Antonescu introduced punitive legislation against the Jewish community across various branches of business, education and law, and issued an official declaration that the majority of Romanian Jews, begrudgingly granted minority status as a sop to the international community in the late 1930s, would henceforth be considered 'stateless'.[34]

Manning left Bucharest for Athens in the early autumn of 1940 and therefore would have missed any first-hand experience of the worst excesses of antisemitic practice in Romania, but she undoubtedly knew of the pogroms of 1937. In *The Spoilt City* Harriet recalls hearing of how Romanian Jews were hung from meat hooks in the city slaughterhouse, and is told by Drucker's sister of the desperate situation for Jews in the city a year later. The novels make frequent reference to social restrictions, persecutions and evictions. Manning was also aware of the course of events after her own departure from the country. Her account of the fate of a Jewish refugee ship, the *Struma* (discussed further in Chapter Five), details the plight of the Jews under Antonescu's dictatorship and the Iron Guard brutality, which increased dramatically during the winter of 1940/1. In this piece (published in 1970) Manning summarises a history of the confiscation of property, arrest, imprisonment and torture, and of the many Jews who simply disappeared following Guardist squad raids on their households. She also discusses the events of 1941 when the Guardists, in their attempts to seize power for their leader Horia Simia, embarked on a two-day massacre in Bucharest, driving Jewish civilians in their thousands to the city slaughterhouse, where they were mutilated and then murdered as the synagogues burned down.[35]

Again, Manning's treatment of this subject involves her careful avoidance of hindsight. She traces in the novels a historical increase in antisemitic practices without regard for a distanced, post-war narrative of condemnation. Hence the two Romanian novels in the sequence establish a climate of anti-Jewish prejudice, even paranoia, on a number of distinct but subtle levels. Yakimov, in order to entertain his vehemently anti-Jewish landlady, for example, engages her in a ribald conversation about a 'Jew-shoot' orchestrated by his former aristocratic friends, while Harriet hears from Sasha Drucker the tale of how his friend Marcovitch was thrown off a train to the wolves, the latter incident confirmation of worsening anarchy in the country with regard to the treatment of the Jewish minority (*BT*, p. 204). Guy, meanwhile, criticised by Bella Niculescu because he 'cultivates Jews' (*BT*, p. 534), is seen as being in danger because his school is now mainly attended by the young Jewish community; he remains committed to his teaching partly because his classroom in the British Institute provides teaching for Jewish students desperate, as Harriet points out, to prepare themselves for flight to English-speaking countries.[36]

Yet Manning's tactic is not to solicit an unconditional sympathy as such for the Jewish community. Her choice of the wealthy banking family, the Druckers, as representative of the Jewish element (and fate) in wartime Romania offers instead what amounts almost to caricature, even stereotype, in the novels. Her ambiguous treatment of the family seems to fly in the face of Reggie Smith's left-wing, pro-Jewish activities. The Druckers (who were probably based on a family of Manning's acquaintance in Bucharest) are depicted from the very beginning as an erratic phenomenon in this society, racially and culturally resistant to integration within a Romanian national identity. When the Pringles are invited to lunch with them in *The Great Fortune* (Guy having met them previously through his pupil, their son Sasha), their home appears to Harriet as yet another instance of a bizarre Balkan exoticism: the women are lavishly attired but curious and alien, the men of a type, dedicated to their common financial interests above and beyond the issues of place and nation. Harriet watches as the Drucker brothers-in-law return home for lunch from their offices extravagantly and expensively dressed. 'Teitelbaum wore several gem rings, a gold watch bracelet, diamond cuff-links, a diamond tie-pin and a broad gold clip to hold down his tie. His elderly, humourless manner made this jewellery seem less an ornament than a weariness of the flesh' (*BT*, p. 96). These men – German, Austrian and Pole – have, it seems, bought their way into Romania, where their *raison d'être* is simply and selfishly business, to the extent that Guy's talk of Germany's imminent financial collapse throws them into theatrical panic.

The representation grows in ambivalence with regard to Drucker's three sisters, who, largely indistinguishable from each other, appear as rapacious, crude and demanding in the novel. Lassner argues that Manning's portrait of the Drucker women, which should in theory recuperate their lost identity, ends up by reinserting them in a narrative of marginalisation (replaying the predicament surrounding the objectionable Frau Leszno in *School for Love*). We never learn their fate, Lassner complains, 'but their grossly stereotypical representation reflects only too painfully the process of dehumanization which made the Jews the irremedial alien'. In Manning's aggressive portrait these women, with their chubby fingers, heavy jewellery and greed for the cream cakes served up after an over-rich lunch, are nauseating rather than sympathetic. 'Set in contrast to Harriet's reserved femininity', Lassner continues, 'the aunts are a cultural gloss on the feminized Jewish man and on Manning's representation of European anti-semitism'. Rightly, too, she queries whether the representation is framed by Manning's political consciousness or simply by Harriet's, but ultimately is led to a negative reading of the portrait: in the end, the Druckers are 'a serious critical problem in an otherwise masterly epic of the war'.[37]

Does Lassner's reading in turn miss Manning's *real* intentions with the portrait? The author does make sympathetic claims on the Druckers' behalf, largely through their reports to the Pringles of the persecution they have already suffered in Romania, including physical assaults on family members, and of the fear of the Iron Guard which they now must endure in the city. At the lunch party, Guy's attempts to outline a plan of Russian and socialist economic redistribution fall on justifiably cynical ears. And from the stereotype the Druckers seem to fulfil, Harriet (and Manning) retrieves as symbolic the meaningful and deeply sympathetic figure of the family's young son, Sasha:

> Watching the boy, Harriet thought that were one to meet him in any capital in the world, one would think not 'Here is a foreigner' but 'Here is a Jew'. Though he would be recognizable anywhere, he would be at home nowhere except here, in the midst of his

> family. Despite the fact that he did undoubtedly belong – as though to prove it his aunts had each as he passed given him a pat of welcome – there was about him something so vulnerable and unprotected that Harriet's sympathy went out to him. (*BT*, p. 97)

It is Sasha who, following the imprisonment of his father, the seizing of the family's financial assets and the flight of his relatives, turns to the Pringles for help. When he hides out in their apartment as the city plunges further into chaos, he becomes an ally for Harriet, a companion on the periphery of a war not of his making. Discussing in detail the function of this relationship within the terms of the military plot as a whole, Lassner sees Sasha, the Jewish presence, as a reinforcement of the position occupied by Harriet, the oppressed female partner. In their passive alliance the two characters in turn subvert the masculine war epic: 'Manning narrates their relationship as a counter-discourse, both in relation to the fascist takeover which threatens their lives, and to the rhetorical force of the war stories playing out around them. The combined perspectives of the hopeless Jew and depressed woman deconstruct and mock the war epic as it is implicated in the historical movements of fascism.'[38]

Perhaps, however, Lassner overemphasises their similarity: while both, in effect, play out the role of refugee in the climate of fear and exclusion, it is Sasha who claims protection and Sasha whose life is in actual danger following his desertion from the Romanian army. In the description Manning provides as he appears outside their flat, Sasha represents the Jew anachronistically (the author conceding an element of hindsight here) as a figure familiar from a post-war narrative of Nazi extermination. Again, the Gothic mode is used by Manning to underline the force of repression and anxiety shrouding his appearance:

> He was tall, skeletal, narrow-shouldered and stooped like a consumptive. His head, that had been shaved, was beginning to show a yellow stubble. The face, grey-white, with cheeks clapped in on either side of a prominent nose, would have seemed the face of a corpse had not the close-set, dark eyes been fixed on her, alive in their apprehension of need. (*BT*, p. 318)

If there are echoes of Orwell here in the closeness of the portrait to Winston Smith as he emerges from O'Brien's torture sequence, there are louder echoes of Belsen and the images of Jewish prisoners emerging in 1945 from the camps.[39] The portrait outweighs, emotionally, the apparent prejudice shown in Harriet's earlier response to the vulgarity of the Drucker sisters. In what is an implicit rather than a stated connection, Manning foists on to Sasha a broader European Jewish plight and through Harriet's reaction to his miserable appearance suggests a non-Jewish response combining sympathy with disgust: 'She was repelled by such misery. She wanted to get out of sight of it. She shook her head' (*BT*, p. 319). Through such conflicted imagery and detail, she thus positions the Druckers, and Romanian Jews in general, at the heart of a Chinese box of the country itself – its social whole broken up into gypsies, peasants, beggars, old aristocrats and ethnic minorities – caught in a desperate struggle for security on the edge of a fragmenting Europe.

The writer Geoffrey Household, who was engaged in undercover military missions in Romania during the first year of the war, later recalled how the country at that time, on the eve of occupation, staged a final flourish of its legendary glory and beauty. His eloquent descriptions, with their elegiac images of a people and landscape on the threshold of disaster, could easily be passages from Manning's *Balkan Trilogy*:

> Bucharest put on a high summer, which I drank from the balcony of a delightful rent-free flat, taken over from one of the most deservedly exiled, high above the boulevards. The monks chanted in the dark-panelled monasteries. The willows continued to cascade over streams racing down to the Danube with the last of the snow water, while the frogs sang and the buffaloes wallowed. The restaurants which jewelled with their flowers or lights the chain of lakes around Bucharest – all marshes when I was young – still offered white wine and gipsy music, while the night air breathing up from roots of rushes cooled the exquisite complexions of the women. Never was there such a country as the Wallachian plain for shade and water in the savage heat. Those summer months of 1940 were the last blossoming of Byzantine civilization.[40]

This is the great fortune of Manning's title, the fortune lost irretrievably as Romania's neutrality came to an end. For the Pringles, the fall of Romania is perceived not as a vertical descent from high to low but rather as a horizontal collapse, west to east. The growing panic experienced by the citizens of Bucharest as they view film footage of the German invasion of France is predicated largely on the knowledge that the advances in civilisation they had gained since independence from the Turks will now be sacrificed: Romania will be returned to a Balkan darkness and primitivism, its eastern origins victorious over its Western aspirations. 'With France lost, there would be no stay or force against savagery', Harriet comes to understand. 'The truth was evident even to those who had invested in Germany: the victory of Nazi Germany would be a victory of darkness. Cut off from Western Europe, Rumania would be open to persecution, bigotry, cruelty, superstition and tyranny. There was no-one to save her now' (*BT*, p. 265).

The future of the country is bleak; there is no salvation ahead. As Klein comments to Harriet, 'You are watching a history, *Doamna* Preengal. Stay, and you will see a country die' (*BT*, p. 314). But Romania is not falling in isolation; it is quintessentially at the heart of the European project now threatened irretrievably by the war. The final chapters of *The Spoilt City* are a catalogue of Guardist expansionism, in raids, kidnappings, torture, beatings and executions, along with demonstrations of power, leading to the raid on the Pringles' own apartment which eventually forces the couple's departure from the country. But Romania's destruction is symbolic of a larger degeneration, its chaos the chaos of a continental structure which held promise but fell to clashing incentives, ambitions and greed. The final emphasis of Manning's Romanian novels is simply on concepts of depletion. Within the space of the year the Pringles spend there, the country cedes Bessarabia and some of Bukovina to the Russians, Transylvania to the Hungarians and, in a further round of diplomatic expediency, the Dobrudja region in the south to the Bulgarians. Overall, Guy points out to Harriet, this is some 40,000 square miles of Romania's territory and six million of its population (*BT*, p. 459).

Towards the very end of her time in Romania, looking at the lake in the Cişmigiu gardens, Harriet thinks back over her year in the country as, in itself, a fall from richness into poverty, harmony into abjection. 'She seemed to remember the water, beneath its haze of heat, as translucent as crystal. Now it smelt of weed. The crusted surf round the café held captive floating bottles, orange-peel, match boxes and paper bags. As for the café itself, it reflected in its greyish weathered timbers, its crippled chairs, its dirty table papers, the decay of the whole country' (*BT*, p. 459). She and Guy, their marriage straining and cracking under the clashes of interest and personality, are also party to this historic loss. Here they were, she realises, 'wrecked together on the edge of Europe as on an island' (*BT*, p. 459). The brief European dream has finally exploded; the nightmare of its long-term disturbance has begun.

CHAPTER THREE

From Athens to Alexandria: The contexts of Personal Landscape

As the long spring twilight fell we watched the Peloponnesus change from their sunset colours to purple. Behind us in the evening blue the Acropolis glimmered white and faded from sight. The darkness became complete. We went down to the lowest deck where we shared a two-berth cabin with six friends – two other married couples and two bachelors. The ship had been used to transport Italian prisoners, and every way of escape was boarded up. That meant no escape for us too, so we took off our life-belts.

Olivia Manning[1]

'All through this beautiful summer', wrote Manning to her fellow novelist Jocelyn Brooke in September 1964, 'I have been closeted in my small back bedroom struggling with part three of the trilogy. A difficult book to write because it means a drawing together of all the threads in the previous books, and a final settlement of everyone concerned.'[2] *Friends and Heroes* was not to be the 'final settlement', just a further stage in the wartime narrative as it tracked the eastward journey of the Pringles from Bucharest towards Cairo. But through its location in Athens, where the Smiths settled in the winter of 1940 after their flight from Romania, the novel does function as a caesura, at least, in Manning's fictional sequence. Greece was a recognisable classical refuge in an alien

Balkan landscape, its culture reassuringly penetrable in contrast to a Romanian exotic. '"Athens," Harriet thought. "The longed for city." Bucharest had been enclosed by Europe, but here she had reached the Mediterranean. In Bucharest, the winter was just beginning. In Athens, it seemed, the summer would go on for ever' (*BT*, p. 591).

The Greek capital in wartime was not exactly idyllic but it was familiar, not least in cultural terms. *Friends and Heroes* picks up on long-ingrained British Romantic treatments of Athens and its surrounding region and Manning launches the novel with a series of predictable classical and literary allusions. Harriet Pringle's plane flies over the Acropolis in the evening glow, 'the moment acclaimed by Pindar' (*BT*, p. 595), while in Athens she notes appreciatively the commemorative plaque to Byron on a nearby house (*BT*, p. 661). There are more recent literary echoes too: this is the landscape venerated by Virginia Woolf's Jacob Flanders during his European tour immediately before the cataclysm of 1914, and his enchantment with the Greek city and its distinguished ruins underlies Harriet's meanderings through the same topography in 1940.[3] Greece, in this respect, offered a certain degree of security despite the war, simply because of its literary familiarity. 'If Manning's descriptions of Romania reflect a sense of the discovery of an unknown world', Vesna Goldsworthy suggests, 'Greece is, as in Lawrence Durrell's descriptions of it, always "longed-for", dreamed of, already known and locked into the imagery of "returning home". For Manning, as for so many other English writers, descriptions of Greece consist of defining the terms of that "recognition" – the ways of finding a long-lost home.'[4]

The brief sojourn which began in Athens in the autumn of 1940 and continued through the hard winter of that year also provided space for significant developments in Manning's literary life. In Greece she first came into contact with those members of an expatriate literary coterie – Lawrence Durrell, Bernard Spencer, Robin Fedden – who would help her towards shaping more self-consciously a 'refugee' sensibility, accentuated by the loss of Greece to the Nazis late in the following spring and hardened into aesthetic practice by these, the *Personal Landscape* poets, as they subsequently resettled in their default home in Egypt. Through her close contact with Greek poets George Seferis and Elie Papadimitriou, she gained imaginative access to the political hinterland of a Greek identity still burdened by painful memories of the Anatolian disaster of 1922, when the Greeks were put to flight from their homeland in Smyrna by a vengeful Turkish army. Though Manning remained largely on the periphery of these two overlapping literary communities, she was clearly influenced by their respective treatments of exile. Her critical article on the *Personal Landscape* venture, published in *Horizon* in 1944, was, as we shall see, more a defence of a refugee mentality among her literary associates than a technical validation of their verse, while her contribution to the first volume of the *Personal Landscape* journal, her poem 'Written in the Third Year of the War', combines a bitter meditation on the experience of leaving Greece – 'exiles from a country not our own', as she described it – with a respectful gesture towards Elie Papadimitriou's anguished recitative *Anatolia*, an epic treatment of Greece's historic loss, in composition during the early years of the war.

In Greece, there is for the fictional Pringles, meanwhile, a gradual apprehension of how things have come to stand in their relationship. During the course of *Friends and Heroes* Harriet Pringle undergoes a personal evolution of sorts, and is stirred from her marital despondency towards a tentative pragmatism and a greater degree of independence. Where previously she had retreated into passivity and self-pity, she now begins to assert herself, to see the world more clearly and her place within it. 'It had seemed to her then that she had left behind not only her friends but her individuality. Now she began to feel the absurdity of this' (*BT*, p. 649). Disillusionment emerges too in her revised understanding of the marriage contract. She realises that Guy, in his reckless sociability and left-wing propagandising, is, at heart, insubstantial, even insecure. Recognising his exertions on behalf of others as 'a form of selfishness', Harriet comes to apprehend her husband's psychological limitations, 'beginning to fear that he was a man who in the end would achieve little. He would simply waste himself' (*BT*, p. 672). If the affair she tentatively pursues in Athens with the military liaison officer Charles Warden is ultimately unfulfilled, its *potential* is enough to confirm the enervation of her relationship with Guy and the flaws endemic in the marital arrangement: 'She had found no release in marriage. It had forced her further back into the prison of herself. Acutely conscious now of the passing of time, she felt she was not living but being fobbed off with an imitation of life' (*BT*, p. 791).

Again in this, the final volume of the *Balkan Trilogy*, the marital relationship between the protagonists dovetails with broader political transitions; in this case, the move from ill-founded optimism about the war to the bitter, brutal realities of conflict and defeat. Harriet's change of perspective with regard to her husband reflects the parallel political transitions charted in the novel from idealism to crippling disillusionment. Initially the Greek capital is a paradise of sorts, tranquil and safe after the insecurities of life in Bucharest, but, in the course of the Athens-set narrative, Harriet's impressions of a romantic and heroic culture are undermined by a wartime actuality and the country's less than heroic slide from petty dictatorship into humiliating occupation. The collapse of the Greek dream is in turn mirrored in the dissipation of the British presence in Athens, manifest in the corruption, in-fighting and sycophancy of the expatriate community grouped in the capital. In the staff of the British Legation, the Information Office – headed now by the odious Professor Lord Pinkrose – and the British School where Guy attempts to pursue the duties of the Organization (the name Manning gives to her version of the British Council in Greece), there is a prevailing sense of degeneracy. In ironic contrast to the noble Greek civilians, the British are exposed as lacking in integrity and wanting in self-respect, *Friends and Heroes* incorporating in its chronological account of the conflict in the region a damning indictment of an overseas mission that failed to meet the challenges of the war.

The material of *Friends and Heroes* is carefully positioned along a discernible trajectory of British literary responses to Greece. Concepts of the Greek idyll developed by generations of travellers steeped in classical literature and history, and enhanced by the iconic status of Byron as the country's major celebrant among the Romantic poets, were elaborated in the first half of the twentieth century by a modernist *literati* drawing on forced contrasts between a coherent Hellenic past and a contemporary fragmentation. In his critical account of the treatment of Greece in British writing, David Roessel records the efforts of an interwar generation to shore up an image of Greece as a repository of the 'unspoiled' in a contaminated civilisation, an investment visible in the writings of Lawrence Durrell and Henry Miller during the period or in eulogistic works like Compton MacKenzie's *South Wind of Love* (1937).[5] By the 1950s, following the damage done in succession by occupation, communism and civil war, Byronic representations of the country were no longer possible and Greece became instead the lost dream of a British imagination. Writers such as Louis MacNeice (appointed to the Directorship of the British Institute in Athens in 1950) now came to regard Greece as emblematic of a cultural decay, a ruined homeland. MacNeice's poems 'The Island' and 'Athens', for example, are laments for a fallen civilisation and admissions at the same time of Western neglect of a once-favoured region. From his Greek collection *Ten Burnt Offerings*, compositions such as 'Cock o' the North' and 'Poor me, poor Greece . . . ' are haunted by the wartime ghosts of refugees and exiles, as can be seen in this extract from 'The Island':

> Idyllic? Maybe. Still there is hardly
> Such a thing as a just idyll. The sanguine visitor dreams
> And finds himself on the run with barking
> Dogs at his heels who turn into wolves, into men, and each of them
> seems
> To be running with creaky shoes; before him
> Brood vast grey rocks, turtle shape, cottage-loaf, rubble of dried up
> streams. . .[6]

The novelist and classical historian Rex Warner, who preceded MacNeice at the British Institute in Athens, similarly tracked the disintegration of Greek political culture in his allegorical *Men of Stones* (1949); so too did Manning's close friend and contemporary Francis King, who, having lived in the country for a short period, reflects frequently in his work on its lapsed condition. In his 1956 story *The Firewalkers* (first published under the name Frank Cauldwell) and *The Dark Glasses* (1954) – novels set in Athens and Corfu respectively – King portrays the grievous decline of a landscape which the British visitor must now confront in its true form, a location of suffering and social deprivation in the wake of wartime occupation.

Initially, in her own novel, Manning's vivid descriptions of a picturesque landscape and society coincide with the intense infatuation with the country developed by her immediate expatriate circle in the late 1930s and throughout the war. This group of philhellenes was dominated by Lawrence Durrell, who overlapped with the Smiths in Athens in 1940, having arrived there from Corfu in the wake of the German invasion of Poland.[7] Durrell was initially employed in the Greek capital by the British Embassy's Information Service and put to work on an official bulletin aimed at countering German propaganda, before being taken on by the British Council to teach English. In the city, he met the two fellow writers who would in turn become his closest colleagues in the *Personal Landscape* venture, Bernard Spencer and Robin Fedden. These men, like-minded devotees of Greek culture and landscape, were already engaged in documenting the last days of the British love affair with the country. For Fedden the initial meeting with Durrell securely grounded the origin myth of the entire *Personal Landscape* enterprise – along with Durrell himself as its defining personality – in an Athenian locale and sensibility relished long afterwards in the memory. 'His exuberant vitality kept us talking on a bench in Syntagma Square until it grew cold and late', he later recalled. '*Personal Landscape* was for all three of us in some degree the extension of moods and relationships to which from our exile we often looked back.'[8]

The outbreak of war in Europe inevitably threatened the attempts of writers like Durrell, Spencer, Patrick Leigh Fermor and the novelist Robert Liddell (who was also in Athens writing a book on Crete) to maintain the Greek dream. The transition into a new phase of Britain's Hellenic attachments is evident in the work of another familiar figure on the Greek horizon, the journalist and society legend Derek Patmore, who preceded the Smiths in Romania and who had spent the initial year of the war as a news correspondent covering the collapse of Poland and the invasion of Yugoslavia.[9] Patmore's Balkan journey was dominated by his attachment to Greece. In 1944 he wrote the introduction to *Images of Greece*, a book of sumptuous black-and-white photographs of the country, produced by various noted photographers and published by *Country Life*. This work, 'an evocation of what Greece was like before the present war and what, surely, it will be like when the war is over', was to provide reassurance, he claimed, for anxious lovers of Greece languishing back home in England. In 1946, Patmore was the editor of the first (and, in the end, only) volume of an English literary quarterly, *Greek Horizons*, with Durrell leading a list of contributors affiliated to the country including John Waller, Rex Warner, Steven Runciman and Ian Scott-Kilvert, together with a number of Greek writers and illustrators. Patmore himself contributed an effusive 'Pages from a Greek Journal', setting the tone for the issue's melancholy tribute to an enduring Anglo-Greek relationship.[10]

Last, and importantly for Manning's perspective on the circles of cultural diplomacy in *Friends and Heroes*, Anglo-Greek relations continued to build on connections forged and consolidated during the pre-war decade through academia. The strong academic relationship between the two countries was cemented by the appointment in 1938 of classical scholar Professor A.V. Routh to the Byron chair of English Literature at Athens University. Routh, who also acted as press attaché for the British Embassy in Athens during the war itself, was much disliked by those who knew him: he suggests a further source for Manning's Professor Pinkrose, who, having also relocated from Bucharest, spends his time in the Greek capital neglecting his duties at the British Legation's Information Office in order to work on his lecture, 'Byron: the Poet Champion of Greece' (*BT*, p. 753). The literary scholar and historian of Greece A.R. Burn, meanwhile, took over from Routh as head of the *actual* British Institute in Athens early in 1940, with Lord Dunsany, redeployed from Romania, succeeding Routh in the Byron Chair. When the Germans advanced on the city, Burn left Athens on the same evacuee ship as the Smiths, along with the literary scholar Harold Edwards, an early contributor (with a rather idiosyncratic review of *Finnegans Wake*) to the *Personal Landscape* journal.[11] As individuals, such figures were insignificant, perhaps, but, as a coterie of numerous minor literary figures of the period, all passing through Athens, the Greek mainland or the islands, they amounted to a distinct entity, representative of cultural, scholarly and literary investment in a country still firmly embedded in British affections.

Characteristically, Manning's treatment of a rampant British Hellenism is double-edged in *Friends and Heroes*. Her ambivalence about this subject is played out in the novel through the Pringles' relationship with Alan Frewen, the enigmatic director of the British Information Service in Athens (and, as a character, a compound of figures such as Derek Patmore, Patrick Leigh Fermor and, perhaps too, Bernard Spencer). Frewen has immersed himself in the landscape and history of his adoptive homeland. Having originally travelled to the Aegean before the war to try his hand as a photographer, his ambition is now to record for posterity the lush scenery and traditional peasant culture of the Greek countryside, and the work he shows to an enchanted Harriet evokes all the clichés of this theme: 'pictures of rocky islands, olive trees, classical temples outlined against the sea, and chalk-white churches and houses taken at midday when the shadowed walls shimmered with reflected light' (*BT*, p. 776). Despite his large and gout-ridden physique, Frewen leads the company's walks into the hills bordering the capital, claiming the territory as his own. His attachment to Greece cannot be shaken even in the shadow of invasion. Like so many of his real-life counterparts (notably Durrell and Spencer), Frewen has translated Cavafy, the poetic figurehead for the Greek-based British poets, and in the face of the Axis advance on Greece's borders he launches into an evocative recitation of Cavafy's 'The Barbarians', in a vain but romantic expression of literary heroics against the force of the German machine, before the air-raid siren brings him to a halt.

For all that Frewen is a sympathetic character, he is set up in the novel as a target for those with more prosaic responses to the contradictions of the Greek situation. It is Guy Pringle, predictably disinclined to join the Byronic cult of the country, who issues an outright and even aggressive challenge to Frewen's faith in a picturesque Greek peasantry at one with the idyllic Mediterranean landscape. Guy's scepticism forces Frewen to examine the political realities of the country. Since the death of the Greek statesman Eleftherios Venizelos in 1936 – an event marking the end, effectively, of transitions towards full democracy – the country had been run under the veteran royalist dictator General Ioannis Metaxas. If the Metaxas government, which ostentatiously declared itself to be the 'Third Hellenic Civilisation', represented at least a 'soft' totalitarianism in comparison with other Balkan regimes, it nevertheless held a deeply conservative grip on a population desperate for economic development. For Guy Pringle, the notion of 'unspoilt' simply means 'underdeveloped', and Frewen's attempted defence of Metaxas as a 'paternal despot', acceptable in the terms of classical antiquity, inevitably clashes with his adversary's faith in a modern industrial socialism. Under the stress of their polarised viewpoints, a British Hellenic tradition begins to unravel:

> Guy, assessing and criticizing Alan's limitations, said: 'You prefer the peasants to remain in picturesque poverty, I suppose?'
>
> 'I prefer that they remain as they are: courteous, generous, honourable and courageous. Athens is not what it was, I admit. There used to be a time when any stranger in the city was treated as a guest. As more and more strangers came here, naturally that couldn't go on; yet something remains. The great tradition of

> *philoxenia* – of friendship towards a stranger – still exists in this country and on the islands. It exists here, in a little café like this!' Alan's voice sank with emotion; he had to pause a moment before he could say:
>
> 'A noble people! Why should anyone wish to change them?'
>
> Guy nodded appreciatively. 'A noble people, yes. They deserve something better than subsistence at starvation level'. (*BT*, p. 659)

For Guy, the tension inherent in British attitudes to Greece finds release in the community of like-minded leftists he tracks down in the Café Aleko. Harriet's position remains more ambivalent, merging with the broader sense of contradiction maintained throughout the trilogies between the pull of a communal but abstract democratic socialism – the philosophy pushed at every opportunity by her husband – and an individualism steeped in a more conservative, indeed apprehensive, view of both society and culture. For all his humanist principles, she gradually comes to realise, Guy's abstractions represent a failure of commitment as much as dedication to a cause: 'To someone so enamoured of the general, could the particular ever really mean anything?' (*BT*, p. 756). Increasingly now, Harriet discerns that, in figures such as Alan Frewen, the particular must be allowed to survive, and ultimately it is Frewen, the loner, the individualist, the carrier of the philhellenic torch, who will simply disappear into the Greek hinterland when the arrival of the Germans forces the rest of the British community to take flight across the Mediterranean.[12]

The ambivalence experienced by Harriet Pringle in her response to Greece is replicated in the novel's treatment of the country's passage into war, a treatment that shows more than anything else in the two trilogies Manning's continuing determination to splice the tropes of epic and romantic history with the responsibilities of contemporary political and realist commentary. In *Friends and Heroes*, her self-consciously 'painterly' style, depicting the country in a series of framed, impressionistic vignettes, deliberately plays on the traits of British philhellenism discussed above. It is worth noting that Manning herself painted extensively while in the country, meeting noted Greek artists such as Nikos Hatzikyriakos Ghikas – later championed in *Personal Landscape* by Durrell and in the British journal *Encounter* by Patrick Leigh Fermor – while she was in Athens.[13] Aspects of this visual investment are employed in *Artist Among the*

Missing, where Major Geoffrey Lynd's nostalgic attachment to his prior posting in Greece is largely expressed through his memories of painting its glorious landscapes. Manning's narrative attention to scenic and visual detail is both a means of recreating a sense of place and an ironic allusion to ingrained British habits of overseas myth-making.

In the same vein, romantic depictions of the country going to war are initially framed as visions of heroism harking back to classical precedents – Greece is 'collecting its legends', Harriet reflects, as Athens prepares to enter the conflict (*BT*, p. 719). With deference to the concept of Greece as the cradle of civilisation, Manning represents the beggars in Athens as civilised, respectful and picturesque (in marked contrast to her metonymic depiction of a Gothic and alien Romania through the grotesque mendicants of Bucharest, in the two preceding volumes). Similarly the Greek army is celebrated as a heroic resistance movement emerging from the heart of a resilient and ennobled population. After Metaxas' defiant (and subsequently legendary) refusal of the Italian ultimatum, the mobilisation of troops in Athens is treated as a mass celebration, and Harriet is 'transported by the glory of war' as she bids farewell to the Greek conscripts on their way to the train station (*BT*, p. 629). In the same mood early Greek victories against the Italians in Albania, during the winter of 1940, are reported in a litany of joy. At the fall of Koritza, crowds dance the *Zeibekiko* in the streets; the city is 'intoxicated' with its own glorious spirit (*BT*, p. 672). Church bells ring again for the capture of Muskopolje, Konispolis, Pogrodets, each battle invested with romance: 'After Pogrodets, there came the capture of Mt. Ostrovitz; then Premeti, Santa Quaranta, Argyroskastro and Delvino. The *evzoni* captured the heights of Ochridia in a snowstorm. The attack lasted four hours and the Greek women, who had followed their men, climbed barefooted up the mountainside to take them food and ammunition' (*BT*, p. 691). Harriet is carried along on the emotions of heroic sacrifice, her visions of Greece clouded with sentiment. As Goldsworthy observes, '[t]he notion of the Greeks as a race of noble warriors permeates Manning's descriptions of their dignified dances and their love of music, her portraits of *evzones* in their *fustanellas*, and even the accounts of Harriet's encounters with old men who regret their age because it does not allow them to join in the battle.'[14] British troops, meanwhile, from the airforce pilots to the regiment of Scottish Highlanders depicted arriving in the capital, are immediately taken to the

Greek heart in an overwhelming show of comradeship and shared purpose, the entire city and its expatriate inhabitants succumbing to a vain and precarious wartime romance.

The value of *Friends and Heroes* as an intervention in the war epic lies in the counter-narrative pursued by Manning (and gradually too by Harriet) when the reality of war intrudes on this heavily visual display. Such undercutting is in itself a cliché of war writing, predictable in any account of conflict, but it none the less serves as a means of unsettling the grip of a British hold on heroic and increasingly obsolete images of the Greek. Again, in a characteristic dovetailing of individual relationships with overarching political themes, Harriet comes to undermine a Greek mythology of war through the progress of her relationship with the officer Charles Warden. Initially Charles is transfigured through her infatuation into a war hero, 'one of those sacrificial youths of the last war whose portraits had haunted her childhood'. To Harriet he appears as 'a romantic figure, marked down for death' (*BT*, p. 752); he is described in the same terms of ennobled heroic virtue as the Greek resistance campaign itself in the newspaper reports flooding the city. When Charles escorts her to the Parthenon, now a restricted zone for the military only, Harriet is enchanted when he is ceremonially saluted by the soldier on guard:

> Detached from limiting reality, lifted into a realm of poetic concepts, she saw Charles not as an ordinary young man – she had, after all, known dozens of ordinary young men, some of whom had been quite as handsome as he – but a man-at-arms to whom was due both deference and privilege. She was her own symbol – the girl whose presence heightened and complemented the myth. (*BT*, p. 741)

The language here both inflates and undermines simultaneously: in the same moment that a mythology of a wartime romance is evoked, it is deflated, with Harriet's recognition of a prosaic irony undercutting the reaches of the poetic and symbolic. 'Enchanted, she was almost immediately disenchanted; was, indeed, amazed at finding herself dazzled by the cantrips of war. She was against war and its trappings' (*BT*, p. 741).

Through the same process the Greek campaign against the Italians will reach its *own* turning point, its metaphors reversing into those of destruction and suffering. In Athens, the atmosphere of festival with girls throwing flowers to the departing soldiers is replaced by one of anxiety and silence when martial law is declared. The public mood changes and the imagery of Greece follows suit. Harriet, looking at a propaganda recruitment poster, sees through its gladiatorial pose: 'The civilian image of the fighting man was much like that of the war posters that showed the Greeks in fierce, defiant attitudes, exhorting each other up snowbound crags in pursuit of the enemy. Now, she thought, she had seen them for herself, the heroes of Episus . . . The enemy had not had much hand in killing them. The dead had died mostly from frost-bite and cold' (*BT*, p. 909). In turn Manning's painterly depictions of the capital and its surrounding landscape give way to portraits of the defeated and battle-wounded making their slow and painful journey to a hospital that has already run out of medical supplies. There is a revised version of the Anglo-Greek encounter in Harriet's witnessing of a soldier struggling by on crutches: 'The Pringles, as they approached the soldier, gazed at him with awe and compassion. He met their pity with indifference. His gaunt face was morose with pain. He was intent on nothing but making the next move' (*BT*, p. 706). And the British soldiers who pass through the city, lauded and celebrated by the Greek citizens, return only weeks later from the front, dejected, stupefied with fatigue, 'so chilled by despair that a sense of death was about them like a frozen mist about an iceberg' (*BT*, p. 884).

Idealism in the novel fragments under the combined pressures of wartime disenchantment and actual physical hardship in the Greek capital. Civilian suffering during the war in Greece, including widespread starvation as food supplies ran short, has been well documented by historians.[15] That the British also suffer the restrictions of wartime is increasingly the focus of the narrative as Manning details the characters' daily struggle for food amidst the general deprivation of the city. Harriet, who has volunteered in the British servicemen's canteen and is forbidden to touch the supplies set aside for the soldiers, almost breaks down in tears as she serves fried sausages to the combatants. On a bitterly cold Christmas day the expatriates walk, ravenous, along the beach, to be saved from their hunger only by the generosity of a Greek café owner who cooks for them the mullet he had managed to secure for his own family. Frequently the only vegetables available are potatoes; protein comes in the form of animal intestines or the sea urchins which Yakimov encourages a reluctant Harriet to try; in the formerly well-stocked restaurants of Athens, the only item on the menu is lung stew. Along with material deprivations, the British now share too with the Greeks the very real dangers of physical injury and bombardment. In the middle of the night Harriet and Guy are thrown out of bed and on to the floor in shock by the force of an explosion in Piraeus harbour; in the city they must run for shelter regularly as the air-raid siren sounds. A British sympathy with Greece is now made real as the expatriates experience the suffering of ordinary civilians and endure, alongside their hosts, the restrictions of martial law, a degradation brought home violently in the sudden and banal death of Yakimov, shot by a Greek policeman for failing to extinguish his cigarette during a blackout.[16]

As in all the novels of the trilogy, Manning's strength as a writer of war is her ability to draw thematic and metaphoric capital from the basics of historical fact. In the case of *Friends and Heroes*, this process is concerned with the representation of the British presence in Athens in terms which render it symbolic of a broader national constituency. The British community is *not* cast in the same heroic light as its Greek host: rather, for all its deprivations and suffering, it is condemned in this novel and, to a greater extent than anywhere else in Manning's writing, subject to charges of indolence, self-absorption, vanity and corruption. In the scheme of the trilogies as an epic on the decline and fall of a British imperial culture, this element conveys Manning's will to observe a dysfunctionalism at the heart of the British foreign mission, an idea similarly expressed by her contemporaries Anthony Burgess, Evelyn Waugh and (in *Burmese Days*) George Orwell, but given an added vehemence by the closeness of her fictional representations to the actual community in which she lived.

Thus Harriet Pringle, surprised by the vacuity of the expatriate British community in Athens, suggests to Alan Frewen that the city has become home to foreign parasites, attracting the kind of people 'who live abroad and do nothing' (*BT*, p. 651), an observation validated by many of the individuals – narcissistic, hysterical, petulant or self-obsessed – whom the Pringles encounter during the course of the novel. While this criticism of Athens society echoes aspects of Manning's vampiric configuration of Romania, her primary target in Greece is a foreign, not a native, constituency: the corps of diplomats, journalists and teachers involved in the nexus of the British Legation and the 'Organization', few of whom seem to have the ability to rise above petty squabbling and careerism towards a genuine commitment to the country. Through the grievances of the British Institute widow Mrs Brett, she paints a history of corruption and fraud in the Organization's operations and tracks on the back of this the vicious struggle for leadership which ensues after the departure of the enfeebled director, Colin Gracey. The duplicitous and under-qualified teachers Lush and Dubedat, who had earlier abandoned their posts in Bucharest, together with the foppish and ambitious Archie Callard, represent a culture of self-promotion and sycophancy at the expense of a communal effort. The School, under the auspices of the Organization, has become a laughing stock, the lectures hopelessly inadequate and factually erroneous: on one occasion, the Pringles learn with horror, Toby Lush has discussed with his students the possibility that Dante and Milton may have met in the streets of Florence (*BT*, p. 648). The reported scenes of drunken violence at Major Cookson's grandiose party confirm the degradation at the heart of the British expatriate and diplomatic service. In parallel with the actual fall of a heroic Greece, a mock heroic line is traced in the activities of a tangential British presence fast deteriorating into histrionics and bathos.[17]

Manning reserves her strongest condemnation for the character of Ben Phipps, the freelance journalist, writer and socialist who befriends Guy Pringle in Athens. 'Harriet was disturbed, feeling that the atmosphere between them was like the onset of a love affair. She became more critical of Phipps, suspecting he was the sort of man who, though sexually normal, prefers his own sex. He disliked her and he probably disliked women' (*BT*, p. 713). Ten years older than Guy, Phipps is described as an established left-wing figure: 'I have a reputation – you may have heard that I scribble a bit. I had a book published by the Left Book Club. I'm not unknown' (*BT*, p. 713). Now, in the climate of war in Europe, he has turned into an international conspiracy theorist, his extremist views combining with his ego to intrigue Guy but simultaneously to disgust Harriet. Already alienated by his sneering, needy behaviour and truculent personality, she is eventually provoked to outspokenness by Phipps's endless chatter during a group visit to the Parthenon, and the exchange confirms the further deterioration of the tense civic order hitherto maintained around her marriage:

> As the evening went on, Phipps returned, inevitably, to the sources of the world's mishap and Harriet, listening, reached a point of conscious revolt. At the mention of the mysterious Zoippus Bank, she broke in on him: 'There is no Zoippus Bank. I'm quite sure no Jew ever financed Hitler. I know the Vatican was never involved with Krupps and Wall Street and Bethlehem Steel. . .'
>
> 'You know fuck all,' said Ben Phipps. Harriet met the hatred of his small eyes, and said with hatred: 'You ugly little man!' His mouth fell open. She could see that she had hurt him. (*BT*, p. 791)

This intervention in Guy's friendship is not only a signal of her growing independence but also a mark of deep cynicism about the nature of her susceptible husband's associates. Against the grain of a wartime ethos of manliness, honour and self-sacrifice, these characters appear as pathetic and silly, their political views naive and self-serving. Phipps and Guy, enclosed in their own world as they discuss prospects for international socialism, suddenly represent for Harriet not only a failed ideology but also a failed *masculinity*, as they sit giggling together before her, 'like a couple of schoolgirls discovering sex' (*BT*, p. 715).

What did Manning intend with this treatment of the British representatives in Athens? In the context of a heroic and valiant Greek population, her depiction of a rotten inner circle is thrown into relief. Lawrence Durrell described the British Council team in Greece as 'a splendid lot, very popular and efficient', while other reports of the period suggest that the Council's efforts provided Greece and the Balkans generally with a much-loved and necessary morale boost in the lead-up to war.[18] However, Manning's portrayal of the Council and Legation types as shallow and self-serving coincides, in fact, with in-house British Council documentation on certain individuals in Athens at the time of the Pringles' stay in 1940. A year later the pacifist Robin Fedden became the subject of an inquiry launched by the British Ambassador in Egypt, Miles Lampson, who was provoked into action by rumours that Fedden had been 'spreading defeatism' in Egyptian circles.[19] Earlier, in October 1940, a report supplied to British Council headquarters by C.A.F. Dundas, the British Council's Middle East representative, noted the proliferation of negative attitudes to the Council staff in Greece. A committed and highly successful administrator for the Council, Dundas was unwilling to take on staff he regarded as the substandard products of wartime displacement and was particularly suspicious of lecturers and teachers arriving in Egypt from Greece and the Balkans. 'I feel very strongly', he wrote, 'that some of the Council's Greek staff have gained (and a few deserved) a reputation for qualities which make their position untenable in the especially difficult and delicate circumstances of the present time'. Of various Council employees, he continued, it was reported that they were indiscreet, extravagant, badly behaved, lacking in any serious purpose and irresponsible in financial matters. 'It is, too, repeatedly said, however slanderously', Dundas concluded, 'that they are "pansies", "long-haired", or "soft"'.[20]

This reputation found its way to the Middle East, where the Council authorities still suffered 'unwelcome repercussions of it' from time to time. Frances Donaldson, who reports on this episode in her history of the British Council during the war, points out that the somewhat inappropriate terms employed by Dundas were frequently used about 'anyone with the faintest intellectual pretensions'. There was also an element of suspicion from the 'old guard' of the Council towards the 'young Turks', whose activities and behaviour frequently seemed out of line with an official cultural and diplomatic mission, and, certainly, Dundas toned down his language in a report sent two years later, confidentially, to the Council's Director of Education for the region, Ifor Evans. However, his expressions of disquiet remained in his outline of abuses associated with Council staff, according to members of the English community evacuated from the Balkans – charges including maladministration and financial misdealing, public immorality, disloyalty to the Council and a relentless pursuit of internecine quarrels.[21]

In *Friends and Heroes* there are obvious echoes of this situation generally (and the investigation of Fedden in particular) in the confidential report on Guy Pringle prepared for head office by Pinkrose and accidentally overseen by an outraged Harriet. 'In the opinion of Pinkrose, Guy had dangerous left-wing tendencies. He was a trouble-maker who mixed with notorious Greeks. He had become a centre of sedition and was disapproved of by all responsible persons in Athens' (*BT*, p. 829). The terms of this confidential report, so far removed from the trilogy's consistent portraits of Guy as universally admired and respected, suggest a growing gap between ideal and reality in Greece. Manning shows the aims of the Organization in its wartime role to be deeply flawed, its aspiration towards cultural idealism riddled with discrepancies and threatened by conflicts of personality. While, on one hand, the defamation of Guy is bogus, and evidence moreover of the inequities and corruptions against which he has to battle, on the other it suggests that, increasingly, a British presence in the country now has nothing of value left to offer Greece. The British are seen as blinded by outdated social philosophies, distracted by the kind of political fantasy indulged in by Ben Phipps and hamstrung by the baggage of domestic class hierarchies. The dissipation of the imperial centre is nuanced here in the portrait of a 1930s generation lapsing from idealism and purpose into petty wrangling and political posturing, its wayward behaviour sorely heightened by the tensions of the European backdrop.

Towards the end of *Friends and Heroes*, as German troops are breaking through at the Corinth Canal, Harriet and Guy join the last of the British expatriates to flee the country, travelling to Egypt on a rusted and barely seaworthy vessel previously used for transporting Italian prisoners-of-war. The fictionalised journey is intensely dramatic, but so too was the *actual* voyage on which it was closely based, an event that remained central to Manning's recollections of wartime. In 'Last Civilian Ship', published at the end of the war, she described the experience of sailing for several days through submarine-infested waters with only limited supplies of food and drink, eventually to dock in relative safety at Alexandria. Accompanied by various Athens acquaintances, including the novelist Robert Liddell, the Welsh literary scholar Harold Edwards and his wife, and the Greek poets George Seferis and Elie Papadimitriou, she and Reggie made the slow and treacherous journey out of Piraeus harbour, past the cliffs of Crete (where Seferis landed to join an emergency Greek government administration in exile) and on towards the African coastline.[22]

Like her fictional alter ego, Manning was distraught at the loss of Greece to the enemy and at her dislodgement from what had come to seem like a home. In Harriet's mind the passage eastward into Egyptian waters occasions a significant shift, too, in terminology: 'Leaving Greece they had left like exiles. They had crossed the Mediterranean and now, on the other side, they knew they were refugees' (*BT*, p. 924). The transition in status signalled here coincided with the change in geography. Previously the context of expatriate life for the Pringles had been relatively secure, despite the activities of the Iron Guard in Bucharest and the advance of the Axis forces in Greece. In the departure from Athens, however, Manning identifies Harriet with the unsettling, even shocking, reality of a refugee existence and begins to draw on an archive of literary and political reference to the refugee condition. In so doing, she cautiously bridges a British experience to the prevalent terms of a contemporary Greek culture, characterised by a recent history of displacement and exile. While it provided an idyllic sanctuary for the British philhellenes, Greece was burdened during the first year of the war with a growing refugee population, a fact noted quietly but persistently by Manning in *Friends and Heroes*. In the novel, the hotel in which the Pringles manage to secure a room, for example, is described as having absorbed refugees since the start of the war; the trains arriving at the main station in Athens are crowded with refugees from Belgrade fleeing a collapsed Yugoslavia: 'political refugees, religious refugees, racial refugees, and English wives with small children' (*BT*, p. 831). Both capital and countryside seem to swarm with the displaced and the temporary sojourn of the recent British arrivals therefore reads as merely another layer of disturbance and instability.

The effect in the novel is that of a palimpsest, and in this respect Manning's treatment of a wartime Greek landscape cannot help but invoke more distant histories of Greek dislocation, including the 1922 devastation of the Greek community at Smyrna (on the Turkish coast) by Ataturk's forces. The attack marked the culmination of long-term Graeco-Turkish conflict and the incident, during which Greek civilians were reportedly slaughtered even as they attempted to board boats along the quays, surpassed in brutality all previous skirmishes. As a result, Smyrna would become a byword for the cataclysmic destruction of a civilisation and the subsequent emergence in Greece of a modern culture of exile, inspired by those defeated Greeks who survived and struggled back through the Greek mainland over the following months and years. Smyrna became emblematic of modern Greek experience but a defining moment of loss too, in European history generally. Outside the country itself (and despite the fact that the British apparently turned a blind eye to the event in order to safeguard their oil interests in the region), it also had a significant emotional impact.[23] Noting the frequency of references to the atrocity in British and American writing of the period, David Roessel suggests that

Smyrna was adopted in modernist discourse to nuance the death of noble, classical Greece and the end therefore of the philhellenic legacy in general. It marked the close of one civilisation and the imminence of its threatening replacement: it represented, in Lawrence Durrell's apt phrase, 'a lost peace of mind'.[24]

Manning too was aware of this legacy: the Athens hotel in which the Pringles stay in *Friends and Heroes* is already full to capacity, overloaded not only with recent arrivals since 1939 but 'a backlog of Smyrna Greeks' (*BT*, p. 615). More important, she was close to Greek poets still engaged in writing specifically on this chapter of their history, and, indeed, her knowledge of Greek literary material on the exilic theme generally emerges as a significant resource for her own writing on British wartime itinerancy. The poet George Seferis, whose work she knew well, was born in Smyrna, and though he missed the violence of 1922, he was inevitably caught up in its emotional residue. His self-definition as a refugee poet would shape many of his major works in the period, including his contributions to *Personal Landscape*. His long poem 'The King of Asine', which describes how a minor hero of the Trojan wars returns to haunt his former home on a ruined acropolis, is fraught with dark allusions to displacement, insecurity and alienation:

> Here where we live now unsubstantially entangled
> Like the withes of horrible willow bound up in the length of our
> hopelessness:
> While yellow streams bring down rushes uprooted with mud:
> Image of a face petrified with a decision of sharp bitterness.
> And the poet a void.[25]

A translator of Eliot, Seferis sought to fuse communal Greek memories of territorial and political loss with a modernist aesthetic of dejection. Manning recognised in this combination his distinctive strength as a poet. In 1944, she heralded him as a writer who should be known widely abroad, not least because he represented a new kind of literary identity, both modern and displaced. 'As a result of his awareness of himself as a product of mixed cultures', she wrote, 'he is preoccupied with the necessity of finding a myth that will express a ruling unity over our unstable civilization'.[26] While she would seek no such myth in her own writing, her recognition of Seferis as central to a formative contemporary poetics of 'refugee-ship' thus endorsed (from outside a British literary authority) the directions she had begun to contemplate in her wartime compositions and formative narrative sequences.

Closer still to Manning, and another fellow passenger on the evacuee ship from Piraeus, was Elie Papadimitriou, a Marxist writer who, unlike Seferis with his official Greek government position, had long been marked out as an undesirable communist by the Metaxas regime. Pursued by the authorities even after she settled in Egypt, she eventually found sanctuary of sorts in a monastery in Palestine (a situation that is perhaps alluded to by Manning in the character and plight of Maria, in *Artist Among the Missing*). Throughout the disturbances of the war years Papadimitriou managed to maintain her writing and Robin Fedden would single out the publication in *Personal Landscape* of the second and third recitatives from *Anatolia*, her long work-in-progress on the Asia Minor disaster, as one of the journal's significant achievements. 'Even through the opacity of translation', he wrote, 'the originality, the poetic confidence of the poet and the poem, come shining through'.[27] *Anatolia*, which was issued privately in Cairo in 1940 and eventually published fully in Athens in 1952, provided an extensive, detailed and brutal account of the purging of the Greeks from Asia Minor and the build-up to the disaster of 1922, when 'all Anatolia was ablaze' and the Greeks were chased into the sea. 'One country – whom to pity?' asks the poet, in the midst of harrowing details of the attack:

> The face of the land has changed
> Trees bowing with hanged men.
> On the waters float women's hair
> And the villages burn slowly by the roads
> Like abandoned chalk kilns.
>
> There was no more Smyrna in the bay – gone.
> Gone the streets with the balconies – the taverns,
> The churches and the shops of Fassoula,
> Merciful launches alongside are sunk:
>
> From the craziness of this land:
> At every military cordon men are sorted out

And hidden valuables come to light here:
All the desperate appeals:
Their lives part with one glance.[28]

Manning, who later translated Papadimitriou's work for the literary journal *The Windmill*, was clearly very much taken with this talented and courageous woman writer.[29] Praising her for enduring conditions of extreme poverty during her first months in Cairo, she acclaimed her in 1944 both as an exceptionally gifted poet and as a valued political activist, before quoting the final two stanzas – the Cairo section – of *Anatolia* itself.[30] Meanwhile, in its entirety *Anatolia* stood as the ultimate expression of cataclysmic loss and exile, experiences replicated for many by the German invasion of Greece in the spring of 1941. The critic Roger Bowen suggests that this work would become a seminal text for the exile experience, 'its power derived from an unheroic sympathy with the texture of people's lives, the history and endurance of a community, and the appalling brutality of religious nationalism'.[31]

Manning's connections to these poets and their work had a significant effect on her sense of Greece. In *The Great Fortune* and *The Spoilt City*, she had depicted Polish refugees in Bucharest as an abject but distanced presence; in *Friends and Heroes*, by contrast, British and Greek subjects coincide in suffering the refugee plight. Perhaps this was to some extent vicarious, the writer borrowing from her contemporaries a hinterland which lent depth to her own more limited, if none the less harrowing, experiences, and credibility to her formative literary context. Crucially, too, the identification of a literary 'refugee-ship' via the Greek community in exile would shape her approach to a landscape even farther east, in Egypt. Writing in 1944 on the sense of exile which affected every aspect of life in the Middle East, she presented the expatriate Greek literati as a romantic, spirited and cohesive unit, in sharp contrast to her novel's depiction of the jaded, effete British community in Athens. 'One chilly night in Jerusalem', Manning recalled, 'while the Germans were at El Alamein, half a dozen of us sat in the poor light of a hotel dining room, reading poetry to each other. "Think of it", said the Greek Seferis from his dark corner, "exiles reading poetry to each other."'[32] A fictional version of this reminiscence occurs in *Artist Among the Missing* when Geoffrey Lynd, recently displaced from a Greece in which his artistic talents had flourished, is temporarily drawn back into that lost world by the vibrant cultural conclave of Greek exiles in Jerusalem. In a dark hotel room in the city, the poet Demetrios (a thinly veiled version of Seferis himself) recites in his native tongue to the assembled community of refugees:

> Geoffrey, understanding only imperfectly, watched Demetrios, who, with his eyes hidden, seemed too sombre, too discouraged a man for a poet. Only when he lifted his sloe-black glance his spirit was visible. Geoffrey covered his own eyes with his hand as though absorbed by the poetry and there came into his mind a picture of a taverna on the lower slopes of Pendele where he had gone with Demetrios to a party in spring. He was conscious of the sun on his hands, the sound and clarity of running water, the taste of retsina and the smell of the pine-trees that grew distorted on a windy hillside. There were cyclamen flowers dotted over the ground and tortoises of all sizes moved across the paths in the pine woods. Far below, the salt-white city sparkled under a mist of heat. (*Artist Among the Missing*, p. 50)

As with Lynd, whose imagination is thus suddenly released, the Greek alliance provided Manning with creative energy and a validation of a refugee sensibility grounded in concepts of exile, nostalgia and loss.

For Manning and the other British writers who came to be associated with the *Personal Landscape* venture, the strong connection with Greece was twofold in importance. First, it offered them an archive of imagery and metaphor, based largely on classical tropes of the sea, the ship, the journey or the ruined homeland, on which to build a contemporary aesthetic. Secondly, Greece provided a unity of values and sensibility for those cast into the alien landscape of the Middle East. The Greek link enabled a British literary coterie to distinguish itself somewhat from a broader expatriate wartime culture, which, though catered for by sister publications such as the army-based *Parade*, or *Salamander*, was in some respects alien to what was in effect a predominantly leftist and (with the exceptions of military men like George Fraser and Keith Douglas) largely non-combatant circle, with certain pacifist leanings.[33] Following the lead of a Greek literati which had responded evocatively to Smyrna, those writers who regrouped in Egypt after the fall of Greece itself were self-consciously and rigorously attentive to the theme of dislocation; they launched their new journal, *Personal Landscape*, as a study of cultural deracination stimulated by a Greek template. The first number, predictably enough, was dominated by reflections on their former Aegean home.

This is not to suggest that the initiative was apolitical. Rather, the sense of alliance with a refugee mentality opened up an intriguing and complex position for *Personal Landscape*. Exploring the history of the journal in the context of Egyptian transition from British protectorate to independence, Jonathan Bolton suggests that its affiliates were in a 'unique situation in which writers who were bound to the Empire by citizenship were also bound to the archetypal postcolonial subject by virtue of their migrant status, the fragmentation of national identity and by their heterogeneity'. Perhaps this overstates the case and pre-empts a later Egyptian history, but the observation none the less conveys the importance (and ambiguities) of the refugee context for the poetic association. Discussing the position of Lawrence Durrell, the critic Richard Pine gestures with more subtlety towards a similar idea of the writer's Janus-faced condition, 'embarrassed by Europe yet still part of it', a *déraciné* still carrying, reluctantly, the historical burden of colonialist baggage.[34]

Durrell's position foregrounds in many ways the temper of the group as a whole. He was the individual who carried most tenaciously to Egypt an identity forged in Greece. Evacuated in April 1941 (having made his escape via Crete in an open caïque along with his wife and new baby), Durrell was initially taken on as a British Embassy foreign press officer in Cairo. His strongest attachments in Egypt were to Alexandria, however, where he was subsequently sent as a press attaché. For Alexandria remained at the time a quintessentially Greek city, culturally defined through its close identification with a classical Greek heritage and a 'homeland' community across the Mediterranean. Here Durrell shared a flat with novelist Robert Liddell, both pining for Greece (the loss of which Durrell, in the wake of the occupation, would describe as 'an amputation') and making occasional forays to the livelier haunts of the Egyptian capital.[35] Later, in the *Alexandria Quartet*, Durrell would celebrate the eponymous city, transformed into a densely symbolic realm through the terms of his high-modernist aesthetic – the 'heraldic universe' – as an iconic locus of diversity: polyglot, inter-racial, multi-devotional, erotic and deeply sensual.[36]

In their literary identification with the city, the British Alexandrines had long been inspired first by E.M. Forster, whose *Alexandria: A History and A Guide*, originally published in 1922, remained the standard source for Westerners in search of the city's evocative cultural and architectural treasures: Durrell, in a new introduction for a 1982 edition, wrote of his arrival in Alexandria in 1941 that '[f]or two years, I was able to walk about in the pages of this guide book, using it as piously as it deserves to be used.'[37] And secondly, the *Personal Landscape* writers held up as a talisman the figure of Constantine Cavafy, the Alexandria-born poet whose own creative life had engaged a constant creative tension with the Greek hinterland of his origins. In so many respects Cavafy, who died in 1933, was the inevitable father-figure for the *Personal Landscape* company and its attachment to Alexandria during the war: Durrell would later use him as the basis for the figure of the poet in the *Alexandria Quartet*; Liddell drew on him for the character of Christo Eugenides in his Alexandria novel *Unreal City* (1952) and would later write Cavafy's biography. For the *Personal Landscape* group as a whole, Cavafy was a mythological but exemplary presence whose antecedence made Alexandria a meaningful, if provisional, creative home. Fedden would write of him, in his 'Anatomy of Exile': '[t]he last representative of Hellenism, he passed his life in a town of cotton kings, a vague solitary, living over a brothel and carrying, under the straw hat that he always wore, passionate thoughts of Antiochus Epiphanes, and of the tragedy of the Hellenistic world – a tragedy that seemed to him clearly to be repeating itself in his own time.'[38]

An exilic literary sensibility provided the determining context, therefore, for the emergence of the *Personal Landscape* journal, founded in the late summer of 1941 by Robin Fedden, who drew in his friends from Athens days, Durrell and Spencer, and various others similarly relocated to diplomatic or educational positions in Egypt. The journal, which ran to eight issues over the course of the next three years, was distinctive and successful within the immediate expatriate British community, but beyond this it represented for its contributors a means of securing function and identity within an increasingly vulnerable European–Egyptian relationship. Bolton decribes how 'it was *apropos* . . . for the exiled writers' own interior struggles with their circumstances and the processes by which they resisted isolation and *accidie*'.[39] Above all, it pursued the concept of the *personal* (defined by Robin Fedden's short poem in the first issue), endorsing the elevation of individual and private desires over and above the demands of a chaotic and unpredictable political horizon (and implicitly rejecting therefore a school of pre-war poetry rooted in the pressures of social commitment). The group that emerged under the flagship of *Personal Landscape* in the early 1940s was characterised not by the war as such but by a plangent sense of individual and scenic loss. Grief for a vanished Greece, laments over the country's fall and recollections of its stolen beauty were the characteristic topoi of those writers who gathered at the journal's unofficial headquarters, Cairo's Anglo-Egyptian Union, to reflect on their situation. 'From the moment of its inception', observes Bolton, 'the magazine was foremost a cure for boredom, loneliness, and isolation, and consoled the writers against an overwhelming sense of homelessness'.[40] Manning herself also recognised the extent to which the enterprise was characterised by its prevailing backward look. 'The creative force of the early 40s was nostalgic', she later wrote. 'Cairo's civilian poets, Terence Tiller, Larry Durrell and Bernard Spencer, had started a poetry magazine which chiefly expressed longing for times past, places lost and friends who would not come again.'[41]

Manning was appreciative, then, of Greece's literary tradition of exile, and was keen to follow its traces in the movement fostered by the British literati in Athens, Alexandria and later Cairo. She remained very much on the edge of the *Personal Landscape* initiative, and her relationships with Lawrence Durrell and his colleagues appear to have been strained by various personal animosities. The poet George Fraser was disgruntled when she derided his verse and Durrell was similarly unenthusiastic, referring to her privately as 'the hook-nosed condor of the Middle East'.[42] Frequently, those recalling her presence within the group were cynical about her motives. Nor, of course, was she exclusively attached to this one outlet, being involved at the same time, for example, with *Citadel*, the British Council magazine edited from January 1942 by Reggie Smith and the economist David Hicks (another former Athens associate), and very probably with other wartime publications, such as *Desert Poets*, emerging from Cairo's British expatriate contingent.

Beyond personality clashes, there was perhaps a sense within the inner circles of *Personal Landscape* that Manning, already a published novelist, was never going to produce poetry of the standard the journal required. George Fraser was certainly disparaging about her *husband's* efforts in verse-writing: Reggie Smith, he recalled, was a particularly inept war poet, out of touch with the new climate and aesthetic created by the conflict. 'For Reggie', he wrote, 'there had not really been a poet worth talking about since Auden and MacNeice, and he felt that poetry had gone off the rails since it had ceased to concern itself primarily with the social situation and the political struggle'.[43] If Manning, too, had felt the sting of rejection, she was able at the very least to take revenge in the *Levant Trilogy*, with her portrait of Bill Castlebar, the boisterous, crude and womanising poet whose presence in Cairo's expatriate drinking venues so frequently irks Harriet Pringle. As suggested earlier, Castlebar is probably based on more than one of Manning's acquaintances from the period – a fusion of Durrell, Bernard Spencer (the basis for Durrell's Johnny Keats in *Clea*), Robin Fedden (who, like Castlebar, had a pronounced stammer) and perhaps too Keith Bullen, editor of the literary journal *Salamander* and another larger-than-life fixture in the Anglo-Egyptian Union in Cairo, whose sudden death in 1945 may have inspired Castlebar's equally unpredicted demise in *The Sum of Things*.[44] Whatever his biographical origins, he is reconfigured in the fiction as a buffoon and a grotesque, a writer whose vulgar limericks are deemed to be too obscene for publication in *Personal Landscape* (*LT*, p. 485). Yet more serious is the implication that his approach to his own craft is casual to the point of becoming fraudulent. In the 'mists of alcohol' at his hotel in Beirut (to which he has retreated with Angela Hooper, now his mistress), Castlebar describes to a quizzical Harriet his daily work routine:

> He took out of his pocket a page from a small, ruled notebook. 'I have it here. Before lunch, when I'm shaving, I put it up on the shaving-mirror and look at it, and I alter a word here and there, and gradually it builds up. In a couple of weeks it will be a poem.' (*LT*, p. 486)

Despite reservations on both sides, however, Manning did begin to engage with the *Personal Landscape* cohort, and contributed to the journal a piece which illustrates the impact of her experience in Greece – both lived and literary – on her imagination. 'Written in the Third Year of the War' is a long-line poem in three non-rhyming sections, reading almost, one might suggest, as a prose piece. With what Roger Bowen describes as its 'nervous, hypnotic rhythm', it is at once grandiose and unassuming in its ambitions towards a descriptive statement on the conflict.[45] Its theme, the fall of Greece and the exile of the British community, overlaps with several images finding their way into *Friends and Heroes*: the soldiers leaving Athens to vanquish the enemy, returning on lorries, bandaged and defeated; the sunken ships in Piraeus harbour after the explosion and the guns poised ready on the quayside – all elemental material, for Manning, of what she encapsulates in the verse as 'a thing unknown to our generation, the sorrow and terror of defeat'. With its titular reference to Thucydides and the 'ancient wars' of Greece, the poem draws in requisite classical antecedents but echoes, too, the language and sentiments of her Greek contemporaries, as discussed above:

> When the brilliance of the Pelopponese went down in darkness,
> When the night came between us,
> Our friends returned to Athens, excited a little, more afraid.
> We faced the sea
> Knowing until the day of our return, we would be exiles
> From a country not our own.

In the invocation of the exile's sensibility, there is a specific nod to Papadimitriou: Manning's poem, Bowen argues, 'owes some of its inspiration to *Anatolia*, particularly the symbolic hope of the early spring offensive and the imagery of flowers and flags'.[46] However, the evocation of a refugee culture is taken further, mapped on to a newly developed British crisis of identity, the imperial personality having been pushed into insecurity while still enmeshed in historical culpability:

> We, the deniers, have known long denial.
> Alien in a domesticated land, choiceless between the century-planted and the sand,
> We are a long way from childhood, from the wild shore and the mountain wind.

'Written in the Third Year of the War' appeared in the second issue of *Personal Landscape* in March 1942 and was later reprinted in the selected anthology of the magazine produced in 1945.[47] No other contributions from Manning appeared in the journal, but in 1944 she published in Cyril

Connolly's *Horizon* a defence of the *Personal Landscape* venture in an article entitled 'Poets in Exile'. Connolly had been favourably disposed towards the Cairo-based group, believing that Durrell and his fellow writers, 'steeped in the Aegean civilization', would provide a disciplined and tasteful antidote to the 'windy nothings' currently being submitted to him in England. He wrote to Robin Fedden offering to sell copies of the magazine, putting in a request at the same time for contributions on Egypt to his 'Where shall John go?' series in *Horizon*, with which Fedden helpfully complied.[48]

How exactly Manning came to be given priority as the voice of the enterprise is not exactly clear. She had already flattered Connolly in print – 'an essayist of high order, and one of the few reviewers whose reviews are worth preserving between stiff covers' – and it was also rumoured that her article had arrived safely at the *Horizon* office only by misuse, through a friend, of the diplomatic bag.[49] Regardless of its provenance, the article was in keeping with various essays on the poetry of the moment appearing in *Salamander* and *Oasis*, and in keeping too with the series of meditations on the current state of verse which ran in *Personal Landscape* itself. There was a difference in status, however, in that this essay marked a return to London as a critical centre and sought specifically to answer a previous journalistic criticism, supposedly directed from the capital, that the poets in Egypt had become, through their long sojourn abroad, 'out of touch'. Manning's rejoinder was systematic. With the wartime closure of the Mediterranean, she argued, those in Cairo had met the necessity of forging new, local literary circles and of establishing new relationships with place. 'Whether willingly or not, they have become cosmopolitan', she claimed of her fellow writers; 'they have met and been influenced by refugee writers of other countries; they have learnt foreign languages not commonly learnt by English people and so absorbed new literatures'. In a snipe at the insularity and stagnation displayed, in comparison, by a *domestic* idiom, she added: 'The character of poetry written out here may suffer from being outbred as that written in England during the same period may suffer from being inbred.'[50]

The aggressive tone here, together with the critical weakness of judgements passed by Manning on some of her contemporaries (Durrell's verse is dismissed vaguely as 'pretending to be something that it is not', Spencer's decried as being pleasantly 'Georgian', and so on), gives some indication of Manning's insecurity in the poetry field at this level of production. Not surprisingly, there was a backlash from within. As Bowen reports, Terence Tiller was among those perturbed by Manning's opinions, writing to John Lehmann: 'You will have seen Olivia Manning's article in *Horizon* on Middle East writers; and it has given great annoyance to all but the Apocalyptic and Salamandrine locals.'[51] He shared with others the view that her intervention was closer to interference in a territory to which she was, by and large, peripheral, particularly given the fact that by 1944, the year of the article's publication, she had already moved with her husband to Palestine, leaving behind the centre of creative action in Cairo. Durrell was resolutely unimpressed with the article and unconvinced by what he perceived to be Manning's attempts to insinuate herself into the *Personal Landscape* clique.[52]

Manning's was not the only cause of dissent: there was also disagreement over the tone of George Fraser's piece, 'Recent Verse: London and Cairo', published in *Orientations* in September 1943, and some rumblings too over Durrell's 'Airgraph on Refugee Poets in Africa', published in *Poetry* in London in 1944. However, Manning's survey had appeared in the most respected of London-based literary journals and it therefore came under most serious attack, having, as Bowen suggests, 'tried to give a group "identity" to a group that wanted none of it'.[53] The publication of Manning's views on *Personal Landscape* seemed in the end to do her few favours, and doubtless gained her new enemies.

What is clear in hindsight, however, is the extent to which the essay provided her less with an opportunity to discuss poetry, and more with a platform on which to pursue yet further the particular and precise conditions she was beginning to establish as essential to her own creative and personal profile: that of the refugee. Tracing her own route to Cairo as typical of the civilian writers caught up in the same process of transition, she describes here in detail the departure from Athens with Liddell, Edwards, Seferis and Papadimitriou, and confronts at length the slow, painful process of acculturation on which all had embarked on reaching Egypt:

> The first shocking impact of the Middle East numbed everyone. It took months to get over it, and longer to become reconciled to it. Resentment of the squalid shabbiness, the dirt, exposed diseases, beggary, luxury and heat, produced in the refugees an

> overwhelming nostalgia for Greece that filled their writings and began to bore their friends who had not been there.

Gradually, she explains, the new arrivals did become accustomed to their surroundings, making new liaisons with the refugee representatives of other cultures, forging new bonds and contracts and developing an entirely new creative dynamic. Theirs was not the 'rootless, neurotic produce of the expatriate' but a body of material in close touch with the life around it; 'the new work being done here', she concluded, 'may take home a strain that will prove of real value to the stock'.[54]

For the Pringles the onwards move to Egypt throws into a nostalgic, rose-tinted relief the country left behind. Greece, with its familiarity of culture and like-minded literati, had come to feel like home. For Harriet, even its contradictions – the hard facts of its poverty and repression – cannot override the nobility with which the country is reinvested in the hindsight of Egypt. In common with many of her generation, she regards the final fall of this nation, heralded in the closing broadcast from the Greek radio station the Pringles listen to in Egypt, as indicating 'the silence of the civilized world' (*LT*, p. 66). Any loss of faith was not in Greece but in an increasingly jaundiced British element, turning in on itself and against itself under the pressures of expatriate life in wartime. Estranged by now from any coherent imperial war effort and increasingly at odds with a stable sense of British identity, this group appears troubled and conflicted as it gradually moves closer to a precarious refugee condition. There are certainly no heroes in this contingent, and by the time of their journey from Athens on the *Erebus*, amidst the petty wrangling over cabin-space and supplies conducted by their British associates, Harriet can only conclude, desolate, that '[n]ot one of their friends remained.' (*BT*, p. 923).

For Manning, too, the passage yet farther eastwards that she and her husband were forced to take after the German invasion of Greece was, in a sense, a movement towards diminishment. The flourishing literary climate she subsequently tracked in Egypt and experienced within the *Personal Landscape* cohort could never be as accommodating, in its social or emotional resources, as what had been left behind in Athens. If in life the Greek interim represented a short but affecting episode of relative personal security in the context of disturbance and dislocation, in fiction it provided for a more enduring legacy: a penetrating scrutiny of rottenness at the heart of British cultural imperialism. As a novel, *Friends and Heroes* turns on an acute sense of lost richness and missed opportunity, reflecting long after the actual events its author's continuing passage to wry maturity amidst the changing fortunes of the wartime period.

Chapter Four

Egypt, the desert war and the Levant Trilogy

In the Middle East, in 1940, 1941 and 1942, a lot of young men in corduroy pants, suede boots and spotted scarves saved the sum of things. Theirs is the achievement, and let no man question it.

John Connell[1]

The three novels first published together in 1982 as the *Levant Trilogy* are among the most vivid fictional representations of wartime experience to exist in modern literature in English. Manning's descriptions of a British refugee community waiting out the war alongside the diplomatic and military corps stationed in the Middle East positions Cairo as the nub of a soured imperialism: a volatile, intemperate city disturbed not only by the pitched battles staged in the outlying desert but by mounting pressures for nationalist revolution within the country's borders. Egypt, flanked by the Suez Canal, could not be lost, yet between the initial drafting of the trilogy and its eventual publication Egypt *was* lost, Britain's passage to India cut from under her feet and the international order changed irrevocably. Manning's portrait of Cairo is therefore paradoxical: this is a city in the last throes of a decadent imperial indulgence and, simultaneously, in the early stages of a hysterical retreat. Her theme is the fraught interface between two epochs, and the beginnings of a transition to a post-war, post-imperial order.

Though she continues to draw on autobiographical supports, her subtle exaggerations of actual historical experience create an agitated political and cultural landscape, peopled with plausible yet theatrical individuals. In Castlebar the poet, Jackman the war correspondent, Edwina Little the embassy sweetheart, she traces personalities rooted in reality but depicted almost as grotesques, heightened and stretched by the excesses of this extraordinary environment.

The *Levant Trilogy* also succeeds as war fiction because it splices the perspectives of a non-combatant community with those of an active military contingent. Cairo was the centre of Middle Eastern operations for British and Allied forces during the war, including the North African desert campaign and the decisive battle of El Alamein in 1942. An important departure in this sequence, comprising *The Danger Tree* (1977), *The Battle Lost and Won* (1978) and *The Sum of Things* (1980), is the creation of a male parallel for Harriet Pringle. The experiences of Simon Boulderstone, a young British officer dispatched to the desert and into battle at El Alamein, provide a narrative that interrupts and amplifies Harriet's own, with episodes of each interwoven in a strategic counterpoint of circumstance. At the initial meeting of the two characters on a sightseeing drive to the pyramids, Simon is attracted to Harriet as 'a pale, dark-haired girl . . . not much older than he was' (*LT*, p. 19); she, in turn, though momentarily taken aback by his youth and political naivety, recognises him as a companion of sorts, at odds like her with a wartime culture of swagger and false *bonhomie*. The parallel works very much to her benefit – Simon's character serves to obscure Harriet's less appealing traits and she regains an integrity of spirit by virtue of his innocence and purity. But Manning also establishes through Simon a purposeful dovetailing of masculine and feminine plots, gaining a means of passing beyond a female and domestic environment into the theatre of the military campaign in North Africa.

The impact of the *Levant Trilogy* derives fundamentally, however, from the vividness of its settings, which stretch across the Middle East from Alexandria and the Egyptian desert to Jerusalem and Damascus. Cairo dominates this historical landscape as the enervated centre of expatriate life for the Pringles. The Egyptian city to which they flee in 1941, disorientated and almost destitute, provides Manning with a natural meeting-point for her prevailing themes, enlarged and expanded since her rather poetic treatment of the same city as an Allied forces playground in the second half of her 1949 novel *Artist Among the Missing.* In the trilogy, there is a heightened consciousness of Cairo as a precarious refugee haven, temporary home to an assortment of exiled monarchs, homeless Greeks and deracinated European Jews, surviving alongside the Pringles' coterie of wandering English lecturers and writers, and a greater sense, too, of a city under genuine threat as Rommel's eastward sweep across the desert continues. The vulnerability of the Egyptian capital is underlined here in its geographical proximity to the war, with losses reported back from the battles at Tobruk, Kidney Ridge and El Alamein, but also in its symbolic proximity to the death of a civilisation, represented by the pyramidal tombs which frame the action and remain, for Harriet, always visible on the near horizon.

In assembling this picture, Manning was adding to an expansive catalogue of portraits of the city, both ancient and modern. To a greater extent than Bucharest and perhaps even Athens, Cairo was already familiar in the public imagination, already represented to a British reading public through a sequence of imperial records, military memoirs and tourist travelogues. By the time of her trilogy's publication, wartime Cairo and Alexandria had been well established as notable literary locations, as part of the itinerary for a fraught Guy Crouchback in Waugh's *Sword of Honour* and the setting for novels by three of Manning's contemporaries in Egypt – Robert Liddell, D.J. Enright and P.H. Newby.[2] Shortly after the end of the war Manning had reviewed several accounts of Cairo for the *Palestine Post*, including Pennethorne Hughes' illustrated memoir of the city's landmark Shepheard's Hotel, *While Shepheard's Watched* (1943), and (less favourably) *For the Rest of our Lives*, Dan Davin's Cairo-based military *roman à clef*, published in 1945.[3] In its wartime dress, Cairo featured heavily in popular material ranging from Cecil Beaton's military and airforce photographs to Evelyn Waugh's diaries, and in numerous memoirs and correspondence produced by the various figures stationed there during the conflict. By the time of the trilogy's composition the city's major landmarks had become redolent of Egypt's *belle époque* and the glory days of diplomatic balls, villa parties, polo and horse racing. Manning's depictions of Cairo's legendary Shepheard's Hotel, home to the multitude of wartime generals and foreign correspondents stationed in the Middle East, or of the Mena House Hotel at the foot of the Giza pyramids – the secret location in November 1943 for talks between Churchill, Roosevelt and Chiang Kai-shek – build on the existing notoriety of these landmarks. Similarly her descriptions of the luxurious Gezira Sports Club with its gardens stretching down to the Nile, or of the more downmarket Anglo-Egyptian Union and its welcoming bar trace a cityscape which, despite its initial strangeness to the Pringles, is both familiar and suggestive in terms of what Egypt had come to signify to a British reading public in the years between her fiction's conception and publication.[4]

Beneath the apparent richness of this portrait and the compression of the city's landscape into sites reaffirming a history of European – specifically British and French – domination, Manning interposes a seam of political irony, darkening her previous highly romantic treatment of the city in *Artist Among the Missing*. In the earlier novel, for example, Geoffrey Lynd pauses to appreciate the way in which the military barracks at Zamaleck are tinged with the quality of a Victorian print: '[T]he palms, the still water, the square, low-lying buildings, the Empire, the Queen-Empress, the opulent East' (*Artist Among the Missing*, p. 253). In *The Sum of Things*, this Victorian allure has become a crippling hangover and the same barracks appear to Simon Boulderstone as a mausoleum, turned by the evening light to the colour of dried blood. 'The long, low building, so bug-ridden that only fire could disinfect it, was hazed by river mist and looked remote, a Victorian relic, a symbol of past glory' (*LT*, p. 427). Through such redrafting, the narrative sweep of the *Levant Trilogy* frames Cairo's noted sites in the context of a long and now pressing political chronology: the city, for all its continuing opulence and indulgence, is seen as jaded, tainted by its own excess.

The country, meanwhile, and the Middle East in general will slip the ties of a British connection in an inexorable movement towards political and cultural independence. In Manning's trilogy it becomes clear that Cairo now stands on the brink of a radical disengagement from a Western imperial system. Her presentation of the clubs and hotels of the city undercuts an expatriate extension of the glory days of a British diplomatic and military ascendancy with pointed allusions to the threatened disruption of western authority in the country. Though less precise on this trajectory than Durrell, whose complex reading of Egypt's internal ethnic and religious contradictions drives the tension of the *Alexandria Quartet*, Manning is none the less attentive to the country's imperial counter-narratives of nationalist and fundamentalist insurgency. In particular, elements of the *Levant Trilogy*'s final volume, *The Sum of Things*, revisit the political territory of her earlier Palestine-set novels but with an ominous sounding of cultural fracture in the Middle East as a whole. By the time of the author's own arrival in Cairo in 1941, an Arab resistance in some form seemed imminent. The publication of the Christian Arab George Antonius's book *The Arab Awakening* in 1939 signalled for some a newly confident Arab nationalism, and for others flagged the pressures mounting around questions of both secular and religious autonomy in the Middle East. During the brief interim between the Anglo-Egyptian treaty in 1936 (formally marking the end of a British High Commission) and the coup that ushered in a republic in 1952, the fragile monarchy of King Farouk – the figure so viciously mocked in the trilogy by Jake Jackman and his cohorts – held the country in a precarious tension and Cairo itself in a volatile condition. At home, the outbreak of war fragmented still further the illusion of Egypt as a British 'safe house' overseas: '[A] general suspicion of the West is current throughout the Middle East', Robin Fedden wrote in *Horizon* in 1945, 'a suspicion which primarily expresses itself in the strong reaction of Islam against our influence and ideology'. In his view, Egypt had become a lost and much-lamented indulgence, with the modern traveller no longer insulated from its brutality and aggression. If anything, Britain's military presence during the war had succeeded only in exacerbating and consolidating Egyptian discontent. '[T]he lasting importance of the Occupation was the spirit of nationalism that it provoked', he concluded. 'It could be said that the most valuable contribution of British rule was the corporate resentment it ultimately aroused.'[5]

Olivia Manning had become interested in the imperial history of Egypt some time before her actual arrival in the country during the war. After the completion of her Irish novel *The Wind Changes* in 1937, she had begun to compile material for her historical account of journalist Henry Morton Stanley's infamous rescue of the besieged governor, Emin Pasha, from the province of Equator, following the fall of Khartoum and the assassination of General Gordon in 1885. The book which resulted from her research, *The Remarkable Expedition*, is in most respects a fairly straightforward adventure narrative based largely on late Victorian journals and records, including Stanley's own 1890 memoir *In Darkest Africa*, but her introduction, 'The Egyptian Empire', written between the end of the war and the book's initial publication in 1947, hints at more current concerns. Here, Manning reviews Egypt's thwarted attempts to expand its territory into Sudan – attempts inevitably complicated by tensions between British and Turkish interests – with a sequence of asides on the country's limited capacity for national self-determination, its predisposition to 'an Oriental chaos of despotic inefficiency and official dishonesty', and its deep-rooted 'love of the old muddle which everyone understood'.[6] In the context of imperialist historiography, this was standard supremacist discourse, a language infected with the terminology of the author's Victorian predecessors and a predictable reflex perhaps, in the context of Britain's own 'old muddle' of the war years. At the same time this historical view provides an ironic frame for Manning's confrontation with *modern* Egypt in the trilogy, highlighting her awareness of the terms of contemporary Anglo-Egyptian relations and her recognition of Egypt's centrality to a broad and convoluted imperial project of economic, strategic and cultural authority in the Middle East.

In the *Levant Trilogy* a split perspective emerges over the issue of Egyptian insurgency, an ironic double-take which foregrounds a comedy of hesitant native unrest shadowed by the obscure but discernible threat of outright rebellion. The ordinary Egyptian civilian is presented as a vaguely disaffected subordinate lacking the initiative to take up arms. When Harriet broaches the question of the country's independence with her colleague Iqal, a clerk in the American Embassy where she works, his response is predictable if perhaps disingenuous: '"But to govern ourselves! – that we have forgotten, so how do we do it?"' (*LT*, p. 74). In the burlesque episode of the assassination of Lord Pinkrose in Cairo's lavishly decorated Opera House, the students who initially leap forward shouting threats to all 'enemies of Egypt's freedom' quickly retreat from any claim of responsibility: this is not Palestine, they remember, and the politics of resistance are not – or not yet – to be taken too seriously. By contrast, Egyptian nationalism is afforded intellectual credibility and recognition through the character of Dr Shafik, Harriet's physician at the American hospital and a member of the Nationalist Party. Shafik scorns the war effort on both sides, the European armies 'going backwards and forwards in the desert, chasing each other like fools', while neglecting their own impoverished citizens. 'You know', he remarks simply and more than a little menacingly in quiet reproach to Guy Pringle, cutting across the latter's attempts to foist a Marxist agenda on to their discussion of Egyptian freedom and social responsibility, 'there are many of us' (*LT*, p. 343).

At a more subtle level Manning recognised that nationalism was not just a question of two rival wills. Behind the façade of a homogeneous Arab and Muslim Egypt lay various competing political, religious and ethnic interests stranded across the country's Armenian, Greek, Jewish, Coptic and Christian communities. The critic Michael Diboll has persuasively read Lawrence Durrell's *Mountolive* (in the *Alexandria Quartet*) as an allegory of Britain's failure of nerve in removing support from the secular and pro-Western nationalist Wafd party at the expense in the end of a multicultural and cosmopolitan nation.[7] Manning too was aware that beneath the immediate threat of insurgency lay a schism between a secular, democratic Egypt and the pull of a pan-Arab Islamic alliance. In *The Remarkable Expedition* she had underlined the historical dangers posed to Egypt and British imperial interests in the region by the rise of a Muslim Sudan, a territory galvanised in the period by the *Mahdi* or spiritual leader Mohammed Ahmed. Religion, not nationalism, she asserted in her preface to the book, would eventually work as a uniting force to lead the English into 'ignominious defeat' in the Middle East.[8] Her perspective in the 1940s would be endorsed and confirmed by subsequent violent events and by the founding of a fundamentalist Arab Egyptian state under Gamal Abdul Nasser after the revolution in 1952. By the time of the *Levant Trilogy*'s publication in 1982, the region's power struggles with Muslim fundamentalism had escalated to yet more grievous levels and the diverse identities of Durrell's Egypt further obscured.

Manning gestures towards a political future for the Middle East in one of the most important, yet perhaps most opaque, sections of the trilogy. In the final novel, *The Sum of Things*, Harriet, now estranged from her husband and wandering through Syria alone, comes under the protection of a Christian Arab businessman, Halal. Treated in the context of a conventional romance plot, their subsequent friendship might be read simply as a repetition of the pattern in which Harriet engages with various masculine figures (other than her husband) throughout both trilogies. In political and cultural terms, however, her liaison with Halal is an important illustration of cross-cultural encounter. In Bucharest (during the course of *The Spoilt City*) Harriet allied herself with Sasha Drucker –

sidelined spouse paralleling threatened Jew – both surviving on the periphery of European war. Now she becomes the wandering wife who finds a natural ally in this affluent and educated Arab, a former student of the American University and a member of what he humorously terms an 'advanced circle'. In the home of Halal's close friend Jamil, a Circassian Muslim, there is pride in the fact that the guests, who include an assortment of Muslims, Christians and Jews, mingle freely (albeit that their freedom is limited to men, as Harriet's awkward meeting with Jamil's sequestered wife reminds us). Halal takes Harriet to visit the sites of a Damascus split between religious affiliations, and in his commentary on this landscape upholds a vision of Christ and Mohammed coexisting as divine avatars in an ideal spiritual and civic harmony. Yet such harmony is already in retreat. Even as they return to Harriet's hotel, the sound of gunfire in the streets signals popular resistance to the British and the Free French. In the future this educated, liberal businessman, who carries his college diplomas in his briefcase, will be forced to the periphery of a fundamentalist ideology in his own country and in the region as a whole. The romance he briefly offers Harriet is therefore the romance of a liberal Arab heritage – poetic, spiritual and multi-denominational – now foundering on the rocks of an Islamic nationalist incentive.[9]

These layered elements within wartime Egyptian political culture are nuanced rather than profiled directly in the trilogy. Characteristically, Manning simply gestures towards Egyptian resistance and revolution on a distant horizon as the background to her close-range Tolstoyan study of an expatriate, military and diplomatic community failing to recognise (or choosing to ignore) that narrative and its implications. In this respect her prevailing theme is simply imperial vanity and the decadence that accompanied it, her novels an almost documentary reading at times of British Cairo's profile in 1942. Undoubtedly, the war intensified the Raj mentality separating European from Egyptian, and in its isolation the British community fell back on its own increasingly vapid social and cultural resources. Tracing the fates of the various expatriate communities present at the time in Cairo, historian Magdi Wahba has suggested that, to a far greater extent than the Italians, French or Greeks, the English became fossilised in their own complex structures of rituals and pageantry: the searchlight tattoo at the polo grounds at Gezira in honour of the Prince of Wales; the Armistice Day airshows at Almaza airport;

the church parades in Garden City; the changing of the guard outside the Residency – all these represented 'a world of ceremony sufficient unto itself', artificially extending the lifetime of the city's jaded British community.

> First, it went into a sort of discreet hibernation period between 1936 and 1939, when nationalist riots occurred with disturbing frequency. Then came the War, and the emergence of an entirely new, largely male British community in uniform, with its own ENSA shows, NAAFI stores, and short-lived literary reviews, such as *Personal Landscape* and *Salamander*, its own popular press modeled on *Picture Post* and *Lilliput*, its own dance bands, its own academics in Intelligence Units – and its own feeble gesture of friendship towards the Egyptian intelligentsia (then teetering on the brink of Nazi sympathies) . . . The old community was dying, its children sucked into the War, its security shaken by anti-British riots and the crippling infirmities of age.[10]

The *Levant Trilogy* is a portrait of this society in retreat, experiencing the endgame of its glorious Middle Eastern adventure and beginning to consider its likely fate if, in Harriet's teasing words to Simon, 'the gyppos turned on us' (*LT*, p. 24). At the same time it is a critique of a short-sighted and ultimately doomed imperial project. Simon Boulderstone's naive belief in the structures of Empire – '[W]e've shown them how people ought to live' – is met by Harriet's more worldly take on the expediency of a British mission which has ignored a peasant underclass while making a minority of Egyptians rich, a protectorate whose protective instincts are geared entirely towards the maintenance of Suez and the eastward oil and trade routes (*LT*, p. 24). Imperial pride in the Egyptian jewel will lead inevitably to a grievous fall and indeed, by the time of their composition and publication, the novels of the trilogy detailed a world that no longer existed. Many of its glamorous locations were destroyed in the riots of the 1950s, while in 1956 the nationalisation of the Suez Canal, beside which Simon Boulderstone disembarks in the opening paragraphs of *The Danger Tree*, effectively ended privileged trade access through the region and European tenure in Egypt. In the course of the same novel, Harriet comes to recognise that an endgame is in process:

> She saw the Middle East cracking between the pincers like a broken walnut and asked herself: what would happen then? She tried to work out on the map the strategy of defeat. The British troops, she supposed, would retreat into Iraq and make a last stand in defence of the Persian Gulf. But suppose there were no troops? Supposing the whole Eighth Army was caught between the converging pincers and not one man remained to retreat and defend what was left? What would they do then? There was almost relief at the thought of it. Responsibility would cease. (*LT*, pp. 80–1)

The Pringles' arrival in Cairo following their precarious sea voyage from Greece and train journey from Alexandria marks a transition from the reassuringly familiar environment of Athens to a city that is in so many ways beyond their comprehension, and a country which evokes in them 'disgust and a fear of its strangeness' (*LT*, p. 56). From the roof of the cramped pension where she and Guy initially manage to secure a room Harriet struggles to order her panoramic view of this intractable place, built on land reclaimed from the sea, its pyramids standing upright on the horizon 'like little metal pencil sharpeners' (*LT*, p. 54). Walking through Cairo's baking hot streets, almost overwhelmed by the smell of urine from its waste lots, she notes the ways in which a modern city is beginning to emerge in the confused chronological space between subjugation and independence. On the crowded pavements of rush hour the citizens push their way back to the city's offices. 'Some of the men were so new to commerce that they still wore the *galabiah* but most of them had managed to fit themselves out with trousers and jackets. Some had even taken to wearing the fez. Many were pock-marked or had only one seeing eye, the other being white and sightless from trachoma; many were enervated by bilharzias, but they were all rising in the world, leaving behind the peasants and the back street *balani* from whom they derived' (*LT*, p. 81). Like Guy's students in Alexandria, who press their teacher for 'commercial English' rather than the comic abstractions of *Finnegans Wake*, these are pragmatic and modern Egyptians; like Eastern Europe, this region is in transition beneath the surface vignettes of picturesque antiquity and tradition.

In *The Danger Tree*, the perambulations of Harriet and later Simon through the streets of Cairo are a means of exposing the gradual detachment of the city from its former imperial ties. The Egyptian capital had long been established as a fashionable winter resort for European royalty and a British aristocracy, as Trevor Mostyn describes: 'The Turf club, the Shepheard's Hotel, the Khedival Sporting club – these were the pivots of Britain's effective rule in Egypt. Life's pleasures were cheap for the British at the beginning of the century. You could sit and drink coffee and eat sickly sweets and cakes at Groppi's, or by 1919, see the latest American films at the Metro or the Miami cinemas.'[11] But the topography the new arrivals' encounter is ersatz, its baroque effects a poor imitation of European grandeur, its landmarks faked and then run to seed. Simon emerges from the train station into the seething mass of beggars, street-sellers and British troops 'marooned' by sheer boredom, to find a city modelled on Paris and Haussmann's famous boulevards, but somehow lacking a Parisian authenticity: 'here, it seemed to him, was another Paris, not quite real, put up too quickly and left to moulder and gather dust' (*LT*, p. 15).

For the Pringles, Shepheard's Hotel is still the centre of expatriate life but has become tarnished by time, reminding one of the visiting soldiers of the interior of his local Putney Odeon. Mena House Hotel at Giza, where Harriet and Simon are abandoned by their tour party after climbing the great pyramid, retains its decadent and shabby interior of reproduction log fireplaces and imported English furnishings. And Groppi's, Cairo's famous garden café where Harriet takes tea with diplomat Dobbie Dobson, is merely a stone-floored yard with little more on offer than a strip of imported earth and a creeper. As a young officer remarks in disappointment to Harriet: 'The chaps in the desert think Groppi's is the Garden of Sensual Delights – but, good grief, it isn't even a garden!' (*LT*, p. 132). Cairo's glories are now further diminished by the fact that the war has put an end to its place on the itinerary of the English traveller's grand tour. Looking through the window of a closed-down tourist agency, Harriet sees, 'dusty and cracking with heat, the posters that used to draw the rich to Egypt: the face of the Sphinx, the lotus columns of Karnac, the beautiful and tranquil Nile with the feluccas dipping in the wind. "Goodbye Egypt", she thought' (*LT*, p. 81).[12]

Underlying the death of a British presence in Egypt is the pervasive sense of death which Manning recruits from the tourist landscape of Cairo and maps on to the trilogy, undermining both traveller's dream and imperialist fantasy of the Middle East within the context of deep-seated wartime anxiety. Major Clifford's guided trip to the pyramids, which Harriet and Simon join at the opening of *The Danger Tree*, sees a group of half-hearted individuals, distracted by rumours from the desert campaign and fumbling with confused fragments of Egyptology, confronting, as they descend into the best-preserved of the tombs, not richness and antiquity but mortality itself:

> The tomb was empty except for a stone sarcophagus of immense size. Everything else had been looted, even the sarcophagus lid. Not only was there nothing to see but Simon realized that to enter the place was foolhardy. The apex of the pyramid was breaking through the roof plaster and poised over their heads with several tons of bricks that could be brought down by the slightest earth tremor. Clifford, moving imperturbably beneath this peril, flashed his torch on to the decayed walls, saying, 'Wonderfully fresh, these colours. Book of the Dead, y'know!' (*LT*, p. 23)

This tour of the pyramids acts as a prelude to the trilogy as a whole in heralding a narrative punctuated by death. With its topography of ruins, tombs and cemeteries and its ancient mythologies of the dead, Cairo represents the inevitable dominion of the grave over the living.

And only in death are true connections forged between British and Egyptian. All the deaths in this trilogy become related in some way and all are prefigured by the death which provides without doubt the most disturbing incident in this or any of Manning's novels. Shortly after leaving the pyramids, Clifford's tour party descends on the house of Sir Desmond Hooper, on the outskirts of Cairo, hoping for news of the campaign. During their visit, Hooper's wife Angela arrives home distraught, her servants carrying in with her the dead body of the couple's eight-year-old son. 'One eye was missing. There was a hole in the left cheek that extended into the torn wound which had been his mouth. Blood had poured down his chin and was caked on the collar of his open-necked shirt. The other eye, which was open, was lacklustre and blind like the eye of a dead rabbit' (*LT*, p. 35). The assembled company comes to understand that the boy has accidentally picked up a live grenade while out in the desert on a sketching party with his mother, and now, transfixed by shock, they watch as his uncomprehending parents attempt to feed their dead son with gruel through the hole blasted through his cheek. At once tragic and grotesque, this extraordinary event will become for the expatriate community the talk of Cairo.

As noted in the introductory chapter, the death of the Hooper boy was based on a real incident – the death of the son of diplomat Sir Walter Smart and his artist wife Amy in 1943 – and Manning's use of the event proved highly controversial, but her reconfiguring of this small moment of individual destruction in the panorama of conflict in the Middle East is far from gratuitous. Symbolically it outlines the invasion of a civilian space by the destructive power of war, and through its positioning early in the Cairo sequence, it initiates a chain of interrelated deaths, instigating a cumulative weight of mortality and a deep pessimism in the trilogy. Simon Boulderstone remembers the dead child before he himself is unleashed into the theatre of war in the desert. Once in action, he will confront the first dead bodies (other than that of the Hooper boy) he has ever seen; later, he must also confront the death of his older brother Hugo, killed in a mortar attack while serving in a neighbouring desert unit. As friends and fellow soldiers fall around him, the culture of death operates like an infection, working itself back behind the lines of the military units to the civilian front. In the course of the trilogy Aidan Sheridan's suicide, Pinkrose's assassination, Castlebar's sudden death from illness, the death of a young Egyptian in a car accident, the drowning of evacuee wives and children after the sinking of the *Queen of Sparta*, the countless bodies Harriet sees being taken for burial after the outbreak of plague in Luxor, all coincide with the deaths of the thousands lost as the desert campaign intensifies, British and Egyptian ironically united in mortality.

Manning's focus on death in the trilogy maps the historical and mythological apparatus of Cairo on to the morbidity of a generation experiencing the cataclysm of war and the death on a vast scale of young men like Hugo Boulderstone. As with the army tanks decorated with the eye of the god Horus, the figure representing death and reincarnation in Egyptian myth, there is a constant crossover from ancient culture into modern trauma, symbolised by the presence of the pyramids but also by repeated reference to Cairo's Muslim cemetery, the City of the Dead, where the Pringles join a mourning ceremony for one of Guy's students. Meanwhile, the dominating symbol of the opening novel, the 'danger tree', is explained in a discussion about the mango tree outside the window of the Pringles' room in Dobbie Dobson's villa. Every year, Dobson explains, some unfortunate individual dies as a result of choosing a mango contaminated by the natural poison in its own stem. Like the grenade picked up by the Hooper boy from the desert sand, the fruit is both temptation and damnation, and even supposedly safe domestic spaces in the city give way to the all-pervasive claims of mortality. Cairo becomes in a literal sense the death zone for Manning's sequence, its morbid topography attuned to the pessimism sounded by her trilogy as a whole.

The Egyptian setting draws in other themes too. Cairo in the period of the Second World War was legendary for its glamour. The existing British community expanded significantly when the city became the centre for British and Allied operations in the Middle East, the huge numbers of military and diplomatic corps stationed there for the duration of the war adding to its allure. Its social élite sparkled. British commando Fitzroy MacLean recalls flying in from an undercover mission in Yugoslavia to dine with Anthony Eden and an array of Foreign Office officials at the exclusive Mohamed Ali club: 'Round us at the other tables sat the collection of Egyptian pashas, Greek millionaires, exiled princes, high-ranking British officers and cosmopolitan beauties that constituted Cairene society during the war. They gave the impression of great wealth and considerable elegance. It all seemed faintly improbable.' Freya Stark, engaged at the time in Allied propaganda work throughout the Middle East, also celebrated the glossy wartime aura bestowed on Cairo by virtue of its centrality to military operations. 'It had returned to the days of the Ptolemys when Egypt was the gate to Parthia and India and all the spice trade', she wrote. 'Exhausted as we all were at the end, the threat was an enhancement, and no-one can forget the gaiety and the glitter of Cairo while the desert war went on.'[13]

Not surprisingly, perhaps, it has been suggested that writers of the period played up this atmosphere. The critic Mark Rawlinson, for example, suggests that Manning and Durrell, in particular, indulged in a 'romancing of expatriate wartime culture' in their fictions of the militarised city.[14] Yet thematically Manning's trilogy is far from indulgent; rather, her version of Cairo treats the city's social effervescence as a nervous reflex, a superficial symptom of its grievous and deep-seated insecurities. Continuing her focus on the development of a refugee culture in wartime, she emphasises the composition of Cairo's wartime society as quintessentially transient, a volatile conglomerate of expatriates and exiles. Egypt in this respect was the 'dumping ground' of Europe, as the British Ambassador in Cairo, Miles Lampson, complained frequently at the time, and the constant arrival of fresh transients created a pattern of disturbance, the resultant squeeze on space and resources fuelling greed and competitiveness at every social level. Harriet, catching a train westwards to Alexandria to warn Guy about Rommel's advance, observes the crush on the opposite platform when the city's European refugees, packed together 'in a state of agitated anxiety, expecting tumult', push for the train in panic as they flee eastwards to Palestine. The sweltering heat of the city seems intensified by the suffocating effects of its temporary population:

> Cairo had become the clearing house of Eastern Europe. Kings and princes, heads of state, their followers and hangers-on, free governments with all their officials, everyone who saw himself committed to the Allied cause, had come to live here off the charity of the British government. Hotels, restaurants and cafés were loud with the squabbles, rivalries, scandals, exhibitions of importance and hurt feelings that occupied the refugees while they waited for the war to end and the old order to return. (*LT*, p. 93)[15]

Life here cannot settle, with civilians constantly on the verge of evacuation or flight from a home that is, at best, provisional. Whereas in Greece the Pringles experienced a relative security, in Cairo their situation is governed by instability: here, a 'jittery' Harriet represents the condition of an entire community riddled with nervous tension. The terse exchanges and vulgar conversations Manning stages between her major characters at the Union Bar reflect this precarious state as the pressure of war erodes a normal civic ethos, while the obvious childishness of so many minor personalities – Cookson, Tootsie, Jackman – similarly underline the collapse of a mature and rational society.

Perversely, then, in Manning's account, the city so acclaimed for its glamour and vivaciousness enshrines at its heart alienation and enervation. The British expatriate element expresses itself, in turn, through a behavioural excess, a recklessness and self-indulgence generated by the pressures of their compacted position. In *The Battle Lost and Won*,

Harriet's evening at the Extasé Club with various acquaintances, including Castlebar and Angela Hooper, pitches from banter and sniping towards drunken aggression and violence; in *The Sum of Things*, the war correspondent (and probable spy) Jake Jackman embarks on a drunken rampage during which he destroys the interior of Mrs Rutter's lavish Gezira mansion. Such behaviour points up a dysfunctionalism in this wartime expatriate community, a level of damage and disintegration far more serious than the petty wrangling which characterised social interaction in Athens. Additionally, Manning conveys in her Cairo sequence a dislocated society which, having lost its grip on any securities of national identity, now gives itself over to self-dramatisation and theatricality. In the expatriate haunts of the Egyptian capital, Castlebar, Jackman, Cookson and even Guy Pringle constantly play to a gallery of hacks and hangers-on.

This relentless tendency towards *performance*, often at the crudest level, is endemic in the *Levant Trilogy* as a feature of wartime expatriate existence, commented on at one stage by Harriet to Aidan Sheridan: 'The English do become odd here. Ordinary couples who'd remain happily together in Ealing or Pinner, here take on a different character. They think themselves Don Juans or tragedy queens, and throw fits of wild passion and make scenes in public . . .' (*LT*, pp. 112–13). The poet George Fraser, in the city at the same time as Manning, describes in very similar terms the inevitability of this behavioural transformation. Cairo was a complete assault on the senses, he recalls, the heat and confusion contributing to the state of 'inner exhaustion' suffered by his contemporaries. The result was an exaggeration of normality into levels of self-caricature, grotesquerie – an extravagance of being:

> In fact, against the background of Cairo, about so many of my friends, as I remember them, there was a garishness – a flourish and ostentation of every eccentric quality, that had often a deadness about it, exactly like that of posed waxwork figures. That inner exhaustion from which we all suffered affected that side of each of us that can be called the actor – the side of critical self-awareness – rather than the other side, that can be called character. We were all too much 'in character', predictable in our responses; and these tended to be violent and shallow. Cairo was a place of

> quarrels and the making up of quarrels, of rows at parties, of little rival gangs, not a matter of those quiet and steady dislikes, and settled loyalties, that are a normal part of the British character.[16]

In Manning's trilogy this condition is exhibited throughout, so that Cairo itself becomes a heady, atmospheric stage for the self-dramatisation of an exaggerated British personality, increasingly vulgar, garish and conflicted as it begins to disintegrate.

Manning extends the theatricality noted by Fraser from the public to the private domains of civilian life and, specifically, to the arena of sex and sexuality. In her earlier account of Cairo in *Artist Among the Missing*, her portrayal of the off-duty British military community underlined its indulgence in highly sexualised (even sexually depraved) behaviour. An expatriate party that takes place in the city during the second half of the 1949 novel, for example, is orgiastic and explicit. All the guests are inebriated, the women shed their clothes and dance naked, couples lie together and caress each other in full public view and the scene appears 'as though a pin had been pulled from a piece of machinery so that some parts had fallen out, static, while others whirred without meaning in eccentric circles' (*Artist Among the Missing*, p. 173). In the *Levant Trilogy* Harriet notes the same pattern of exhibitionist behaviour as she considers her expatriate companions:

> The climate changed people: it preserved ancient remains but it disrupted the living. She had seen common-place English couples who, at home, would have tolerated each other for a lifetime here turning into self-dramatizing figures of tragedy, bored, lax, unmoral, complaining and, in the end, abandoning the partner in hand for another who was neither better nor worse than the first. Inconstancy was so much the rule among the British residents in Cairo, the place, she thought, was like a bureau of sexual exchange. (*LT*, pp. 336–7)

The observation suggests at one level that Harriet herself suffers from sexual inhibitions or insecurity brought on by the deteriorated condition of her own marriage. At another, and in a broader respect, however, the volatility of sexual and marital relationships generally in the trilogy parallels the instability of political circumstance and the constant disturbances of a refugee existence, with concepts of sexual fidelity and restraint eroding under the pressures of transience and dislocation.

Combining Cairo's expatriate theatricality with its licentiousness, Manning suggests that this transformed community is further degraded by its indulgence in both sexual voyeurism and exhibitionism. In the *Levant Trilogy*, the public display of sexual congress and the repeated witnessing of congress which forms a motif in the novels is an indication of the damage done by war to concepts of privacy and moderation. The dominant sexual liaisons or partnerships are heightened and theatrical. This is particularly the case with Edwina Little, whose reputation as 'the most gorgeous popsie in Cairo' serves to embed her within a public aura of wartime desirability, undercut with darker hints of sexual menace. Edwina's lovemaking with Peter Lisdoonvarna in the embassy flat leads the jealous and semi-naked Percy Gibbon to bang furiously on her door in a state of obvious sexual arousal, to the amusement of the sniggering Egyptian servants and the consternation of Harriet herself. Later, accompanying the lovers on a trip to Saccara, Harriet observes the brutal nature of their dalliance in the shadows: 'Edwina, giving a scream, broke away from Peter and he pursued her round the huge sarcophagi, then, seizing her, he pushed her down on to a slab of black granite and threw himself on top of her' (*LT*, p. 289). Later still she overhears the lovers again as their deteriorating relationship brings actual violence into the bedroom: 'The sobbing grew louder and gave rise to a slap and scuffle and Peter's voice, contused with sexual intent, spoke hoarsely: "Come on, you little bitch. Turn over"' (*LT*, p. 322).

A similar exhibitionism characterises the other major sexual relationship of the trilogy, that which develops between Angela Hooper and Bill Castlebar. Their alliance is initiated in the most public of circumstances, Angela teasing Bill in the Union Bar as he shows off his copy of a lewd book entitled *The Golden Member*, and pursued in similar episodes of public display. Given its flouting of social conventions and adulterous context on both sides, their liaison quickly becomes Cairo's *scandale du jour*, but their sexual relationship is also allowed to overflow the boundaries of the intimate into a public arena as if intended to be witnessed and validated by an audience. On one occasion, shortly after Angela has moved into the embassy flat, Harriet hears a glass breaking and finds her mopping up water from her bedroom floor:

> 'Bill knocked down a dish of water. He keeps it by the bed because he's inclined to come too soon so, when he's over excited, he dips his wrist in the water and it cools him down.'
>
> This explanation, unblushing and matter-of-fact, took for granted Harriet's acceptance of the situation and she could only say, 'I see.' (*LT*, p. 265)

Partly such encounters serve to force a contrast with the increasingly distant relationship between Harriet and Guy, as the latter becomes yet further absorbed in his own theatrical enterprises and the administrative duties of the British Institute. At the same time, in elevating the sexual encounters and liaisons of the expatriate community to this staged and public level, Manning replicates and then reverses the prevailing narrative of Oriental licentiousness for which Cairo itself is celebrated. In *The Battle Lost and Won*, the Extasé Club's belly dancer looks down at her rotating abdomen 'as if it were an unattached object which she swirled like a lasso': she is no more than a passionless blank canvas, reflecting the sexual tension and voyeuristic energy of the group of expatriates watching her (*LT*, p. 191). It is made clear that sexual extravagance can no longer be treated as characteristic of Egyptian society. Rather, this reputation has been imposed on Egypt from without by a British element which has warped into sexual exhibitionism and even degeneracy. This theme is pointedly developed in the set-piece scene of *The Battle Lost and Won*, in which several characters – Angela Hooper, Castlebar and Jake Jackman, together with the less enthusiastic Simon and Harriet – visit the Berka, Cairo's infamous red-light district. Here, Castlebar and the doorman of one of the brothels solicit from the waiting queue of Egyptians a man who agrees to participate in a live sex-show for the 'English visitors'. The stage is a seedy downstairs room which stinks of sweat and garlic, where an elderly and indifferent woman lies on a bunk:

> The young man from the queue entered, wearing his shirt. He held his trousers in his hand and, giving the audience a sheepish glance, stood as though he did not know what to do next. The woman, having no time to waste, muttered, '*Tala henna*', and held up her arms in a caricature of amorous invitation. The union was brief. As he sank down, spent, she pushed him aside and,

> throwing the wrapper round her shoulders, made off on flat, grimy feet.
>
> 'Is that all?' Angela asked. She sounded defrauded but Simon felt they had more reason to feel ashamed. (*LT*, p. 231)

In fact, the young man turns out to be one of Castlebar's students, but, far from being embarrassed in front of his professor, he is merely dismayed when Castlebar enquires if he is a regular performer in such shows. '"You see," he replies simply in consternation, '"we Egyptians are not like you Europeans. We are liking to do such things in private"' (*LT*, p. 232). The humiliation is on the side of the voyeurs; ironically it is the British who are implicated here and in the trilogy as a whole as sexually incontinent and exhibitionist. The exchange confirms their role as the sponsors and instigators of a sexual excess foisted throughout history on to their Egyptian hosts but rebounding now on the expatriates themselves as they collapse into moral and cultural freefall.

Inevitably the incursion of army troops into the streets exacerbated significantly the sexual tensions of the British presence in wartime Cairo. The city's close proximity to the battlegrounds, remarked on with some surprise by Simon in his first trip into the desert, reinforces the repeated collision of military and civilian, active and passive, war and domesticity. 'It was a common experience in those days', Durrell noted in his account of the life of desert-war poet Keith Douglas, 'to hear the doorbell ring at any time of night and day and to find some duty officer on the doorstep, fresh from the desert front, begging for a bath and a whisky'.[17] A less civilised note is sounded in other accounts of how British soldiers assailed the city streets as if in a kind of reverse invasion or assault. In his memoir of service with the desert army, Cyril Joly recalls the impact of the military camps on the outskirts of Cairo when ordinary troops from the infantry battalions swarmed in their hundreds into the city on recreational leave: 'They crowded the streets, the bars, the cinemas. They got drunk and fought. They broke up the dance-halls and night-clubs. They violated the virgins, appropriated the professionals and encouraged the enthusiastic amateurs. Cairo was a seething, swarming mass of soldiers, swindled, cajoled and cursed by the crowds of impoverished and grasping Egyptians.'[18] Accordingly, in her sequence Manning portrays the intrusion of British soldiers into domestic life in the Egyptian capital as a continual rupture of strained attempts to maintain a sense of moral normality in the city: Simon Boulderstone, arriving with his romantic visions of Edwina, is taken aback to be considered as yet another British soldier intent simply on visiting 'Mary's house', one of Cairo's notorious brothels.

Manning's treatment of this subject is concerned with spatial as much as with sexual relationships. The intrusion of the military into the domestic arena is a challenge to the normal politics of place. The young British soldier abandoned by his comrades in a Cairo bar finds himself adrift in the city with no place to go, following Harriet with the look of an 'eager dog', estranged and directionless (*LT*, p. 79). A similar sense of displacement strikes her when she sees on the pavement opposite 'a very tall man with a grave, handsome face and a broad brow'; on this occasion it is General Auchinleck himself who threatens the fragile sanctity of a civilian thoroughfare (*LT*, p. 158). In parallel (and the feature that makes this trilogy significant as an account of war) is the reverse movement, however, from the domestic arena into military territory and indeed the battle zone. From the perspective of Simon Boulderstone, Manning offers a vivid portrait of the North African desert, with its sandstorms, flies, heat and dramatic open spaces, a landscape depicted with the same precision of detail as the complex sequence of battle manoeuvres leading up to the engagement at El Alamein itself.

Again, as with the descriptions of Cairo, Manning pushes towards an authenticity in the campaign scenes, having for reference by the time of her trilogy's composition numerous published first-hand accounts of the operation in the desert and the kind of existence endured there by British troops. Along with Dan Davin's autobiographical novel *For the Rest of Our Lives* (on which she probably drew more heavily than she might have admitted), these included, as cited above, Cyril Joly's *Take These Men*, first published in 1955, which provided intricate descriptions of tank and shell warfare, together with details of the tedium, discomfort and anxiety attendant on daily military routine in the desert. Noted war correspondent Alan Moorehead's *African Trilogy*, published in 1945, also covered the battle preparations and action of Montgomery's campaign as it advanced from Egypt through to its culmination in Libya, while Montgomery's own *Memoirs*, meanwhile, were one of Manning's obvious sources, less for specific details of military strategy perhaps than for the script of the stirring address delivered by the distinguished military commander to the battalions of the Eighth Army (and in the novel, to an enraptured Simon Boulderstone) on the eve of El Alamein: 'The battle which is now about to begin will be one of the decisive battles of history. It will be the turning point in the war . . . The Lord mighty in battle will give us the victory.'[19]

Other celebrated evocations of the desert war included photographer Cecil Beaton's book *Near East* (1943), which gives a startling insight into the ravaged scenery of the battlegrounds. These, he suggested, had, in the sheer incongruities they presented to the eye, been anticipated by the surrealists before the actual conflict: 'The carcasses of burnt-out aeroplanes lying in the middle of a vast panorama: overturned trucks: deserted lorries: cars that have been bucked by machine-gun fire, with their under parts pouring out in grotesque, tortured shapes: some unaccountable clothing blown into the telephone wires, or drapery in a tree: the shattered walls: the sunsets of bright, unforgettable colours. All these have been faithfully reproduced by Dali, Max Ernst, Joán Miró, long before the war.'[20] As always, the flood of cinematic depictions produced after the war may well also have contributed to Manning's vision, in particular, perhaps, the defining images of the North African desert produced for two landmark 1958 film treatments of the conflict, *Ice Cold in Alex* and *Sea of Sand*.

As general background for Manning's fiction, such material provided much in the way of atmosphere, period detail and tone. Key elements of her narrative may have emerged, however, from very specific individual sources, and for details of Simon Boulderstone's experience she almost certainly drew on aspects of the poet Keith Douglas, who became, for a post-war public, a romantic embodiment of the desert soldier. Douglas was called up in 1940 and served in the Middle East with the Nottinghamshire Sherwood Rangers, keeping a notebook of his campaign experience. Manning was familiar with him through the *Personal Landscape* group and came to admire his writing; perhaps too, in his tragic early death, he evoked a heroic version of her own brother, killed in action in October 1941, and anticipated the slain Hugo Boulderstone in the trilogy.[21] The posthumous publication of Douglas's memoir *Alamein to Zem Zem* in 1946, following his death in Normandy at the age of just twenty-four, swiftly established him as an influential Second World War writer, lauded by Durrell in Egypt and by various influential members of the literati back in London. In this vivid account of the war in North Africa (which Douglas wrote under the pseudonym of Peter Cameron), the experiences of the conflict are offered with poignancy, candour and, frequently, a distinctly black sense of humour. Several descriptions – a four-day sandstorm, the misery of digging slit-trenches for cover, the uncanny tableau of dead bodies trapped in a shelled Italian tank – are echoed in Simon Boulderstone's experiences as envisaged by Manning. For Douglas, like Beaton, the desert in wartime was essentially a surrealist landscape, giving one 'the impression of having walked through the looking-glass which touches a man entering battle', a distorting effect much in evidence in passages of the *Levant* sequence.[22]

> The patch of desert where they had leaguered was like most of the desert elsewhere, yet it had become hateful to them. They seemed to imagine that, once on the move, their world would change. By the time they set out, the track was under mirage and the convoy went at a crawl. Heat fogged the distance so there was no horizon, nothing to separate the silver mirage fluid from the swimming, sparkling white heat of the sky. They might have been moving in space except that objects – petrol cans, scarps scattered from falling aircraft, abandoned metal parts – stood monstrous and distorted out of the mirage. (*LT*, p. 88)

In general, Manning's account of the desert campaign in the *Levant Trilogy* achieves a balance between the journalistic and the poetic, nuancing, in this respect, certain cultural debates of the 1940s over the question of how, exactly, British writers should treat the subject of the war.[23] Her descriptions respect both the visceral matter of battle and the emotional depth-charge it produced. In terms of evolving the fiction of war, however, Manning also advances a female perspective on the campaign and its social effects. In her eventual composition of the *Levant Trilogy* some three decades later, she created a split structure in which the lives of the two protagonists are systematically paralleled in discrete sections. Simon Boulderstone is more than a vehicle through which the landscape of battle is encountered; rather, he operates in the trilogy in counterpoint to Harriet Pringle as she finds herself alone and adrift in the Levant. This narrative arc illuminates both similarity and difference in tracing each character's experience of the battle zone and its associated displacements; for both Simon and Harriet, oppositions between mobility and stasis, claustrophobia and exposure, confinement and freedom, pattern a journey across the ravaged Middle Eastern landscape. Manning's compositional strategy not only reveals the discrepancies between masculine and feminine wartime experience but links once again to her prevailing theme of the refugee, mapped here as a concept on to the twinned personae of wandering soldier and runaway wife.

Most interestingly, perhaps, in relation to this adjusted focus on the battle experience, Manning forwards an ironic counter not only (and obviously) to a persuasive Second World War popular culture of heroic adventurism but also to a narrative of *movement*. In his 1966 introduction to *Alamein to Zem Zem*, Lawrence Durrell described the campaign in North Africa as a quintessentially mobile affair, well suited to the gung-ho temperament of the young Keith Douglas and, in its heavy reliance on tank-based manoeuvres, in sharp contrast both to battle procedures on other fronts and to the relatively static trench warfare of the Great War. Meanwhile persuasive accounts of the legendary military adventurers of the period – of Randolph Churchill and David Sterling on daring Commando raids, Fitzroy MacLean making night-time parachute drops into Yugoslavia, Patrick Leigh Fermor working undercover in Greece – added to the sense of the territory extending from the Balkans into the Middle East as a playground for the fearless and fast-moving maverick. In the desert, Simon Boulderstone's initial impression of the campaign is also that of the flow and movement evidenced in the continual convoys of tanks, troop carriers, trucks towing broken aircraft, recovery vehicles and armoured cars which pass in procession as his division progresses across the sands towards Alexandria.

What Manning achieves through Simon's perspective, however, is the undercutting of this mobile masculine war narrative, marked out in episodes of action, fire and combat, with a subtext aligning the desert soldier, first, to what might be considered a feminised sensibility and, secondly, to yet another refraction of a trammelled refugee experience. The feminising effects of combat had been observed in war writing from 1918 onwards, with Woolf's shell-shocked soldier Septimus Smith (in *Mrs Dalloway*) one of many treatments of the theme. Waugh, too, had commented on this aspect of wartime experience in *Sword of Honour*, when Guy Crouchback notes the way in which the exclusively masculine society of a military unit seemed naturally to soften, adapting its nature in an attempt to settle into new and difficult surroundings: 'In the years to come he was to see the process at work again and again, sometimes in grim circumstances, sometimes in pleasant domesticity. Men unnaturally removed from their wives and family began at once to build substitute homes, to paint and furnish, to make flower-beds and edge them with whitewashed pebbles, to stitch cushion-covers on lonely gun sites.'[24] Similarly in Manning's detailed descriptions of a desert routine revolving around 'brewing up' and 'leaguering' (or making camp), the sense of the officer's role as essentially maternal and domestic is emphasised, and the need for an actual female physical presence diminished. Once in the desert the troops become, in Cecil Beaton's term, 'sand happy', in an asexual space where women are no longer relevant. For Simon Boulderstone, the desert is a place beyond the distractions of male and female: 'He belonged now to a world of men; a contained and self-sufficient world where life was organized from dawn till sunset' (*LT*, p. 197).[25]

It is the spatial aspect of this particular military experience, however, that Manning develops, transforming her account of the desert battle experience into a study of displacement and alienation. Against the disorientation of the desert space, the 'world of men' can offer little protection. Ironically, it is no longer the tension between masculine and feminine which disturbs Simon but, instead, that between open and closed spaces. Though initially he attempts to sleep in the open on the sand, under the stars, all his instincts drive him to find cover, in a place where shelter of any kind is at a premium. In the desert – that vast expanse of open space – there is, he is repeatedly informed, a drastic shortage of actual living space. The apparent mobility and freedom of the desert soldier is an illusion: his routine is, instead, a constant manoeuvering between the billets, tents, dugouts and trenches which offer some protection. The men's anxiety turns constantly to the sanctity of their next place of refuge, with their existence, as Simon comes to recognise (in an ironic throw-back perhaps to T.E. Lawrence), becoming essentially nomadic.

> In his opinion, they were worse off than the nomad Arabs who sometimes passed the camp. The Arabs had tents, and tents were homes of a sort, but the army men slept under an open sky. For

> several nights, Simon was worried not only by the lack of cover but the intrusive magnificence of the Egyptian night. The stars were too many and too bright. They were like eyes: waking in mid-sleep, finding them staring down on him, he was unnerved, imagining they questioned what he was doing there. And there was the vast emptiness of the desert itself. The leaguered trucks formed a protective pale but as there were only four trucks, they could not join up. Between them could be seen dark distances that stretched forever – and what might not come out of the distance while they slept? Some men found the space around them so threatening, they would seek refuge under the lorries. This was a fool thing to do, Ridley told them. There were freak rain storms, even in summer, and lorries had been known to sink into the wet sand and smother the men while they slept. (*LT*, pp. 120–1)

In Manning's outline, the episodes of combat which Simon experiences serve as spasmodic interruptions to a fraught routine dominated by the quest for shelter. The call to action, when it comes, is almost welcome as a break from the mundane anxieties of constant uprooting and resettlement, the fracturing of fast-formed attachments and temporary companionships, and the uncertainty, at every stage, of the next move.

In this manner, Manning's use of Simon converts the positive sense of mobility to which Durrell refers into a negative trajectory of traumatic displacement. The experience of the active desert soldier not only recalls a feminine passivity but imitates at the same time the quintessential outline of the refugee narrative, with Manning's emphasis on the itinerant condition of Simon and his unit subtly reflecting the transitions charted in the dislocated lives of her civilian characters. This thematic echo sounds again forcefully in *The Battle Lost and Won*, where Manning treats the battle of El Alamein itself in the same adjusted terms of a faltering advance, dominated by the quest for shelter. From Simon's perspective, the glorious charge into battle is simply instead a damp squib: the infantry soldiers are 'stuck in slitties [slit trenches] all day' and when evening comes with the first barrage, the effect of the extraordinary, awesome noise serves to paralyse the men around with fear and shock (*LT*, p. 270). Ordered to take a message to a unit of Royal Engineers up front, Simon – now a military liaison officer – must first locate and follow the correct path, each sector of the field being marked with a different symbol: 'On the main tracks, marked with crude replicas of a hat, a bottle and a boat, cut out of petrol tins, lorries appeared like ships, plunging their bows into drifts of dust and rearing up suddenly over crests like waves' (*LT*, p. 272). Halted by a dust cloud, Simon is confused and disorientated; having regained the route, he next has to pick his way round the trip wires laid in the minefields, but now the smoke from the guns on the front line blinds him as he makes his way towards them.

> As their shapes appeared through the fog, he began to stumble on what seemed a stony beach. Lowering his torch, he saw the mardam was thickly covered with shrapnel fragments, jagged, blue-grey and crystalline from the super-heat of explosion. This shrapnel carpet stretched between the guns and many yards beyond them. There was no question of running over it and he picked his way as best he could until he was out in the open area of no-man's land. The fog still hung in the air and even the moon was lost to sight. The mine fields were here. (*LT*, p. 273)

Every aspect of this battle is based on precarious journeys, treacherous routes, stranded vehicles and lost infantry. The Scorpion tanks cannot function in the dust and stand motionless in the smoke, their crews must 'dig in' to survive, the front line becomes 'less an advance than a standstill'. The emphasis shifts from movement to the securing of shelter, but even shelter brings risk. Days later, weary of battle, Simon directs his driver Crosbie to a resting place in the shade of a palm tree, but the shade is mined and both are caught in the explosion. Crosbie is killed outright and Simon struck down with a psychosomatic paralysis (the condition echoing the manner of his brother's death in the desert, both legs blown off in a landmine explosion), resulting in him being invalided out of action. The mobility heralded by the campaign is replaced by physical collapse, the itinerant experience of the desert militia resulting finally in stasis.

Manning's crossover from civilian war experience into the military domain is ambitious in the *Levant* sequence but pays off, ultimately, in the harnessing of what might otherwise be conventional battleground description to a prevailing thematic concern in the trilogies. Simon's experiences of the desert campaign, with its large-scale troop manoeuvres, transportation routes, tank advances and even its culminating battle, should provide for a militaristic (and masculine) narrative of mobility and autonomy, but the descriptions suggest instead a faltering, interrupted process, intercut with recurrent anxieties about place and disturbance, and ironically reminiscent of a narrative of refugee-ship. This adjustment is systematic without becoming programmatic and finds a parallel in the journey taken by Harriet Pringle in the final volume in the trilogy. In comparison with its predecessors, *The Sum of Things* is a somewhat fragmented work, perhaps in part a result of its very late composition date (when the author's health was in decline), and perhaps too because of its slightly strained incorporation of diverse episodes based on Manning's wartime travel experiences in the Middle East, but its thematic development is none the less significant as a contemplation of a peripheral, female experience of war. Harriet's journey eastwards through Jerusalem and Damascus works in direct contrast to Simon's battle experience, inverting his masculine trajectory towards paralysis and proffering instead a distinct if tentative narrative of movement, freedom and release.

Presumed to have drowned after the torpedoing of the *Queen of Sparta*, Harriet exists in *The Sum of Things* as a ghost of sorts, the novel providing an imagined 'afterlife' to the experiences of Cairo and her faltering marriage. Her journey east, during which she meets up with the now self-exiled lovers Angela Hooper and Bill Castlebar, and with the suicidal actor Aidan Sheridan, provides a necessary period of reflection (and individualism) before her eventual reconciliation with Guy. More than this, however, Harriet's route leads her away from the claustrophobia of her life in Cairo and opens up spaces hitherto closed off to her (including the spaces of an occluded Arab culture). Her experience as a British refugee coming from Europe has been defined by enclosure and overcrowding. The cabin on the ship from Athens, the refugee dormitory (in fact a converted brothel) in which she and Guy stay on their arrival in Egypt, the oppressive, artificially lit rooms of Madame Wilk's pension and the small hot room in Dobbie Dobson's busy embassy flat have constituted the spaces of a constrained and makeshift existence. Psychologically she bears the scars of these confinements: at Cairo zoo, she sympathises with the polar bear in his miserable enclosure:

> The bear was in a circular cage, not very big, an island of concrete surrounded by bars that rose up to a central dome from which

> water trickled constantly. The bear, sitting motionless under the stream, hung its head, torpid in its heavy white coat. Harriet felt its despair and leaning towards it she whispered, 'Bear', but it did not move. She was about to move on but, unwilling to leave the creature unaided, she went closer to the cage and stood for a long time, trying to contact the animal's senses through the medium of her intense pity for it. It did not move. (*LT*, p. 372)

However, the confinement is broken as Harriet, turning back from her passage home at the very last minute, unexpectedly finds herself liberated from institutional and cultural constraints. While the paralysed Simon Boulderstone is confined to the 'Plegics' ward of the military hospital at Helwan, she, in contrast, embarks on a meandering journey eastwards, free from the morbid landscape of Cairo and the constrictions of her difficult marriage.

As an interesting adjunct to this narrative of release, Harriet initially negotiates the landscape beyond Cairo's environs in the company of other women – specifically, the two female military drivers from whom she impulsively begs a lift at Suez. One of the drivers, Mortimer, has previously been introduced to her on the night of her visit to Cairo's Extasé nightclub; on that occasion Harriet was intrigued by descriptions of her work transporting ammunition along the treacherous route to Iraq:

> They tried to vary it, Mortimer said, but however they went, they had to cross the Syrian desert. Sometimes they headed straight for Damascus then turned east. Once they went to Homs so they could visit Palmyra but it had been a rough trip and they had broken a spring. Another time they went by the Allenby bridge over the Jordan so they could see the Krak de Chevalier.
>
> 'The Levant sounds wonderful. I'd love to go to Damascus.'
>
> 'We'd give you a lift. We're not supposed to, of course, but we often pick up people on the roads. The matron says it's dangerous but women alone are safer here than in England. We can thank Lady Hester Stanhope for that. She impressed the Arab world so every Englishwoman has a special status in these parts.' (*LT*, p. 229)[26]

While Mortimer's outline is matter-of-fact, it suggests a confident claiming of territory on behalf of the two women, while its reference to the precedent of Hester Stanhope, the emancipated nineteenth-century traveller in the Levant region, quietly offers an alternative, female exemplar to the dominating masculine figure of Montgomery in the desert. The implication in the trilogy is that the two women are in a lesbian relationship (an implication supported by Angela Hooper's sardonic comment to Harriet that in order to join their outfit '"you have to be a lizzie or a drunk or an Irishwoman"'(*LT*, p. 227)), but the nature of their relationship – its intimacy confirmed to Harriet when she joins them on the journey into Syria in *The Sum of Things* – is less significant than the concept of a female community that they provide in the narrative, as a counter to Simon Boulderstone's all-male society of the military in the desert. Together they are capable not only of entering masculine space but of usurping it. Pausing from the drive at one stage, they enter an Arab café, an exclusively male preserve, in a clear statement of appropriation: 'The men stared in silence, obviously confounded by this female presumption and Harriet felt proud of Mort and Phil and their confidence in the world' (*LT*, p. 405). For a short time she shares in their confidence and in their mobility – ironically reversing in her flight to the Levant the negative experience of displacement that has previously dogged her wartime itinerary.

Harriet's journey and encounters in *The Sum of Things* frequently expose the complexity of female status, partly in relation to the restrictions and customs of the Muslim and Arab world she has entered, partly in relation to her own confused position as a married woman, estranged from her husband and at liberty in a region released from the codes of imperial sexual hierarchy. While many aspects of this particular novel in the *Levant* sequence might, perhaps, be dismissed as the overspill of a tourist itinerary based on Manning's visits to Damascus, Beirut and the Sea of Galilee, there is none the less an important thematic thread running through Harriet's various encounters in the region. Her brief liaison in Damascus with Halal, the Christian Arab lawyer, who wishes only to offer her his 'protection', her meeting with Jamil's wife, hidden away from the party and barely able to speak English, her despair at her penniless and estranged state as she contemplates a night alone in the Baalbek café with its proprietors, three Arab brothers, are events which underline the precariousness of her female identity. Yet at the same time her passage eastwards is, paradoxically, defined by a growing sense of individual self-assertion and self-recognition: this is an interlude of feminine independence which temporarily derails the marriage plot on which both trilogies rely, until Harriet finally returns to the restrictions and securities of Cairo and her husband.

The final novel of the *Levant Trilogy* looks forward, therefore, even in its comparatively fragmented form, to a new kind of identity for Harriet Pringle. While she makes only partial, reversible moves towards independence, whether sexual or economic, she abandons her former self which was entirely relational, inhabiting in its place a formative version of an emancipated woman. While neither she nor her counterpart, Simon Boulderstone, are truly 'refugees' in the full sense of wartime dispossession and imposed statelessness, their experiences at least begin to negotiate the term and its defining narratives of dislocation. Harriet's sense of transformation, in the final volume, may be understood to anticipate a post-imperial space in which hierarchies and conventions adapt to a new order, and in which transience and insecurity dominate as modes of being. Her journey in this volume becomes almost mythical in its Odyssean shape, looking forward to a chronological, political and sexual future, before its subject returns to Cairo and the boundaries of wartime and marriage.

It is significant that Harriet's future contains, even if only vaguely, a note of optimism, in sharp contrast to the pessimistic note on which the trilogy otherwise draws to its post-imperial conclusions. That the *Levant Trilogy* is very much about the end of an imperial project, an endeavour tied up with masculine incentives and strategies, is the theme of several exchanges in the concluding stages of the fiction. Diplomat Dobbie Dobson sets the tone: planning to write his memoirs as the war comes to an end, he recalls to Guy Pringle an anecdote about one of King Farouk's characteristically truculent conversations with the British Ambassador: '"He's no fool. The other day he said to HE: 'When are you going to take the last of your damn troops out of my country.' HE gave him a lecture on Egypt being the front line of defence of the Gulf oil-fields. Farouk listened in sulky silence and at the end said: 'Oh, stay if you must, but when the war's over, for God's sake put down the white man's burden and go'"' (*LT*, p. 513). Accepting the inevitability of this very move, Guy, as the white man's representative, now turns from the heightened excitements of war to look at a future that seems to make no sense and to have no place for nobility of thought and action. Amid the rumours beginning to circulate of a conclusive German collapse, he imagines that nothing may remain in the Europe he left behind but 'rat-ridden, plague-stricken ruins' (*LT*, p. 516). Once back in England, will he become a post-war victim of sorts, like Hugo Fletcher in Manning's *A Different Face* (1953), longing for the warmth of Egypt again in the cold, damp climate of an English coastal town? Will his alienation from home, the displacement so representative of his and Harriet's generation, characterise the narrative of return? The evocative concluding line of Manning's trilogy suggests that a refugee-ship of sorts will indeed ironically persist with an ostensible reclaiming of place; that Guy, and perhaps Harriet too, will be the 'stray figures left on the stage at the end of a great tragedy', relieved of destiny and purpose in the fragile landscape of peace.

Chapter Five

'John Bull's Other Ireland': Manning's Palestine fiction

Olivia sits on Arthur Koestler's lap as he and Reggie play chess, in the otherwise deserted lounge. O rather ostentatiously strokes Koestler's hair. He appears a bit contemptuous about R's chess and to take little notice of O – rather as if her attentions are merely his due; he was given at that time to seeing himself as God's gift to women . . . I thought – still think for that matter – that I would not have put up with O's behaviour if she had been mine.

Louis Lawler[1]

This recollection of Olivia Manning from one of her contemporaries in wartime Palestine provides a telling example of how the intrigues of her marital situation so often distract attention from her political context as a writer. Her flirtation with journalist and writer Arthur Koestler is in fact of significantly *less* interest than the spatial and chronological circumstances of Lawler's rather censorious tableau: the chess game was being played in the King David Hotel in Jerusalem – serving in the 1940s as headquarters of the British administration in Mandate Palestine – as the war in its later stages exposed and exacerbated the fragility of a governing British authority in the Middle East. In this most volatile of landscapes, the relationship between two anomalous and very different writers, one the granddaughter of a County

Down freemason, the other an exiled Hungarian and (at this stage) Zionist revolutionary, might be better read as a reminder of the curious personal dislocations and sudden proximities which marked the physical experiences of wartime and which helped shape in its aftermath a literature of deep political insecurity.

Arthur Koestler had left London for Jerusalem in December 1944 and, at the time of his meeting with the Smiths, was spending six months in Palestine in order to research material for his next book. Published in 1946, *Thieves in the Night* was his semi-fictional portrait of a group of 1930s European intellectuals and idealists attempting to establish an exclusivist Jewish community by the Sea of Galilee, against a swelling tide of Arab resentment and British indifference. Part historical saga, part Zionist tract, the novel (based largely on Koestler's own experience in a Zionist settlement in Haifa in 1926) consolidated the author's thematic pursuit of revolutionaries frustrated in their aims by the clash between the purity of principle and the necessary ugliness of practice. On this, his third visit to Palestine, Koestler was also gathering information for a more direct attack on Britain's faltering administration of the troubled territory. Three years later *Promise and Fulfilment*, his account of the history of Palestine from the Balfour Declaration of 1917 to British withdrawal and the end of the League of Nations Mandate in 1948, would deal systematically and savagely with what he viewed as a series of short-sighted, repressive and ultimately brutal policy decisions surrounding Jewish immigration and settlement in the region he pointedly labelled 'John Bull's Other Ireland'.[2]

Such sentiments were a natural extension of the ideas expressed in Koestler's previous works on the plight of European Jewish refugees: *Scum of the Earth* (1941) and *Arrival and Departure* (1944). In addition, his campaigning on behalf of Jewish exiles in London and his close involvement with the World Zionist Organisation had established him in the period as a leading advocate for the Jewish national cause. At the time of their meeting in Jerusalem, his particular brand of intellectual Zionism would certainly have appealed to Reggie Smith, who, despite challenging Koestler's celebrity status in a 1945 issue of the journal *Orion*, was generally an admirer of the writer and a fellow sympathiser with the cause of a Jewish homeland in Palestine, a position vociferously endorsed by his fictional alter ego Guy Pringle (in the *Levant Trilogy*, Guy is 'particularly impressed by the idea of *kibbutzim*, based he believed on the Russian soviets, and the possibility of turning the Negev into arable land' (*LT*, p. 304)).[3] But to what extent did Reggie's perspective align with his wife's views on the same subject? If Manning was persuaded by Koestler's Zionist ideals, then how did she reconcile them with the growing contradictions of the refugee question in Palestine during the war years, and with British sensitivities to the Arab presence in the country?

Manning's tangential engagement with these issues features in the two Palestine-set novels which emerged shortly after the war, *Artist Among the Missing* (1949) and *School for Love* (1951). In *Artist Among the Missing* (perhaps her most accomplished non-autobiographical fiction) she confronts the ideological assault on inherited traditions of British pro-Arabism, sparked by an unprecedented wartime influx of European Jewish immigrants. Though the novel's backdrop recognises the culture of the region as a convoluted historical palimpsest of religious and cultural traditions – classical and Byzantine, Greek and Syrian, Orthodox and European Judaic, Christian and Islamic – its narrative foreground is dominated by the pressure of a contemporary Arab–Jewish conflict over territory. Against this, through the fate of a British army major posted to Jerusalem, Manning portrays the gradual deterioration of British authority under the strain of competing ideological trajectories, pro-Jewish and Arabist. Similarly in *School for Love* – its middlebrow title disguising a bitter political vein – she highlights, through her quasi-allegorical portrait of a claustrophobic Jerusalem boarding house, the mounting pressures on the concept of a Jewish homeland in Palestine caused by dramatic wartime increases in immigration from Europe.

The second novel also introduces a particular motif – that of the sunken passenger ship – which is recalled and pursued in the later trilogies. In *School for Love*, the use of the 'ship of death' as a narrative element alludes both to a series of contemporaneous wartime military and civilian losses at sea and (indirectly) to the plight of the many Jewish refugee boats arriving from Europe in the early years of conflict which were refused access to Palestine under emergency wartime blockades. The frequently tragic history of the latter was particularly close to home for Manning. In the winter of 1941/2, she was witness to the plight of the *Struma*, a Romanian ship bound for Palestine with a largely Jewish passenger list, which was turned away from a series of Allied safe havens and eventually destroyed (almost certainly as the result of a mine explosion) in the Black

Sea. Almost all on board perished and the event, one of several similar fiascos in the war years, crystallised for Manning the human cost of dislocation and exclusionism. Through a thread of references to death at sea woven into her fiction from this point onwards, she would not only begin to designate a cataclysmic failure of political responsibility in wartime but also to draw unsettling connections between specific refugee experiences and a more abstract imagining of human abjection.

Manning's immediate post-war fiction reads, then, as a cautious but exasperated response to a Palestine which, with its volatile wartime demographics, was fast becoming the Achilles heel of an international British paternalism. Without the strong autobiographical ties of her trilogies, these two works lack by contrast the coherence of an ironic narrative perspective, but they function nevertheless as useful precedents for the later material. What they share, and what they lay down as groundwork, is a configuration of domestic damage as metaphoric of a broader political dysfunctionalism, a narrative vehicle for drawing out the intractable residue of imperialism and the disintegration of Britain's overseas mission. Together, they represent the distinct imaginative response of a compromised expatriate community to the crisis of wartime Jerusalem, and to the unsettling template provided by Britain's 'other Ireland' for a post-war international landscape.

Palestine was the last foreign posting taken by Reggie Smith before the end of the war and the couple's return to England. He and Olivia moved from Cairo to Jerusalem in the autumn of 1942, when Reggie left the British Council to take up an appointment as head of the Palestine Broadcasting Service (a somewhat bizarre choice given his overt communist leanings, the writer Denis Hills would later report acidly).[4] In his new posting, Reggie produced readings of Shakespeare and discussions on the novel, while his wife made occasional contributions to broadcasts on music and verse. He remained with the service until his resignation in 1945, his departure announced in the *Palestine Post* with the waspish comment that '[o]f artistic temperament, he found administration irksome'.[5] Until this juncture, however, the Palestine Broadcasting Service – Jerusalem's English-language adjunct to the BBC's overseas broadcasting operation – provided the couple with a fixed purpose and secure social base for a period of three years, during which time Olivia was able to explore the city and its outlying ancient sites, accumulating material that later supplied the geographical basis for the last volume of the *Levant Trilogy* and, before that, for the richly detailed topography of her more immediate post-war fiction.

Manning's creative development in this period can be linked closely to her various literary and cultural engagements in the city. Some of these were connected to the strong presence of the British Council in Jerusalem (she and Reggie both gave lectures in the Council's 1945 series 'Aspects of the English Novel', for example), others to the journal which emerged from a local British-led cultural organisation, the Jerusalem Forum, established in the city in 1942 by the military attaché John Connell. Connell had been posted to the Middle East early in the war and was initially given responsibility for developing a pro-British propaganda campaign targeted at the Arab population (a project that developed gradually into the aforementioned Palestine Broadcasting Service, or PBS). Increasingly concerned at the lack of exchange between Arab and Jewish communities, Connell envisaged the Jerusalem Forum as a companion to the radio project and as a discussion group of sorts, founded, as he later put it, 'on a tide of expectation and enthusiasm – *amongst people who wanted to think as we did*'.[6] Aware too of the hunger for English reading material resulting from wartime shortages, he launched at the same time a magazine, also called the *Jerusalem Forum*, dedicated to representing a range of political and cultural opinion from all the major communities within Palestine, including expatriates. The journal was more successful than the Forum itself (the latter appears to have met with a degree of resistance from individuals suspicious of its motives) and ran to several issues. 'In its first few numbers', Connell wrote, 'there were poems by Stephen Haggard, first-class desert reporting by Shan Sedgwick, one or two passable translations from the Hebrew and the Arabic, and some book reviews by a formidable lady called Olivia Manning'.[7]

The *Forum* was closely linked to what was to be, for Manning, a very significant and long-term literary and social association with the *Palestine Post*, Jerusalem's main English-language newspaper. Founded by the Russian-born Zionist and former Jewish Legionnaire Gershon Agronsky in 1932, the *Post* (renamed the *Jerusalem Post* in 1950) started life as a relatively inclusive cultural, political and literary weekly, ideologically committed to the principle and reality of a Jewish homeland. The paper quickly developed a reputation for editorial independence. After the outbreak of war in 1939, it began to augment its political profile and position, taking a strong line of resistance to British Mandate policies restricting Jewish immigration to Palestine. It retained none the less a moderate voice, speaking out against a local rhetoric of violence in Jerusalem (and, ultimately, against an increasingly belligerent Arthur Koestler), while challenging the spreading underground and paramilitary elements within the Zionist camp.[8] As the war began to alter the nature of Palestine's population, the paper gradually increased its appeal to a professional Jewish readership and (as indicated by Felix Latimer's casual perusal of a weekly issue in *School for Love*) to the more culturally and politically engaged members of the expatriate British community. It listed among its regular contributors a number of British exiles and Mandate employees in the Middle East and published occasional contributions too from abroad, including a series of 'Letters from London' running through 1944 and early 1945 penned by the emerging British critic (and friend of Reggie Smith, who arranged the contributions) Walter Allen.[9]

For Manning, who continued her contributions to the paper long after her return to England, the *Palestine Post* was a credible and vibrant forum for the processing of new British writing. In more than one hundred book reviews written for the paper during this period, she evaluated with care and enthusiasm the established figures from a British, European and sometimes American literary circuit, praising new work by Graham Greene, Evelyn Waugh, Joyce Cary, George Orwell and Elizabeth Bowen, assessing the impact of journals such as *Horizon* and *Windmill*, and judging the potential (or, just as frequently, damning it) of new and emergent writers. Like much literary internship, this work was often formulaic and, in some respects, creatively limiting. Nevertheless, the criticism Manning provided for the *Post* had significant value in illuminating the ways in which modern writers were beginning to use the war as primary material (and perhaps in underlining, too, the fact that the consensual middle-class medium of the novel was fast emerging as the central cultural barometer of British imperialist disaffection and enervation). It was here that Manning paid heightened attention to early work by Greene, on the one hand, and to Koestler on the other: the influence of both hangs over the two novels deriving from her Palestine sojourn. Like Greene, her instinct was not towards the direct critique of policy – fiction writing had no such capacity, in her view – but her close relationship with the paper (and with the Jerusalem Forum) confirmed a *rapprochement* between literary and ideological engagements. She had allied herself with a British expatriate contingent bound by its interest in the tensions of the region, and it was perhaps inevitable that a politically resonant fiction of some kind would follow.

For this reason the *political* character of wartime Palestine, a character fraught, animated and, as John Connell described it, 'squeezed like an orange', is worth profiling here, briefly, as a very specific context for Manning's late 1940s fiction. In the years before her arrival, the region had grown increasingly volatile: the original terms of the 1917 Balfour Declaration (confirmed by the League of Nations in 1922) in support of the establishment in Palestine of a national home for the Jewish people had come under intense and increasing strain since General Allenby's triumphant march into Jerusalem to lay the foundations of a British administration. During the 1930s, worsening antisemitism in Europe and the large-scale immigration to Palestine which resulted made unsustainable the Balfour *proviso* to protect the civil and religious interests of non-Jewish communities in the mandated region. With the Jewish population rising from less than 10 per cent in 1918 to 31 per cent by 1939 and, until curtailed by Nazi policy, the Palestine economy surging owing to the resultant influx of capital, the balance of relations was clearly under threat. Arab concerns, meanwhile, boiled over into active revolt by the late 1930s, throwing the Mandate into an even deeper state of insecurity.

In 1937 the British government made some attempts to reconsider its role in this arena and in the Palestine Royal Commission report, headed by Lord Peel, confronted the necessity for what was termed a 'surgical operation': the partition of Palestine into separate Arab and Jewish states. However, partition was inevitably a convoluted scheme which failed to solve key aspects of the immigration question and met with resistance from the parties concerned on numerous grounds. Gradually it receded from view as a possibility, to be replaced in policy terms by the 1939 White Paper, the document that in effect offered a holding pattern for the war years. In the White Paper, the government set out plans to administer a combined single state in Palestine based on shared Jewish–Arab authority and directed towards the establishment, in ten years, of an independent Palestine. In an elaboration of these terms, the Land Transfer Regulations were put into operation under the authority of the Mandate's High Commissioner as a means of controlling the sale of Arab land to Jews. Finally, and crucially, with due recognition of the refugee situation in Europe, the British legislation set in place an immigration quota permitting only 10,000 Jewish immigrants to enter Palestine in each of the following five years.[10]

The White Paper was described by its critics as the worst kind of avoidance measure, given the aggravated political circumstances of the period. Immediately, it alienated a disillusioned Zionist community angered by what was perceived as a catastrophic breaking of a promise. It also froze rather than solved the problems of Palestine: it was clear to both sides that a heightened conflict in the region would be inevitable when the country emerged from its 'cold storage' after the end of the war. Despite the relative safety of the city itself, compared to conflict zones elsewhere in the Middle East, those who lived in Jerusalem, particularly those administering the Mandate, endured a wartime existence in which the overarching threat of Axis forces moving eastwards across North Africa towards them was combined with a relentless domestic tension marked by sporadic Arab–Jewish outbursts of violence. Life in Palestine – the effort to maintain a credible social presence against a backdrop of hostility and disturbance – was strained and irregular, and a hamstrung British authority found itself facing a series of irresolvable contradictions.[11]

With the outbreak of war in Europe in 1939, political leaders temporarily and pragmatically shelved the vexed issue of the Palestine Mandate, partly in the interests of maintaining Britain's strategic foothold in the Middle East (with access to the Suez Canal deemed as crucial) and partly in the absence of any workable policy that would satisfy the various competing interests in the region. In tandem with a crisis in political affairs (and central to Manning's fictional treatments), the war years marked a companion disintegration in the *cultural* relations of the Palestine question as deteriorating diplomatic relationships threw into relief divided traditions of Arabism and Zionism within the British camp. Many of those still invested in the legacy of T.E. Lawrence, including several notable Foreign Office stalwarts, continued to adhere to romantic visions of Araby based on concepts of ancient attachment, on projected ideals of Arab loyalty and nobility, and, frequently, on conventional images of the country as represented by the rural *fellahin* or itinerant Bedouin.[12]

Under the pressures of war, the cherished British–Arab relationship would come under intense strain, however, and the Arabist school was obliged to stretch its Orientalist affiliations to an increasingly insubordinate Arab population poised for insurgency.[13] Meanwhile, pro-Zionist members of the British Cabinet had in their turn to adapt their Balfourite visions of sympathetic protectionism to embrace a largely unknown quantity in the Eastern European Jews arriving *en masse* with what many suspected to be Bolshevik alliances. Inevitably, the fall-out from Auschwitz would change radically the nature and claims of a Jewish identity and, again, the frameworks of 1917 would simply not suffice in the difficult climate of the 1940s, but there was no new direction to be found at this juncture. Disillusionment combined with the distractions of war to produce a stasis. 'The emptiness in Arab affairs was something more than a dearth of personalities', recalls John Connell in his memoir of Jerusalem in the period. 'It was a void of spirit; idealism had become agitation, and the fire of purpose a smouldering smoke of intrigue. Uncertainty or hesitation had come upon what had once been a certain, clear, issue'.[14]

With this as her political backdrop, Manning's fiction of the period can be read as part of a broader review not only of the British role in Palestine specifically but also of the ramifications of Britain's dwindling imperial capacity across the Middle East. In *Artist Among the Missing*, she offers a study of political responsibility foundering on a historical legacy of cultural (and visual) misrepresentation and misappropriation, an accusation levelled at the long-term British–Arab romance noted above, but countering at the same time the false promises of integrated Jewish settlement. This theme is carried chiefly by the protagonist of the novel, Major Geoffrey Lynd, a character burdened by a prevailing awareness of his own inadequacy, both as an individual (and husband) and as a wartime officer. Posted to Jerusalem in 1942 and thus estranged from his gregarious wife, left behind in Cairo, Lynd's brief is to accompany to safety a group of ten miscellaneous European refugees across the canal from Egypt into Palestine. In this task the fragile nature of his authority becomes apparent: a horde of refugees attempting to make the same crossing swarms about him in a 'compact, sweating mass'; one of them steals his porter, another shouts abuse at him, none takes heed of the authority implied by his military standing. He overhears even his own small group of charges questioning his ability: '"Major Lynd is nice, but he is not competent"'

(*Artist Among the Missing*, p. 15). The refugees crave his help and attention as they attempt to settle amidst the confusions of Jerusalem but their presence in the Jewish cafés and bars of the city threatens his peace of mind, until he eventually pleads with them, violently, to be left alone.

Lynd shares in the refugees' plight and his rejection of them derives from his recognition of this fact. He too is effectively displaced, not only from the security of his marriage but also, as an office-bound administrator, from the action of the battlefield and the sense of legitimacy this might have provided. The Alamein campaign is in full swing and Lynd eyes the ordinary sunburned soldiers passing in trucks to the desert with feelings of desolate inferiority, despite his superior military office. Even his body comes to be perceived as inadequate: 'He felt that his whole appearance was one of guilt, not only for this rank but for his physical difference. He was too thin in face and body; too elegant in person; he felt his Celtic darkness to be a reproach' (p. 46). Lacking vindication, he is plagued by an awareness of 'his own vacancy', the insubstantial nature of his presence. Convincingly drawn as a wartime anti-hero, he combines an existential crisis of personality with the collapse of the imperial self, grounding both in a context that highlights a grievous failure of authority and responsibility. His is a failure of stamina and political nerve, his refrain – '"I can't pity anyone any more. It's too much for me"' (p. 42) – a representative abnegation of moral and political duty.

Lynd's fragility is emphasised, meanwhile, through its contrast with the solidity of his companions in Jerusalem: two British army officers who, in their rigid political opinions, represent the prevailing ideological trajectories of the period. Through their clashing personalities and perspectives, Lister and Clark operate as Manning's means of strategically and systematically tracking the polarised condition of British attitudes to Palestine and the homeland question, under the stress of war. Major Lister is fat and effeminate: a sceptic and reactionary, he indulges in visions of an Arab world still conceived of in terms of Orientalist romance. His rooms at the King David Hotel are depicted as a Foreign Office idyll of Arabia, 'papered with enormous photographs of old Arabs, old Jews, Arabs on horseback, healthy Jewish girls holding bunches of Palestine oranges, Palestine scenery and camels' (p. 55). Trained as an antiquarian, he enthuses over the ancient Assyrian and Byzantine ruins in the Holy City but instinctively condemns the Orthodox Jews parading its streets –

these are Pharisees, as he sees them, 'asking to be persecuted' (p. 73). By comparison, in the virile, handsome, womanising Nicholas Clark, Manning creates a ruthless pragmatist who responds quickly to the rumours now trickling into the city of Jewish persecution in Europe with plans for rescue and resettlement. Clark complains of 'the smell of the Arab world', is impatient with its ruined landscapes and disgusted by its 'filthy, ignorant, empty-headed and half-starved' Arab youths. Denying the inherent nobility of Palestine's nomads, he states his belief instead in the modernising capacity of the region's new Jewish settlements. As Lister complains of him, 'He's all for those gross Jews with their backsides bulging out of khaki shorts. The Jews drive tractors and make the desert bloom with Brussels sprouts. He'd give Transjordan over to the Zionists, if he could' (p. 105).

Manning's polarisations here have an obvious crudeness: Clark is rather one-dimensionally the progressive rationalist, Lister the sympathetic romantic. The vulnerable Lynd is predictably repulsed by Clark's overbearing masculinity, feeling him as 'a shadow on his life as he had once felt the school bully' (p. 74), and drawn instead to Lister's ramshackle accessibility. Yet it is the latter's unreflecting Arabism that comes in for closest scrutiny in the novel. Denying that he is an antisemite, Lister admits none the less to his instinctive preference for an Arab culture and sensibility, which he defines in standard Orientalist cliché: 'They're ruffians, but they're consistent ruffians. Once you've got their behaviour pattern, you know where you are with them' (p. 73). Though tempered by his begrudging acknowledgment of the destructiveness and cruelty of the Bedouin, his outlook is still grounded in the romance of the Arab relationship, and in his local staff he inspires a depth of loyalty and affection which emanates from a bygone era of British–Arab relations. At the post-Alamein party thrown in his honour by his young Arab secretary Jamal, for example, Lister is celebrated as a hero and lavished with attention. As one of the hosts explains to a bewildered Geoffrey Lynd, '"He is a man with a heart," the young man placed his hand tenderly over his own heart, "To us he is an Oriental. He feels with us"'(p. 89). Yet there is now a discernible hollowness in the Arab–British attachment. Jamal admits privately that he is learning German, even in the immediate aftermath of Montgomery's victory (the scene anticipates the similar exchange between Harriet Pringle and Iqal, in the *Levant Trilogy*, where the clerk is unashamedly learning German in expectation of an Allied retreat). In *Artist Among the Missing*, this small act of betrayal is symbolic as much as pragmatic, as Jamal explains to Lynd: 'You promised us freedom in our own country; you betrayed us. We do not betray you – but we must look after ourselves' (p. 89).[15] His sentiments undermine the euphoria of the victory celebrations, a subversive note sounding in the novel to indicate the closing stages of the British–Arab love affair.

Manning's positioning of Geoffrey Lynd as a bystander caught between the conflicting ideological positions caricatured in the novel is strategic in view of the 1940s *realpolitik* that lay behind its design. Lynd operates at a point of rupture in the chronology of British relations with Palestine. While Clark's Zionist sympathies anticipate developments in an unpredictable future, Lister's Arabism is clearly suggested to be a romantic indulgence already moving into obsolescence. Moreover, its basis in a tradition of romantic encounter with Araby is thrown into question by the manner in which Lynd himself responds to the landscape of both Palestine and Jordan. In the manner of Greene, this novel interrogates the deeper fault-lines of British foreign administration by tracking a version of the literary 'voyage into the interior', an ironic take on the imperial adventure story spliced with the kind of contemporary tourist itinerary familiar to visitors to the Middle East since the turn of the century. In its central section, the novel moves from its superficial critique of British administrative inadequacy (represented by Lynd's paralysing failure of nerve) to a penetrating analysis of historical British responses to and *visual* representations of the landscape of the Levant, a venture that queries the conventionalism and sustainability of the British–Arab romance in historically and culturally resonant terms.

Desperately hoping to be returned to Cairo, Lynd sweats out his days at British headquarters in Jerusalem's King David Hotel, until he is invited to accompany the two officers on a visit to the ancient site of Petra, in Jordan. As he and Lister plan the journey, he recalls a picture he once owned, of an island in the Gulf of Aquaba:

> He described the picture as he saw it in his mind: the island small and jagged like an iceberg, was crowned with a medieval castle and set in a sea as flat and colourless as glass. In the foreground was the mainland sand that might have been snow. It was like an

> arctic plane, frozen into silence – and yet across the sand went Arab drivers and a string of camels with all their trappings.
>
> Lister leaned towards Geoffrey, looking slightly to one side of him, and listened with a smile. His eyes, usually flattened by sadness, seemed to deepen. He whispered: 'I wonder if we could get there,' and stared beyond the walls of the bar to some other sight distant in time and place. Geoffrey smiled, feeling in his relationship with Lister an excitement that had almost a quality of romance. (*Artist Among the Missing*, p. 64)

The picture Manning's novel alludes to here is 'The Isle of Graia, Gulf of Akabah', an engraving of 1832 by David Roberts, the nineteenth-century Scottish landscape artist whose paintings, sketches and lithographs of Egypt, Palestine and the Levant were to provide generations of British travellers with preconceived images of the Holy Land and its ancient sites. While the picture itself – a charmed, ethereal landscape with a picturesque grouping of nomads in the foreground – is typical of Roberts' work, its particular quality, emphasised in Geoffrey's memory, is in the appearance of the sand dunes and cliffs as ice and snow. Frozen in time even at its moment of depiction, this scene is already outside a political and cultural reality, and Geoffrey merely indulges vicariously in Lister's fading Arabian dream. Later, at the victory party which signals for him the collapse of this romance, the scene recurs in his mind as he stands in the unusual cold, fusing now with a sudden memory of childhood: 'Now, with the wind glancing at his side, he was nostalgic for a region beyond reality. He saw, as though in a childhood delirium, the picture he had described to Lister – the robed Arabs, the camels with their trappings passing through a world so glass-still with frost that their tread might snap it' (p. 85).

Manning's use of the Roberts engraving is key to how *Artist Among the Missing* operates politically, how it pursues a systematic deconstruction of British configurations of Palestine and its surrounding regions. In civilian life Geoffrey Lynd has been an accomplished painter, and in his previous military posting to Greece he had been inspired by the landscape and had painted furiously. Yet in Cairo, then in Jerusalem, he finds himself frustrated and impotent. While the landscape around him, both urban and rural, constantly presents itself to him (or, rather, is perceived by him) in aesthetic compositions of people and place, he cannot bring himself to paint it. The journey through Jordan to Petra is a picturesque itinerary of ancient nobility and ruins, of colour and feature, but Geoffrey cannot return what it offers, cannot represent it in art.[16] If his artist's block can be taken initially as a facet of his increasing depression, it gradually becomes symptomatic of something broader, the dilemma of a British presence positioned in a world it no longer has the capacity to represent.

A vivid confrontation with this fact occurs in the second half of the novel, when Lynd, safely back in Cairo but psychologically very unstable, attempts to bring normality back into his life by taking up his sketchbook and crayons. Finding himself in the servants' quarters of his house, he comes across his servants taking their afternoon sleep and is astonished by this unexpected yet touching encounter with the hidden life of the household. Observing the men for some time, he notes their potential as subjects to be painted: in particular, his cook, lying snoring on his back, has the potential of a nude, 'his open mouth exposed the inner lip and gums and tongue, pink like a part of the body too intimate for exposure'. But with sudden mental clarity Lynd counters the impulse to paint with a sense of his own ignorance about the reality of his subject. His servants' lives, apparently so simple, are yet far beyond him. 'He was a superior – but what had the others beyond their work and sleep and hope of paradise? In the evenings before dinner and after, they would gossip, vivaciously, with much laughter – but about what? What was the real content of their lives? He knew nothing' (p. 217).

Geoffrey Lynd's individual crisis embodies a wider crisis in the relationship forged by British or Western versions of the Oriental world, a collapse of the cultural and scenic imagery which traditionally provided a bridgehead from London-based policy to Middle Eastern execution, policy now unravelling in Palestine as Lynd and his contemporaries begin to experience the fracturing of the Mandate. As Phyllis Lassner writes, '[t]he depression that drives Manning's vision in 1949 and that overwhelms Geoffrey Lynd also serves as a critique representing Britain's sense of its "unsustainable" Empire in the Middle East'.[17] And, indeed, Lynd's descent into a paranoid psychosis in the second half of *Artist Among the Missing* may be read as signalling the neurotic endgame of an imperial hold on Palestine. Beyond his collapse as an artist – signifying the collapse of British representative domination of its subordinate regions

– his mental disintegration as an individual must be seen in terms of a damaged imperial psyche haunted by its own predicament. At Petra, with Lister and Clark, Geoffrey is bitten on the hand (in fact, simply touched – there is no actual puncture) by a dog which he fears may carry rabies. Despite the absence of any wound, he is nagged by the feeling that his skin has been penetrated. Is he contaminated by the heart of the Levant and all that the ancient site of Petra might represent? Or is the sensation of pressure in his hand (a sensation exacerbated by his subsequent spiralling descent into acute paranoia) related to something more, a register of guilt and failure, a mark of internal corrosion? The indeterminacy of what has actually happened at the tomb generates an uncanny legacy, and the sense of the bite persists even long after his return from the trip:

> In a misery of disgust, he was conscious of an ache in the palm of his hand and he knew it had been there all the time. He gave himself up to examining it. He could not have said by what process he had decided exactly where the dog had touched him, but now he could put his finger on the exact spot. When he touched it, it was tender. There was no mark; not a scratch. Nothing to worry about – and yet it was always reminding him of what had happened. (*Artist Among the Missing*, p. 131)

Rabies, Clark had cheerfully informed him at the time, can have an incubation period of several days to several years. His imagined sickness is thus a blight on the future as much as the present; his fate is always now to be troubled, insecure, haunted by the dog even as he battles against the worst of his illness and as the war itself begins to move towards its concluding stages.

Artist Among the Missing was published in 1949. Its years of gestation paralleled the deterioration of civic life in Palestine and its completion coincided with the end of British control in the territory. The King David Hotel, where a miserable Geoffrey Lynd sits trying to concentrate on a copy of Gibbon's *The History of the Decline and Fall of the Roman Empire*, and where Manning herself had flirted with the chess-playing Arthur Koestler, was bombed in July 1946 by the Jewish terrorist organisation, the Irgun. Almost one hundred lives were lost in the explosion and the atrocity was taken to signal the approach of a political collapse. 'The abject end of British rule in Palestine', A.J. Sherman suggests, 'a revelation of impotence not lost on independence-minded nationalists in the remaining Empire, both engendered and reflected a mood of exhaustion and disgust that coincided with the dismal icy winter of 1947 in which British morale sank further than in the darkest days of the war'.[18] On 13 May 1948, Sir Henry Gurney, the last serving High Commissioner of the Mandate, bade farewell to his remaining staff and the following day departed from the bomb-damaged government office headquarters. Gershon Agronsky's *Palestine Post*, richly sarcastic in its moment of vindication, ran the headline 'Blaze of Glory' over a dejected message of thanks from the Prime Minister.[19] The failure of this particular mission would indeed be, as Manning sensed, a haunting one, shadowing the region's continuing power struggles for several decades in the post-war era.

The second half of Manning's *Artist Among the Missing* includes a scene in which a fragile Geoffrey Lynd, now back in Cairo, climbs one of the pyramids with a fellow officer, Joe Phillips, who is severely shell-shocked after fighting at the front at El Alamein. The two men clearly mirror each other in their nervous condition, and the physical setting of the episode adds a further note to the theme of a British spiritual decline. Looking down from the top of the pyramid, they observe that the hole hollowed out of the rock on which the structure is built appears as the shape of a ship's hull. This feature, known locally as the 'Ship of the Sun', is sardonically renamed by Phillips as 'The Ship of Death', a reference, as Lynd recognises, to D.H. Lawrence's poem of 1930, written as the poet succumbed to tuberculosis. Acknowledging that death is close, that the time to leave one's mortal being is near, the poet urges the reader to build a ship of death to carry the dying body towards oblivion. In its implicit position in Manning's scene, Lawrence's personal lament becomes a universal expression of grief for a civilisation in its own death throes. The image of the stricken officers standing on the pyramid – an ancient tomb of the dead – is already a stirring one, and the poem's shadowy presence between the lines of the text adds to the prevailing mood of morbidity:

> We are dying, we are dying, so all we can do
> is now to be willing to die, and to build the ship
> of death to carry the soul on the longest journey.

A little ship, with oars and food
and little dishes, and all accoutrements
fitting and ready for the departing soul.[20]

Though the Lawrence allusion here is incidental, it contributes to an accumulation of reference and imagery in Manning's writing on the theme of the 'ship of death'. Specifically, this conceit linked for the writer the crisis of Palestine as a contested homeland to a greater crisis of spirit bound up with the casualties of the war. Through various images of the ship carrying refugees or evacuees, refused safe harbour, excluded, torpedoed or foundering on the shore, Manning creates a trailing motif of failed responsibility, one bound pertinently and emotively by the actual events of the conflict and rendered again in allegorical form in her 1951 novel *School for Love*.

As noted above, the British government's 1939 White Paper had established quotas on Jewish immigration to Palestine which maintained an official line of restriction, in deference to its Arab territorial commitments. However, as the pressure of antisemitism in Europe increased and the Nazi eradication campaign advanced towards the Balkan countries, the numbers of illegal Jewish immigrants began to swell dramatically, most arriving via hazardous routes across both land and sea to be installed immediately in internment camps. It was soon apparent that the territory could not accommodate these unprecedented numbers. The British launched a series of protests against countries such as Panama and Liberia, under whose flags of convenience illegal immigrant ships found passage, and, together with the Americans, began to pursue other locations across the Empire for the dispersal of Jewish refugees (eventually deciding on the founding of an enclave on the island of Mauritius, a drastic and clearly unsuitable compromise). The outbreak of war led inevitably to a further tightening of policy on refugees and an intensification of diplomatic blockading. On the pretext that illegal immigrants from occupied countries might be harbouring Nazi spies among their numbers, the government set out to police systematically the major sea routes from Eastern Europe and to repulse, with force if necessary, the tide of immigrant ships arriving in Palestine's waters.

This policy, highly controversial in the context of the worsening crisis for European Jews, led to a sequence of distressing and shocking events as attempted landings were foiled by government troops or by the Palestine police force. Inevitably, several such incidents were publicised, the press drawing international attention to the contradictions of Britain's political judgement and to the desperate plight of Jewish refugees enduring dangerous conditions on cramped and faulty vessels, only to be refused entry to their supposed homeland and abandoned to a desperate fate. In November 1940, for example, two barely seaworthy steamers, the *Pacific* and the *Milos*, arrived at the port of Haifa carrying 1,800 refugees. They were refused entry to Palestine and transferred to a British steamer, the *Patria*, for deportation to Mauritius. Just outside the harbour, however, the *Patria* exploded and over 200 refugees were killed. In December of the same year the *Salvador*, carrying 350 refugees, was refused entry by Palestine and sent back to the seas off Turkey, where the ship was wrecked in a storm, with the death of 231 of her passengers.

Late in 1941, the case of the *Struma* brought this situation to a head and to widespread international condemnation. A converted yacht with capacity for 100 people, the *Struma* left the Romanian Black Sea port of Constanța in December 1941 carrying 769 passengers (almost all of whom were Romanian Jews), to set sail for Haifa. In possession of extortionately priced tickets but no immigration papers, these refugees eventually reached the harbour at Istanbul, where they remained at anchor while the ship's engine was repaired and international diplomatic wrangling over their fate intensified. Conditions on board were described as appalling: the passengers included numerous children; there were virtually no sanitary facilities, and several cases of dysentery were reported, but British officials remained resolute on their blanket ban on illegal immigration into Palestine. After two months at sea and despite a series of pleas from various international representatives on their behalf, those on board the *Struma* were informed by Turkish police that they were to return to Romania. The ship was towed some ten kilometres off the Turkish coast into the Bosporous where, following an explosion probably caused by a mine or torpedo, it sank. All on board were lost except an eighteen-year-old Romanian amateur athlete who managed to swim to shore.[21]

The *Struma* episode marked what was described as a psychological watershed for Jews in Palestine.[22] It cast serious doubt on the British policy of forced repatriation for would-be immigrants, a policy further darkened as news of Nazi extermination camps began to filter through from Europe.

In Jerusalem itself, posters appeared calling for the arrest of the High Commissioner Sir Harold MacMichael, while beyond Palestine a sympathetic international community voiced its outrage in the press.[23] More than almost any other event, the loss of the *Struma* threw into relief the continuing ideological and territorial pressures under which Palestine laboured during the war years. Meanwhile, even in the wake of the disaster, illegal Jewish immigrants continued in their desperate attempts to reach their homeland, until the Nazis effectively closed down Europe's remaining exit routes.

In March 1970 the *Observer Sunday Magazine* published Olivia Manning's lengthy account of the *Struma* episode. This piece, one of her relatively small number of forays into mainstream journalism, is marked by both grief and outrage at the plight of the unfortunate ship's passengers. For Manning, the *Struma* was a connection on a personal level, after all, between Romania and Palestine, the two locations that meant so much to her in her life and her writing. Arguing in her article that the belated inquiry into the sinking should never have been closed (the issue of blame having been left unresolved), Manning sets out to illuminate the chain of circumstances which led to the ship's destruction. First, she traces the background to the position of Romania's Jewish households, suffering under the dual threat of the Nazis and the Romanian fascist Iron Guard. She then relates how the passengers in flight from this regime and embarking on the *Struma* were deliberately misled, both on the capacity of the ship and the availability, once in Jerusalem, of immigration visas. Those who signed up for the voyage were ignominiously relieved of most of their cash and possessions at customs before they finally boarded what was clearly an ill-equipped and seriously overcrowded vessel. Many slept four to a bunk, she reports, food and water were strictly rationed, and when mines were spotted in the water there were outbreaks of hysteria on the overcrowded deck. For the passengers, who were predominantly middle-class Jews, conditions on board the ship were physically and psychologically hellish.

Manning's account took note of the various factors that had complicated the situation. She observed, in particular, that the confused international affiliations of the *Struma*, with its Bulgarian crew sailing under a Panamanian flag, had exacerbated the diplomatic crisis caused by the ship's arrival at Istanbul. She also elaborated on the wider historical context of the Palestinian situation and evaluated various British attempts at control of the region. But while maintaining a fairly even balance in her outline of the competing claims of Arab, Jew and, indeed, British for international understanding, Manning allowed her particular sympathies to emerge forcefully on behalf of the refugees. Beyond the contortions of diplomacy and territorial conflict, the humanitarian disaster represented by the *Struma* comes to the fore with a spectral intensity in the author's recollection of how she herself had seen the stricken ship as it languished in Turkish coastal waters at Christmas in 1941:

> On Christmas night, the officers of a Royal Navy cruiser on a goodwill mission to the Bosporous, invited their British and Turkish friends on board. There was music and dancing. A searchlight, switched on for the fun of it, played over the city and the harbour; and, at one moment, as the ray swung round, it came to rest on a ship crowded with human faces. The ship looked derelict; the faces, row upon row of them, stared white and unsmiling at the cruiser. Shocked by the sight, the guests asked one another 'Who are they? What are they doing there?' Someone said it might be a prison-ship and so, in a way, it was. The light shifted and the party forgot its grim audience hidden in the dark.[24]

Written after the completion of the *Balkan Trilogy* and before the composition of the *Levant* sequence, the *Struma* article reveals the extent to which the plight of Jewish refugees and the saga of their misfortunes at sea as a result of failed diplomatic policies remained on Manning's mind in the war years and after. This would be one of the many ships of death haunting her post-war fiction, an image not only of suffering and terror but also of a grievous failure of protective duty.

It is in the context of this specific international humanitarian and territorial crisis that Manning's 1951 novel, *School for Love*, makes most immediate sense. In *Artist Among the Missing* she had begun to touch on the predicament of an overcrowded Palestine, in the fears voiced, for example, by Lister's servant Jamal: '"This is my country. It is a small country. There would be more room for them elsewhere"' (p. 89). Her second novel on the subject elaborates on the territorial squeeze that the region experienced during the war (and on the harshness of British policy towards immigrants and refugees) in an allegorical structure which gestures towards, rather than secures, a line of political critique. In *School for Love*, a Jerusalem boarding house becomes home to a random group of individuals in the final year of the war, but, like Jerusalem itself, a golden city now overflowing with numerous racial and religious groups, each competing for ownership, the house is a contested space. Held together only by the forceful personality of its repressive and scheming British landlady, Ethel Bohun, its stability is threatened from within by the displaced, shifting and frustrated energies of the claimants to its roof. As the novel opens, this pressure on space is further aggravated by the arrival of a fourteen-year-old boy, Felix Latimer, sent to live under the protection of Miss Bohun until he can find safe passage to England at the end of hostilities.

Perhaps with a nod to the German writer George Tabori's novel set in a Cairo pension, *Original Sin*, which she had reviewed for the *Palestine Post* in 1947, Manning establishes the compacted living arrangements – so often a feature of her own life and autobiographical fiction – as a locus of claustrophobia, paranoia and competition.[25] Of course this is also a Dickensian scenario. The use of the orphaned boy, together with the Gothic atmosphere of the house and the caricatured aspects of the manipulative spinster Ethel Bohun, lead Lassner to read *School for Love* in the light of *Great Expectations*, as a Dickensian *bildungsroman* that 'exposes the consequences of colonial power on novelistic romance and the face of social and individual mobility'.[26] However, Manning may also have had a more recent model in mind: the work of her much-admired contemporary Elizabeth Bowen, whose modernist studies of the orphaned or displaced child confronting an adult world of suppressed or repressed paranoia, *The House in Paris* and *The Death of the Heart*, had appeared in the late 1930s. Reviewing a Penguin edition of Bowen's 1932 novel *To the North* in November 1947, Manning had singled out the particular skill of that novel's schoolgirl Pauline, seeing her as a 'first sketch' of Bowen's subtly developed child characters in later novels.[27] In this respect the *bildungsroman* is, as with Bowen's characteristic formula, a skewed and pessimistic one. The role played by Felix is not to move reassuringly through his experiences towards maturity, but rather to expose, in a sequence of confrontations and emotional disturbances, the ascendancy of self-interest and the ultimate fragility of human compassion.

The novel's background politics are introduced immediately when the taxi driver delivering Felix to the pension points out from the hills above the city the divided landscape of Jerusalem, with its ancient Arab villages high on the rocks and its new and lush Jewish settlements in the valley. An innocent abroad, Felix makes no connection between this introduction and the inhabitants of the house, yet the connections are brutally apparent. In the pension there are already several residents, including Frau Leszno and her son Nikky – Polish Jews exiled from Germany, who have arrived in Jerusalem on 'refugee coffin ships' (*School for Love*, p. 31) – and an elderly British man known only as Mr Jewel. All are seen as having outstayed their welcome and Miss Bohun, taking advantage of Mr Jewel's illness and subsequent hospitalisation, seizes the opportunity to invite a young British widow, Mrs Ellis, to live in the pension in his place. Torn between his attraction to Mrs Ellis and his loyalty to the ousted Mr Jewel, Felix attempts to negotiate the question of rooms and their allocation, but Miss Bohun is resistant to compassion. Driven only by self-interest, she maintains the charade of a family living together in harmony, her blustering rhetoric on the subject flying in the face of reality.

Territorial pressure is a governing theme here, but the novel's force as political critique lies very much in the caricatured figure of Ethel Bohun.[28] To Felix, she appears as a grotesque; insect-like, she reminds him of a praying mantis, a sinister and intractable figure in a household devoid of generosity or sympathy:

> At meal-times he would feel drawn to stare at her face, which was colourless as plaster, the eyes nearly always hidden behind the thick, plaster-coloured lids. Even when she lifted her face to speak or call Frau Leszno, she would not open her eyes. Her mouth was never more than a minus sign drawn under the thin, drooping tip of her nose. (*School for Love*, p. 26)

Miss Bohun's insinuation into the life of the city is through language: fluent in Arabic, she keeps on her bookshelves primers for Hungarian, Russian and Romanian in readiness for the influx of new Jewish students of English, a linguistic opportunism that parallels her mean-spirited exploitation of the pension's more vulnerable tenants. Meanwhile her position of authority in the house is gradually exposed as illegitimate, the pension having been held initially by the Leszno family (whom she has now usurped) and rented in the first place from its actual owner, an Imam in the Old City. In undermining through this set-up an apparent hierarchy of ownership, Manning again puts her allegorical trajectory into play, embedding the present insecurity of the pension in a complex history of contestation and appropriation. Her critique is intensified through the device of Miss Bohun's affiliation to an evangelical Christian sect, the Ever Ready Group of Wise Virgins, or 'Ever-Readies'. In accordance with this sect's teaching and despite the intense pressure on space in the house, Miss Bohun keeps its front room empty, cleaned and prepared in symbolic readiness for the Lord. This display of vain promise based on hollow religiosity and self-righteousness foregrounds a nebulous idea of future salvation at the expense of present, desperate material need.

School for Love can be read in these terms as a bitter comment on the final years of the British Mandate in Palestine, comment sharpened by the subsequent deterioration of the post-partition conflict into civil war. It evokes, through Miss Bohun, a British presence characterised by a drastic failure of compassion. However, this is not to suggest that its allegorical purchase is straightforward. The correlation of Manning's narrative to a political reality and particularly to the history of Jewish Palestine is frequently difficult to gauge. Lassner takes a scene in which Felix comes across a servant setting fire to live rats, for example, as evidence of how the text establishes 'a searing connection' to the Holocaust and evokes retrospectively an anterior landscape of Jewish persecution,[29] but this interpretation is perhaps ambitious. Manning's treatment of the Jewish characters in the novel and in particular of the whining, petulant Frau Leszno is characteristically ambivalent: there is no romanticisation of Jewish suffering and no claims made on our compassion for the Jewish plight. These Jewish exiles are victims, undoubtedly, but they are also seen as vain, self-interested and prejudiced, their demands resulting only in the exhaustion (like Geoffrey Lynd's exhaustion) of Christian pity. Meanwhile Manning treats with scepticism the city's newly arrived influx of Jews, commenting in the novel on their naivety in the face of untenable ideals. At the Innsbruck café near Jerusalem's Allenby Square, where the middle-aged exiles from Central Europe bend silently over their chessboards, the younger men who gather around the charismatic Nicky Leszno discuss Kafka, Palinurus and Sartre, flaunting their European intellectualism in a vain attempt to distance themselves from Palestine's internecine squabbles: 'No-one here – Jews and Arabs though they were – ever spoke of Palestine's private war that was marking time now until the World War ended' (p. 132). That such a community cannot hold is an occasion of irony rather than sympathy, and Manning's Jerusalem a city of violent, splintering wills, never coherence.

In this respect, however, a major difficulty of *School for Love* is that it sheers off from a Koestler-esque treatise on the homeland issue. Indeed, the novel changes tack in its central section, its focus shifting from the specifics of the Jewish immigrant predicament to a narrative that generalises the experiences of suffering in wartime, locating these in the image of the 'ship of death.' As the narrative progresses, the Jewish characters who might have made a claim for understanding and who might, indeed, have vanquished Miss Bohun in some way, are effectively displaced as objects of sympathy by the English widow who joins the inhabitants of the Jerusalem pension. Mrs Ellis is superficially a source of romantic interest for Felix but at another level she embodies the universal refugee figure. It is her history of suffering which provides the novel's keynote when its horrifying details are eventually disclosed. We learn that on board an evacuee ship headed from Port Said to England she was put in charge of an abandoned and neglected five-year-old girl. When the ship was torpedoed, she picked up the child and began to try to escape, joining the terrifying scramble to abandon ship:

> 'People were throwing the kids up on top of one another like parcels. I heard afterwards that some of the boats sank as soon as they hit the water. I knew I'd just have to jump in. I said to the kid: "Now hold on tight. I'm going to swim to the shore." The town was blacked out, but you could see a glimmer in the distance, two or three miles away. The water was black as hell. I jumped in, not even knowing how far I had to jump. It was icy. At first I thought I was the only person in the water and then, suddenly, there were hundreds of them all splashing about and not knowing what to do, the poor brats . . . At one time I was swimming with half a dozen of them hanging on to me. I almost went under but it was so cold, they couldn't hang on for long. They dropped off one by one, but my own kid hung on to my back without making a sound.' (*School for Love*, p. 144)

Only when Mrs Ellis reaches the safety of a rescue boat does she realise that the girl is dead. With the small body lying still in her lap, she finally breaks down in compassion for this abandoned and unloved child, the incident prefiguring the loss later in the novel of her own unborn baby, whose death in her womb at almost full term comes as the result of a fall Miss Bohun causes during a row. Recalling the desperate failed passage of the evacuee child, the miscarriage coincides, suggestively, with the end of the war itself; this is a blighted victory, with no means of securing the future.[30]

Manning's use of Mrs Ellis in this way diverts the focus on Jewish immigration into Palestine towards a more universal comment. A specifically Jewish experience, as defined in Manning's vision of the *Struma*, is linked to non-Jewish suffering in the image of the sinking evacuation ship. This represents an early instance of Manning's strategy, further developed in the later fiction, of mapping particular refugee experiences on to general, more accessible narratives (in the same vein in the *Balkan Trilogy*, Guy Pringle wears clothes designated for refugee Poles and Harriet hides on the roof of their Bucharest apartment with the Jewish Sasha Drucker). But it goes beyond this too. In the context of the reference to Lawrence's 'ship of death' (in the scene on the pyramids in *Artist Among the Missing*) the weaving of the shipwreck narrative into her fiction is bound up with the theme of survivor guilt. In the *Levant Trilogy*, Aidan Sheridan is still traumatised by the memory of what happened when the ship on which he was escorting evacuee children to Canada was torpedoed. He recalls to Harriet how he and the children found themselves abandoned in lifeboats in the bitter cold of the Atlantic, drifting for days while the children died, one by one. Sheridan cannot escape the guilt of having survived; haunted by the memories of throwing bodies into the sea to float after the boat, he will eventually commit suicide (*LT*, pp. 318–20). His description continues to trouble Harriet, who, scheduled to sail home on the ship *Queen of Sparta*, turns back at the last minute with a premonition of disaster, only to learn afterwards that only one lifeboat escapes when this ship is subsequently torpedoed and sunk. After the ship is destroyed, she too becomes a ghost of sorts, her absence and presumed death a reproach to her neglectful husband until the moment of her eventual return home to Cairo.

The loss of the children in Aidan Sheridan's story (and possibly also in that of Mrs Ellis) is likely to draw on the sinking of the *City of Benares* in September 1940. The ship, which had sailed from Liverpool, was torpedoed in the Atlantic, with the loss of 73 children and 172 adults. Only seven children of the original group survived and the sinking came to represent a moment of deep despair and spiritual distress in the course of the war. *Personal Landscape* poet George Fraser published in the Middle East army magazine *Parade*, in 1941, an elegy in which images of the drowned children presented spectral obstacles to a kind of spiritual consolation:

> Think what you will, but like the crisping leaf
> In whipped October, crack your thoughts to grief.
>
> In the drenched valley, whimpering and cold,
> The small ghosts flicker, whisper, unconsoled.
>
> *S.S. City of Benares (Drowned Refugee Children, 1940)*[31]

The sinking of the *City of Benares* possibly figures in George Orwell's *Nineteen Eighty-Four*, which Manning reviewed for the *Palestine Post* in September 1949 ('the writing is flat and completely undistinguished', she remarked in an otherwise complimentary if humdrum review).[32] Early in the novel Winston Smith writes in his first diary entry of a film he and the others have been shown:

> *Last night to the flicks. All war films. One very good one of a ship full of refugees being bombed somewhere in the Mediterranean . . . then you saw a lifeboat full of children with a helicopter hovering over it. there was a middle-aged woman might have been a jewess sitting up in the bow with a little boy about three years old in her arms. little boy screaming with fright and hiding his head between her breasts as if he was trying to burrow right into her and the woman putting her arms round him and comforting him although she was blue with fright herself . . .*[33]

The critic Jonathan Rose suggests that Orwell recalls here Alfred Noyes's response to the torpedoing of the *City of Benares*, described in his 1942 work *Edge of the Abyss* as 'a deliberate assault on the human soul'. Noyes's use of the attack (an incident regarded by many as conclusive evidence of

Nazi extremism) is as an act of barbarity confirming the slippage of civilisation over the edge and into another order of modern life. In *Nineteen Eighty-Four* this brutal picture of the 'ship of death' introduces a moral and emotional vacuum, a new order of human failing at the expense of political systems.[34]

Death at sea was inevitably a recurrent subject for wartime writers, with the sinking of Jewish refugee ships echoing the frequent loss of civilian evacuee ships crossing the Atlantic and the bombardment and destruction of military vessels in the maritime war zones. In Graham Greene's *The Heart of the Matter* (1948), for example, the policeman Scobie must deal with a dying girl and a young widow who have survived forty days in an open boat after their ship is torpedoed off the coast of Africa; Louis MacNeice in his wartime radio play inspired by the death of his friend Graham Shepard, '*He Had a Date*', broadcast in June 1944, used the device of a warship hit by a German torpedo; and James Hanley (noted by Manning for what she classed as his 'miserable' stories of the sea and seamen) picked up a similar narrative thread in his novel *The Ocean* (1941), in which five characters are left adrift in a lifeboat after a torpedo attack. In Arthur Koestler's *Thieves in the Night* the central character experiences nightmares with the recurrent image of the blasted, sinking ship and its aftermath: 'He saw the drowning people before his eyes. It was a sharp, short flash which lasted only a split second but was fantastically clear. There were hundreds of them, with arms and legs sticking out of the water, but there was no sound.'[35]

In addition, some of the disturbing force of the sinking ship image can be traced back into Manning's earlier writing. As the daughter of a naval officer, she had been introduced to the ghostly connotations of shipwreck long before the war itself. In her 1938 short story 'The Children', an elderly naval admiral tells his nephew and niece the story of the loss at sea of two nineteenth-century vessels, the *Eurydice* and the *Atalanta*, both shipwrecks overcast with mystery and superstition. A few years later, writing in the *Palestine Post* in 1944, she reformulated this material in an article on her childhood memories of the Irish and English coasts. Here, she recalls being taken as a child to Portsmouth's dockyard museum where she became intrigued by the wooden figurehead of the ship the *Eurydice*, wrecked in the Solent with the loss of all but two of her sailors: 'There, in the museum, was the long, wooden, despairing figure of Eurydice sinking back into hell with her long, painted face, long, up-held hands.' The portrayal of the beseeching mortal being dragged down through the water to the underworld is haunting. For Manning, who would experience her own terrifying escape by ship from Athens to Alexandria, death at sea was a constant fear (increased, perhaps, by the fact that her brother's body had been lost to the sea after the shooting down of his plane in 1941).[36]

The recollection of the torpedoed evacuee ship in *School for Love* has, therefore, a complex history, one which perhaps compounds Manning's childhood visions of maritime disaster with various recent atrocities, and with numerous contemporary literary treatments of the same theme. As with the other accounts of shipwreck in her fiction, it serves here metaphorically. Those lost at sea cry out, like the Eurydice figure, to those left on land, ghosts of condemnation and abjection. Like the faces on the *Struma*, which still silently watch those on the naval vessel in the darkness, the dead children of the *City of Benares* return, in fictional form, in the experiences of Mrs Ellis and Aidan Sheridan. The sinking ship as an image forges connections between Palestine as a failed responsibility and the international collapse of security and safety, a theme played out by the author in resonant and characteristically Gothic terms. The allusion to the sinking ship that Mrs Ellis survives therefore has a deeper resonance for Manning than at first appears. This is not simply the author's journalistic co-option of contemporary material but an episode belonging to a catalogue in her writing, directed towards the foregrounding of suffering and the manner in which that suffering haunts the progress of military and political campaigns.

Despite its profundity in this respect, however, *School for Love* is a less successful and less politically coherent novel than *Artist Among the Missing*. Chiefly, it raises the problem as to whether the persuasive imagery of the 'ship of death' reinforces or dilutes the specific issue of the Jewish homeland which Manning began to confront in the allegory of Miss Bohun's Jerusalem boarding house. In several respects she could be seen to side-step the territorial issue introduced in the first half of the novel. Where Koestler in *Promise and Fulfilment* incorporated the plight of the 'little death ships' into a caustic attack on the Mandate authorities, Manning remains self-consciously oblique. The use of the 'ship of death' motif in her wartime writing expresses deep anguish but is a means to consolidate the specific plight of European Jews with a universal register of human suffering, dislocation and guilt. In the same way, the trilogies later develop the figure of the wartime refugee from its local contexts into a broader conceptual study of a dislocated and abject presence in the reconstitution of Europe. The manoeuvre might be considered on one level as evasive, particularly in relation to the Palestine problem. On another, however, and more positively, it represents Manning's ability to read the demographic, colonial and humanitarian pressures of the time in genuinely sympathetic terms. Palestine is recognised both as a political reality and as a paradigm for deep anxieties within civilisation itself. The Jewish exile slips into the category of the universal refugee, vulnerable and neglected, as a means of establishing 'refugee-ship' itself as a modern post-war condition, a figure for which the wandering Harriet Pringle, at the end of the *Levant Trilogy*, becomes a kind of vicarious prototype.

Palestine remained on Manning's mind long after the war and not only because of her extended relationship with the *Palestine Post*. She would touch on this particular territory again in *The Sum of Things*, the final volume of the *Levant Trilogy*. Here, Harriet Pringle's brief journey through Jerusalem occasions a revisiting of what was still, at the time of the novel's composition in the 1970s, an intractable political landscape, as one of her more sarcastic characters observes:

> 'Ideal climate, this, never too hot, but awful place, everyone hating everyone else. The Polish Jews hate the German Jews, and the Russians hate the Polish and the German. They're all in small communities, each one trying to corner everything for themselves: jobs, food, flats, houses . . . Then all the Jews combine in hating the Arabs and the Arabs and the Jews combine in hating the British police, and the police hate the government officials who look down on them and won't let them join the club. What a place! God knows who'll get it in the end but whoever it is, I don't envy them.' (*LT*, p. 507)

For Manning as a novelist of war, Jerusalem was a compelling location. From here she could analyse the effects on an individual of a humanitarian and territorial crisis, one fast outpacing the best efforts of colonial and cabinet diplomacy back in London. But she was far from propagandist. If she echoed Koestler in her attentiveness to the homeland question and her willingness to engage with the subject of the Jewish refugee plight, she departed from him by avoiding a direct political front and by withdrawing into the more nuanced, sometimes equivocal, thematic and symbolic framework of the wartime novel. *Artist Among the Missing* is certainly intelligible as a study of diplomatic crisis, but it remains, too, a straightforward drama of individual psychological breakdown; *School for Love* is, on one level, tightly allusive to its context, yet perhaps, as suggested, evasive in many respects and, again, shielded by the conventions of wartime fictional romance. One senses that her instinct was towards a subtle underplaying of a difficult political theme. Reviewing the latter novel for the *Times Literary Supplement*, Anthony Powell was sufficiently astute to note this point. 'The political feelings of Jews and Arabs are perhaps rather understated, in the light of the violence with which they were soon to break out', he remarked of the novel, 'but this impression may have been deliberately intended as one true to the moment in Palestine'.[37] True to the moment indeed, not only to the politics of place but also to the purposeful reticence which, more than anything else, might be said to characterise Olivia Manning's earliest novelistic responses to the war.

Conclusion

The Rain Forest

It once appeared to be the handicap of my and Miss Manning's sex that, while many of us wished to and could write, few of us had anything very particular to write about. For Miss Manning, the changes and chances of life and war have put this right . . . Her artistic sensitiveness has adapted itself, without a quaver, to violent movement and spectacular change.

Elizabeth Bowen[1]

In 1945 Olivia Manning and her husband returned from Palestine to an England much changed since their hasty pre-war departure. For their generation, and particularly for those who had served abroad, the sense of disorientation at the conclusion of the conflict was marked. How would they manage the transition to a settled civilian life? What was to be done with the baggage of memories, relationships and material the war had provided? Harriet Pringle notes the peculiar effects of the conflict on the passage of time while in Greece: 'War meant a perpetual postponement of life, yet one did not cease to grow old. She had been twenty-one when it started. At the end, if there ever was an end, what age would she be?'(*BT*, p. 824).[2] With that postponement now over, the nature of time would change again for Manning and her husband. An extraordinary set of experiences had finished and a long process of reflection was about to begin in a London only just starting to pick up the pieces, in the 'precarious peace' heralded by the conclusion of the *Levant Trilogy*.

Not surprisingly, Manning's version of England after the war charts a nation that is dispirited and confused, and where individuals are rendered erratic by the receding tides of the war effort. Her novels of the late 1940s and early 1950s portray her home society as moribund and colourless. In *A Different Face* (1953), the southern coastal town of Coldmouth (a version of her own native Portsmouth) has 'a look of post-war exhaustion and shabbiness', intensifying the sense of desolation which first afflicted its protagonist Hugo Fletcher on disembarking from his ship in a drab, grey Liverpool:

> Through the rain-obscured air there loomed, menacingly near at times, gas-works, kilns, iron-foundries, cement coolers, power stations, goods yards. He felt stifled by them. He had never meant to come back – and yet here he was, unreasonably returned, walking now in a silvery world without brilliance or shadow that he had taken for the natural order of things until he acquired, in Egypt, a taste for space and sunshine. (*A Different Face*, p. 11)

In *The Doves of Venus* (1955), the streets of Chelsea and Pimlico are alienating and wintry, the city like a mausoleum, and here Petta Bellot, growing old, comes to realise that her generation has decayed into a relic of its confident pre-war form, with only mediocrities remaining on an impoverished social stage.

The reality for Olivia Manning and Reggie Smith was by no means as bleak. Walter Allen records in his memoir of the period that the couple took up with various pre-war friends and developed a series of fresh acquaintances, making regular appearances on London's literary and media circuit. Reggie – by now under constant surveillance from British Military Intelligence – flourished at the Features Department of the BBC and in the company of former associates such as Louis MacNeice. He also managed to maintain several international communist connections and travelled back to Bucharest in 1948 for a meeting of the British–Romanian Friendship Association, of which he subsequently became Vice-President.[3]

Manning's focus was decidedly more domestic. She continued her extensive reviewing, initially for the *Palestine Post* and then gradually for the *Spectator*, *Punch*, the *Sunday Times* and occasionally the *Guardian* and *Observer,* in addition to taking on some minor script-writing assignments for the BBC.[4] In 1948 she published her short-story collection *Growing Up*, which was followed by her three novels set in England – *The Doves of Venus*, *A Different Face* and *The Play Room* – and over the next decade pursued numerous other writing commitments, including her Irish travel book *The Dreaming Shore* and a collection of her *Punch* profiles of Reggie, *My Husband Cartwright*, published in 1956 with illustrations by fellow writer Len Deighton. She was a member of P.E.N. and was casually involved in other literary organisations and committees. Apart from some holiday travel within Europe and regular excursions to Northern Ireland to visit her widowed mother, Manning remained for the most part in London in a series of flats and houses, a phase of her life which is relatively well documented both by her biographers and (less sympathetically) by MI5.

Manning's return to England did not staunch her interest in and sense of a changing European and indeed world order, however. Her final single novel, *The Rain Forest*, was published in 1974, after the completion of the *Balkan Trilogy* and before she began compiling the material of the *Levant* sequence. No doubt because it is overshadowed in this way, the novel is usually overlooked by commentators on her work and, despite some positive reviews at the time, it fails to make an appearance in critical accounts of the decade's healthy run of achievement in fiction. Nevertheless *The Rain Forest* deserves notice here, by way of conclusion to this study, not least because of the ways in which it dovetails with the trilogies, echoing and advancing their end-of-empire themes and building once again on the condition of a faltering marriage to survey the precarious state of the international climate. (Indeed, the married couple introduced in *The Rain Forest*, the Fosters, might be taken as another, later incarnation of the Pringles and in turn a version of Olivia and Reggie – 'this was the Manning–Smith marriage to the life', one of their friends has observed of the novel.)[5]

The narrative of *The Rain Forest* follows Kristy Foster, a fiction writer of relative notoriety who accompanies her husband Hugh to Al-Bustan, a semi-tropical island in the Indian Ocean, where he is to take up a minor government position in the residue of the ruling British administration. If the marriage is under strain before the couple departs from England, it deteriorates yet further under the pressures of living in the midst of the jaded and hidebound British community resident in the island's capital.

Almost to the point of caricature, Manning portrays an expatriate officialdom running to seed, obsessing over hierarchy, form and etiquette in its vain attempt to hold together the remnants of control over the political environment of Al-Bustan. Meanwhile the rest of society on the island has little to offer, with the British contingent alienated by squabbling factions of various native and immigrant sects – Muslim, Nubian, Jewish, Arab – each poised to move to power when the British authorities eventually cede control and grant full independence to the territory.

The Rain Forest obviously borrows from a tradition of 'island' fiction penned by various British writers throughout the twentieth century. That said, it is far from generic, and one can speculate on the degree to which it is grounded fairly precisely in a series of recognisable geographical referents, each adding political nuances to the book. While some contemporary reviewers were keen to link the Indian Ocean island to the Seychelles or Zanzibar, where Manning's father had gone as a young naval officer, it seems more likely that Al-Bustan owes key elements to Cyprus, which she and Reggie Smith had visited in October 1944.[6] This trip, intended as a break from the stress of wartime life in Jerusalem, was a miserable event in many respects: Manning was convalescing after a miscarriage and was in the middle of a related episode of depression. Nevertheless, for her fictional purposes the holiday appears to have been useful. With its explosive Greek–Turkish division Cyprus may well have inspired her novel's foregrounding of long-running territorial disputes, fuelled by racial and ethnic tension and exacerbated by the warped legacies of British colonial rule. The conflict between the Turks and Greeks over control of the island, which worsened after the formal granting of independence in 1960 and led eventually to the decisive coup of 1974, undoubtedly kept Cyprus in view as a byword for the kind of internecine tensions presented in *The Rain Forest*.[7]

Manning may well have had other islands in mind too, including Malta, which she visited in March 1970, and, more significantly, Capri.[8] Already highly evocative in British literary culture, Capri had provided the basis for Norman Douglas's semi-fictionalised island of Nepenthe in *South Wind* (1917). This travel-based novel, detailing the life of a small and eccentric British colony on a Mediterranean island, was much admired by Manning and it is more than likely that she took with her on her own visit to the island in 1971 Douglas's last work, his 1952 factual guide *A Footnote on Capri*. Graham Greene, Elizabeth David and Somerset Maugham (in his short story 'The Lotus Eater') were among the many writers who contributed to the island's literary mythology in the wake of Douglas's sojourn there and, in one of her less fortunate ventures, Manning herself almost came to add to the island's cult. In 1969 the film rights to her novel *The Play Room* were sold to the producer Ken Annakin, who, rather indulgently perhaps, chose Capri as the location in which to shoot the book's scenes of the Isle of Wight. Filming began in the summer of 1971, but with production almost complete, the film crew ran out of money. When they were unable to pay their local bills, their equipment was impounded and they became virtual prisoners on the island until further emergency funding arrived.[9] Manning's visit to the set enabled her to see Capri and observe at first hand the kind of subtropical flora and fauna described so eloquently in *The Rain Forest*, but the film project never came to completion. By this stage she was jaded with the experience of travel, writing home to Kay Dick that 'I am beginning to feel I do not want to go abroad again'.[10]

The Rain Forest took some three years to complete and during the period of its composition Manning was also working on the first volume of the *Levant Trilogy*.[11] This timeframe adds a further element to the novel's backdrop. If the two islands of her distant and recent travel history, Cyprus and Capri, provided her with local colour and scenery, a location closer to home perhaps intensified the novel's political tensions and threatening atmosphere. By 1972 when the fiction was in progress (in letters, Manning makes several references to being 'absorbed' in her new novel during this year), Reggie Smith had taken up a lecturing post in Northern Ireland at what was then the Postgraduate College of Continuing Education in Londonderry. His notes towards an autobiography refer to his life there 'at the most violent time', with armed soldiers guarding the open air theatre productions he staged at the city's Guildhall.[12] Indeed that year was one of the bloodiest in the history of the Northern Ireland troubles, marked by a series of loyalist and republican atrocities and attacks on both military and civilian targets. Perhaps for Manning, who did not accompany her husband to Northern Ireland, this context reawakened the fears she had experienced in Jerusalem during the war itself, which Smith had reported to his superiors in Palestine: 'She has terrible feelings of foreboding. She thinks I am going to be blown up in my office.'[13] This point of connection certainly suggests that it was the Northern Irish context that inspired elements of the 1974 novel and particularly its violent denouement in which the island's government offices are bombed by a native pro-independence group, leaving the hospitalised Kristy Foster to fear that her husband has perished in the explosion.

The Rain Forest has, therefore, an interesting composite political and geographical hinterland, bringing together through the device of the Fosters' faltering relationship various evocative strands of Manning's wartime travel experiences and subsequent international ventures and connections. These are drawn suggestively into a novel satirising the end of British superiority in a version of 'abroad' that has become alien, threatening and assertive. Its setting in 1953, the year of Queen Elizabeth's Coronation and the conquering of Everest, purposefully juxtaposes England's would-be domestic confidence at the time with the tensions of the international arena. The small hotel at which the Fosters stay on the island provides a microcosm of an English society fossilised by its long isolation from domestic normality: in its name, the 'Daisy Pension', it conveys a little-Englander triteness; in its quaint, 'mummified' owner, Mrs Gunner (an alternative and less sinister version of Miss Bohun in *School for Love*), it suggests a mock epic version of English royalty whose demise will bring to a final state of collapse the community of English petty diplomats and functionaries held together by 'a refrigeration of the will' (*Rain Forest*, p. 17). This kind of expatriate life is embodied in the grotesque figure of Ambrose Gunner, a man of great intellectual promise now run to fat, to seediness and corruption, his world distorted by sordid transactions with the island's various native schemers and opportunists.[14]

Such elements give *The Rain Forest* a formulaic profile at times, suggesting the author's self-conscious alliance to a canon of 'imperial decline' fiction set by Graham Greene and Malcolm Lowry (and traces of the Mexican jungle setting of Lowry's *Under the Volcano* are surely discernible in Manning's portrait of Al-Bustan's tropical northern territory). In this respect she moves closest, however, to J.G. Farrell, whose 'Empire trilogy', comprising *Troubles* (1970), *The Siege of Krishnapur* (1973) and *The Singapore Grip* (1978), parallels Manning's *Levant Trilogy* as one of the defining sequence fictions of the period. Manning served as a judge on the committee that awarded Farrell the Faber Memorial Prize for his novel *Troubles*, and she had nothing but the highest praise for his achievement.[15] With its highly evocative portrait of the crumbling Majestic Hotel as one of the last outposts of a fading Anglo-Irish Ascendancy class in an Ireland clamouring for independence between 1919 and 1921, *Troubles* combined a violent political backdrop with an elegiac, comic portrait of a vain imperial retrenchment.

Farrell's distinctiveness in *Troubles* derived, furthermore, from the rich symbolic landscape he developed around a series of horticultural motifs and images, in the fading folly of the hotel's tropical 'Palm Court', for example, or the creeping wild vegetation encroaching on the estate's walls.[16] Manning's deployment of very similar elements in her 1974 novel suggests she was strongly influenced by Farrell's method in *Troubles*. In *The Rain Forest*, Kristy Foster learns that Al-Bustan means 'garden', and the novel's concern is with the loss of this Edenic paradise through a combination of rampant tourism, political dysfunctionalism and ecological irresponsibility – the last treated in a complex but innovative sub-plot involving the island's resident mad scientist Simon Hobhouse. The development of horticultural and environmental motifs is elaborate and, as in Farrell's novel, systematically symbolic. Manning conveys the preciousness and fragility of the residual English hierarchy through the quintessentially Farrell-esque image of Mrs Gunner's private 'Lettuce Room'. Under lock and key in the Daisy Pension, hundreds of lettuces are grown in boxes, lit at night by artificial phosphorescent light, 'the small delicate plants glowing viridian green' through the windows, and sheltered by day by bamboo blinds from the tropical sun (*Rain Forest*, p. 91). There is no way in which this remnant of a society can survive against the menace of the primeval forest through which Hugh Foster treks on his journey with the scientist Hobhouse in the novel's closing chapters, a journey that leads him towards a confrontation with the possibility of the destruction of the human species itself: 'The forest came so close that Hugh could peer between the interwoven branches and creepers but he saw only the inner darkness. He felt a nervous dread of the forest coming too close to him . . . He was lost, with no more knowledge of his surroundings than a grub hatched in a carpet' (*Rain Forest*, p. 261).

Connecting all the novel's thematic trajectories, finally, is a miscarried pregnancy – a device replayed from *School for Love* and reflecting yet again on Manning's own miscarriage in Palestine in 1944.[17] In *The Rain Forest*

Kristy Foster miscarries but is obliged for medical reasons to carry the dead foetus for several weeks before its delivery can be induced in hospital, an experience that on one level duplicates Manning's experience and, on another, transforms an individual biological malfunction (and, in effect, a stillbirth) into a potent symbol of an imperial and social disintegration. In a fiction deeply concerned (as was Manning in later years) with fears of overpopulation and ecological disaster, the dismal scenes of her female protagonist wandering through the streets of an overcrowded colonial island town with the dead child in her womb, feeling 'like a walking cemetery' (*Rain Forest*, pp. 140, 222), suggest not only the deep malaise of Britain's colonial parentage but also the disintegration from within of its reproductive mission, all set in the broader chronological context of an impending if indeterminate ecological and biological catastrophe.[18]

With such ingredients it is not surprising perhaps that *The Rain Forest*, for all its vibrant colour and exotic scenery, gave rise to critical charges of thematic over-burdening, and failed to capture a readership as the *Balkan Trilogy* had done. It remains none the less coherent with the rest of Manning's wartime fictional oeuvre and benefits from being read alongside the grander autobiographical project of the trilogies. A damning portrait of a slow post-war decline in the peripheral landscapes of the former Empire, it brings to the fore a sense of a moribund nation that lacks in the aftermath of 1945 the personality and drive that had carried it through the conflict. Through an implied reversal of fortune, the imperialists have now become the refugees in an international space which is no longer 'home' in any respect. When their possessions, their privacy and eventually their spacious hotel room are removed from them during the course of the novel, Kristy and Hugh Foster are left with no place to go on the unforgiving island of Al-Bustan, but nor is their return to an impoverished England an option. They are casualties of a decline illustrated by Manning with neither blame nor sympathy in a work which offers, at the very least, a subtle footnote to her overarching treatment of the British abroad.

The sense of an ending to Manning's writing life was presaged by the deaths of various literary friends and acquaintances from the wartime period and the years afterwards in London. Louis MacNeice's early death in 1963 was a deep shock to both Olivia and Reggie. This was followed by the death of Stevie Smith in 1971 and, a few years later, in 1977, of the novelist William Gerhardi, the latter a more personal blow to his former acolyte. The sudden loss in 1979 of J.G. Farrell, drowned off the west coast of Ireland, must have intensified Manning's sense of a 'closing phase' in her life. That her marriage, too, eventually gave way as Reggie Smith pursued a rival long-term love affair (events recounted by her biographers in more detail than is necessary here) suggests the gradual unravelling of a core structure to her writing project. After several years of ill health, Olivia Manning died in hospital on the Isle of Wight in 1980.

Inevitably one of the paradoxes of war writing is that material of great passion, vibrancy and even beauty is derived from a history of trauma and disruption. For Manning and those of her contemporaries who dealt with the Second World War in prose, the conflict was a challenge demanding new techniques and approaches, the means to defy a prevailing view that this war, unlike its predecessor, would have no defining literature. The body of war-related fiction she produced met this challenge by rewriting the conventional shape of epic sequence built around a male protagonist, and drawing out instead the edgy, liminal viewpoints of a despondent Harriet Pringle. With this adjusted and frequently ironic perspective, Manning skirted the danger of romancing a wartime culture. If biography provided her opportunity, her skills with scene, dialogue and the complex interplay of domestic and international narratives translated the details of circumstance into one of the most engrossing fictionalised treatments of the war to emerge after 1945. Nor should the biographical parameters of the trilogies – the major element of her oeuvre – limit the reader's appreciation of their subtle historical realism, their reshaping of history to compelling dramatic purpose.

It would be a shortcoming, however, simply to praise Manning's achievement on the grounds of its substance and breadth. What this account has tried to suggest is a political astuteness in her work, a tension forged through her recognition of the ideological and ethical uncertainties of those expatriates who were shifted from country to country by the war. For Manning, this compromised community is ultimately shown to be mediocre, even feckless, and defined by the inadequacy of its equivocal response to a changing international order. Comparing her to Storm Jameson in this respect, Phyllis Lassner suggests that for both writers 'the English are omnipresent but impotent in the impossible and misguided task motivated by their self-appointed moral responsibility as empire-builders. Ultimately, they are always hindered from moral resolution by their combined attraction and revulsion to Others.'[19] Primarily in her references to the refugees of imperial collapse and of the conflict itself, Manning emphasises this point, confirming, in characters ranging from Geoffrey Lynd and Ethel Bohun to the Pringles and the Fosters, the debilitating anxieties of leadership and, at the same time, the exhaustion of compassion within a ruling, but receding, culture.

Through her retrospective harnessing of the Second World War, Manning illustrates what is essentially a weakness emerging at the heart of a British war incentive and intensifying from that point. That 'all are damaged', as a character observes in 'Ladies without Escort', her 1972 story of Europe's stagnant and rancorous post-war condition, is the core implication of her writing.[20] At one with her fellow writers of imperial aftermath in this respect, she augments their perspective by adapting the insecurity of a female identity to the particular condition of the wartime exile. Harriet Pringle is no campaigning feminist internationalist but, instead, a wartime itinerant whose abjection offers a paradigm for a despondent and rootless post-imperial personality. This, more than anything else, is Olivia Manning's keynote, painstakingly drawn from the geographical locations of the war as she experienced it – the vulnerable states of the Balkans to the volatile countries of the Middle East – and persuasively voiced in the masterful historical dramas of her fiction.

Notes and References

Introduction

1. Dan Davin, diary entry for 23 May 1942, cited Keith Ovenden, *A Fighting Withdrawal: The Life of Dan Davin, Writer, Soldier, Publisher* (Oxford: Oxford University Press, 1996), p. 158; Maclaren-Ross, in Paul Willets, *Fear and Loathing in Fitzrovia: The Bizarre Life of Writer, Author and Soho Dandy Julian Maclaren-Ross* (Stockport: Dewi Lewis, 2003), p. 199; Holden's sobriquet is noted by Frances Spalding, *Stevie Smith: A Critical Biography* (London: Faber, 1988), p. 105; Anthony Powell, cited from his *Journals* by Neville and June Braybrooke, *Olivia Manning: A Life* (Chatto & Windus, 2004), p. 159; Powell's favourable reviews of Manning included 'Home for an Orphan', *Times Literary Supplement* (12 October 1951), p. 641, which was unsigned, and an untitled review of *A Different Face*, in *Punch* (9 September 1953): see George Lilley, *Anthony Powell: A Bibliography* (Winchester: St Paul's, 1993); John St John, *William Heinemann: A Century of Publishing, 1890–1990* (London: Heinemann, 1990), p. 346; Kay Dick, *The Shelf* (London: Hamish Hamilton, 1984), pp. 10–11. Various other commentators offer similar opinions on the subject in Sue Summers, 'Portrait of the Artist as a Truly Awful Wife', *Daily Mail* (9 November 1987).
2. Kay Dick, *Friends and Friendship: Conversations and Reflections* (London: Sidgwick & Jackson, 1974), p. 35.
3. Manning's papers are housed in two collections, in McFarlin Special Collections, University of Tulsa (hereafter McFarlin), and the Harry Ransom Center, University of Texas (hereafter HRC).

4. OM to Louise Callender at Heinemann, 24 May 1951; cited in John St John, *William Heinemann*, p. 346.
5. Cited in John St John, *William Heinemann*, p. 346.
6. *Northanger Abbey* (London: Pan Classics, 1968): Introduction and Notes by Olivia Manning, p. 5.
7. *Palestine Post* (7 December 1945), p. 7. Letters between John Lehmann and Manning between 1939 and 1959 record a somewhat tense relationship. During this period Lehmann rejected several of Manning's submissions and a request for review work (see, for example, John Lehmann to OM, 25 May 1939, HRC; John Lehmann to OM, 15 June 1943, HRC; John Lehmann to OM, 28 May 1959 and 30 July 1959, HRC); Manning at one stage took legal advice over what she regarded as Lehmann's 'libellous' reference to her, 10 May 1946, McFarlin. By comparison, she had nothing but admiration for Cyril Connolly, from whom she also solicited publication space: reviewing Connolly's *The Condemned Playground* in 1946, she remarked that '[H]e is one of a species now growing sadly rare – an essayist of high order – and one of the few reviewers whose reviews are worth preserving between stiff covers', *Palestine Post* (8 February 1946), p. 7.
8. Again in a review of *New Writing* and other recent periodicals: *Palestine Post* (23 February 1945), p. 7.
9. I refer in particular to Nicola Humble's discussion of the term in *The Feminine Middlebrow Novel, 1920s to 1950s* (Oxford: Oxford University Press, 2001).
10. Manning's remark on Greene was in relation to what she deemed a 'very smartie' review of her book *The Remarkable Expedition* in the *New Statesman*, which she believed to have been written under a false name by Greene, who 'had it in for me for my review of his short stories in the *Spectator*', OM to Kay Dick, n.d., McFarlin (Series 1, Box 1, Folder 1). Lowry is frequently acknowledged by her as a major writer: Manning's husband Reggie Smith had known him in Birmingham and he had, apparently, been 'discovered' by Hamish Miles at Cape. See Michael S. Howard, *Jonathan Cape Publisher* (1971), p. 211. Manning subsequently developed a deep appreciation of the troubled writer. Braybrooke reports that in the 1960s Manning 'often smuggled out from the public library in Swiss Cottage his *Under the Volcano* in the hope of gaining converts for him' (*Olivia Manning: A Life*, p. 57).

11. Manning had high praise for J.G. Farrell, to whose works elements of her late novel *The Rain Forest* are possibly indebted. She wrote to Kay Dick: 'I have been reading the proofs of Jim Farrell's new 600-page novel *The Singapore Grip* – it is a tremendous achievement', 1 August 1978, McFarlin. See also references to Manning's friendship with Farrell in Lavinia Greacen, *J.G. Farrell: The Making of a Writer* (London: Bloomsbury, 1999).
12. Roy Foster, 'Friendly Disdain', a review of *Olivia Manning: A Life*, by Neville and June Braybrooke, *Financial Times* (15 April 2005); Olivia Manning, *The Dreaming Shore* (London: Evans Bros, 1950), p. 123. Manning also attacked here those she termed the 'pseudo-Englishmen' of the country: 'But every race throws up renegades and among the most useless are the English in Ireland engaged in what the Irish call "the retreat from Moscow"', p. 124. Louis MacNeice dutifully reviewed the book but could not restrain his feelings on this topic: 'Sometimes she is too subjective about persons, Irish or English: not all English visitors are boors, and even the relics of the Anglo-Irish "gentry" often retain at least some of the virtues denied to them by Miss Manning but found in them by Yeats, whom she admires', 'Landscape and Legend', *Observer* (17 September 1950).
13. *Millions Like Us: British Women's Fiction of the Second World War* (London: Virago, 1977), pp. 8–12. Hartley counters in this respect the 'traditions' of wartime writing outlined by Adam Piette, *Imagination at War: British Fiction and Poetry, 1939–1945* (London: Macmillan Papermac, 1995), and Robert Hewison, *Under Siege: Literary Life in London, 1945–1951* (London: Methuen, 1977).
14. See Kristine Miller, *British Literature of the Blitz: Fighting the People's War* (London: Palgrave Macmillan, 2009); Gill Plain, *Women's Fiction of the Second World War: Gender, Power and Resistance* (Edinburgh; Edinburgh University Press, 1996), p. 20.
15. Jenny Hartley, *Millions Like Us*, p. 183; Phyllis Lassner, *Colonial Strangers: Women Writing the End of the British Empire* (New Brunswick: Rutgers University Press, 2004).
16. 'Portrait of a Hungarian Doctor', *New Stories*, vol. 2, no. 6 (December/January 1935–6); reprinted in *Growing Up* (London: Heinemann, 1948).
17. *Autobiographics: A Feminist Theory of Women's Self-Representation* (Ithaca: Cornell University Press, 1994), p. 85.

18. *Women's Fiction of the Second World War*, p. 19.
19. *The Tatler and Bystander* (26 May 1948), pp. 246–7.

Chapter One: A life in writing

1. George S. Fraser, *A Stranger and Afraid: The Autobiography of an Intellectual* (Manchester: Carcanet, 1983), p. 125; *The Dreaming Shore*, pp. 55–6.
2. *Palestine Post* (16 February 1945), p. 7; *Palestine Post* (23 November 1945), p. 7.
3. 'A Scantling of Foxes', *New Stories*, vol. 1, no. 5 (October/November 1934); *Growing Up* (London: Heinemann, 1948).
4. 'My mother came from Ulster, and her mother was an American, called MacShane, whose father was a slave owner on the banks of the Missouri river' (in Kay Dick, *Friends and Friendship*, p. 28). Some further details of Manning's background are provided by Mary Salmon, 'Towards a Critical Biography of Olivia Manning', unpublished PhD thesis, University College, Dublin (1985).
5. OM to Kay Dick, 2 July 1954, McFarlin (Series 1, Box 1, Folder 6); OM to Kay Dick, 6 July 1972, McFarlin (Series 1, Box 1, Folder 9).
6. 'A Visit', *Growing Up* (London: Heinemann, 1948), p. 60.
7. *The Wind Changes* (London: Virago, 1988). This novel was originally published by Jonathan Cape. In her introduction to the Virago edition of the book, June Braybrooke (writing as Isobel English) suggested that Manning regarded Ireland as the exception to her general belief that 'in an imperfect world Britain's rule in her colonies had been for the most part a beneficent one' (Introduction, xv). In fact there is no straightforward endorsement of any such view in this novel. In her exploration of Manning's Ulster background, Mary Salmon reads this novel and eight short stories set in Ireland as initial forays into the deformations of racial, national and imperial identity pursued in the later novels; see her article 'Nowhere to Belong: The Fiction of Olivia Manning', *Linenhall Review*, vol. 3, no. 3 (Autumn 1986), 11–13.
8. 'Portrait of a Hungarian Doctor', *Growing Up* (1948).
9. In Derek Mahon (writer and presenter), 'Never a Day without a Line', BBC radio broadcast, 23 July 1981, Ref 42607 (1).
10. Kay Dick, *Friends and Friendship*, p. 34. Manning recalled here to Dick how her ambitions to become a painter were thwarted by the poverty in which the family lived on a naval officer's salary with 'not a farthing to spare' (p. 27),

and also the cruel behaviour of her mother, a situation recalled by Dick in *The Shelf*, where Sophie is given to outbursts of self-pity as a result of her childhood experiences: 'It's that terrible childhood of mine. The insecurity of parents hating each other. No-one knows how it scarred me . . . And the lack of money. Quarrelling over every penny. Can you imagine what it's like for people to live on an ex-naval officer's pension? I couldn't wait to get away' (Kay Dick, *The Shelf*, p. 41). See also Manning's descriptions of the family in a newspaper article in 1975: 'My mother, an Ulster Presbyterian, was firmly against alcoholic liquor and saw through my father's friends. He had found no fault in them but what a collection of schemers and drunken spongers they became when my mother described them to us', 'Voyages around My Father', *The Times* (24 May 1975), p. 6.

11. 'Voyages around My Father', p. 6.
12. See Louis MacNeice, 'Appendix A', *The Strings Are False: An Unfinished Autobiography* (London: Faber, 1965), p. 221; Auriol Stevens, 'Olivia Manning and her Novel', *Guardian* (13 March 1969).
13. *Continuance and Change: The Contemporary British Novel Sequence* (Carbondale: Southern Illinois University Press, 1972), p. xv.
14. Detailed by Manning to Kay Dick, *Friends and Friendship*, p. 30. See also Braybrooke, *Olivia Manning: A Life*, chapter 6, for full details of Manning's early writing under the name of Jacob Morrow.
15. 'The Companionship of Books', *Palestine Post* (14 December 1945), p. 7; *Artist Among the Missing* (London: Heinemann, 1975), pp. 138–9.
16. 'Displacements by a Newcomer', *Times Literary Supplement* (4 September 1953), p. 564. Jeremy Treglown provides some background to this unfortunate literary incident; see his article 'Anthony Powell at the *TLS*', *Times Literary Supplement* (25 June 2006). Arthur Waley's complaint appears on the letters page of the next issue.
17. Braybrooke notes a further element of tribute, that, in Jacob Morrow's *Here's Murder*, Gerhardi's novels are on the hero's shelf (*Olivia Manning: A Life*, p. 44). In addition to Manning's frequent references to the novelist in her journalism and letters (she would always spell his name without the final 'e'), she was later to take responsibility for the scattering of his ashes. See her piece on the author, 'Buried Alive', written for *The Times* in 1961.
18. *The Doves of Venus* (London: Virago, 1984), p. 121. Smith had already drawn on several of her *own* friends as the basis for characters in her 1949 novel *The Holiday*; see the useful account of her fiction by Kristin Bluemel,

George Orwell and the Radical Eccentrics: Intermodernism in Literary London (Basingstoke: Palgrave Macmillan, 2004), chapter 1.

19. On Smith's personality in this respect, see both Jack Barbera's *Stevie: A Biography* (London: Heinemann, 1985) and Frances Spalding's *Stevie Smith: A Critical Biography* (London: Faber, 1988). Numerous letters from Manning to Kay Dick refer to Stevie's malice: OM to Kay Dick, 1954, McFarlin (Box 1, Folder 6); OM to Kay Dick, 7 November 1958, McFarlin (Box 1, Folder 7); the review was published in the *Observer* (23 October 1955), where Smith suggested the book showed a 'moral naiveté' and lacked balance in representation.
20. OM to Jocelyn Brooke, 16 January 1956, HRC.
21. OM to Kay Dick, 21 September 1971, McFarlin (Box 1, Folder 9). See also Braybrooke, *Olivia Manning: A Life*, pp. 64–70, for further speculation on Manning's response to Smith's death and reputation.
22. Walter Allen became a lifelong supporter of Manning as a writer, championing her trilogies in his study *Tradition and Dream: A Critical Survey of British and American Fiction from the 1920s to the Present Day* (Harmondsworth: Penguin, 1965).
23. Walter Allen, *As I Walked Down New Grub Street: Memories of a Writing Life* (London: Heinemann, 1981), p. 116. Reggie Smith had been three years his junior at school in Birmingham.
24. Louis MacNeice, *The Strings Are False*, p. 210. Walter Allen also recalled the wedding, a little differently: *As I Walked Down New Grub Street*, p. 116.
25. From the collection *Mother, What Is Man?* (London: Cape, 1942). On the altered text, see Spalding, *Stevie Smith*, p. 109. Spalding also cites a letter from Manning to Stevie Smith, suggesting her apprehensiveness about the nuptials: 'I'm still undecided as ever about getting married. Marriage is so permanent nowadays, when one has to wait three years for a divorce. What a barbarous law!', pp. 108–9.
26. *The Strings Are False*, p. 208; *As I Walked Down New Grub Street*, p. 111. So enchanted, indeed, was MacNeice that at one point he considered joining Reggie in Romania: 'Had lunch today, darling, with a friend who has a job in Rumania', he wrote to Eleanor Clark; 'he says any time I want it he can get me £8 a week there <u>and</u> all expenses (including drinks, cigarettes & newspapers), so if I can't raise any money in the States this year I might go to Rumania'; Louis MacNeice to Eleanor Clarke, 16 July 1939, in *Letters of Louis MacNeice*, ed. Jonathan Allison (London: Faber, 2010), p. 351. For

other similarly enthusiastic recollections of Reggie Smith, see Anna Davin, 'R.D. Smith', *History Workshop Journal* 21 (Spring 1986), pp. 227–8.

27. *The Strings Are False*, p. 208.
28. See *The Spoilt City*, *BT*, p. 354.
29. R.D. Smith's 'Notes towards an Autobiography' (reference courtesy of the author's estate and Gerry Harrison) mentions his friendship with Anand, Indian author, BBC scriptwriter and independence campaigner. See also the description of Anand by MacNeice, *The Strings Are False*, p. 209.
30. 'In the spring [of 1939], Reggie Smith came back for two or three weeks bringing with him a party of Romanian students for a quick look at Britain. I helped him to organize the programme for the party. We got E.M. Forster to meet them and talk to them. Many of them, as I have only recently realized, were Jews consciously looking for somewhere they could escape to when the inevitable happened' (Walter Allen, *As I Walked Down New Grub Street*, p. 114). Numerous episodes in the *Balkan Trilogy* reflect the closeness of the British lecturer to his Jewish students, including Sasha Drucker, into whose home he is invited. In *The Spoilt City* it becomes apparent that most of the students recruited by the Legation are Jews hoping to improve their English before fleeing to safe havens in England or America (*BT*, p. 103). In the same novel, Yakimov finds Guy's chequebook with stubs recording payments made to London banks on behalf of local Jews (*BT*, p. 324). For comment on individual British engagements with Jewish refugees in the period, see David Cesarani, 'Mad Dogs and Englishmen: Towards a Taxonomy of Rescuers in a "Bystander" Country', in David Cesarani and Paul A. Levine (eds), *Bystanders to the Holocaust: A Re-Evaluation* (London: Frank Cass, 2002).
31. Other notable socialist influences mentioned by Smith in his 'Notes towards an Autobiography' include journalists Philip Toynbee and Naomi Mitchison. (See Manning's use of this university background for Guy's political profile, *The Spoilt City*, *BT*, p. 391.)
32. 'Notes towards an Autobiography'; see also Braybrooke, *Olivia Manning: A Life*, p. 53.
33. British National Archives, Cat. Ref. KV/2/2533; MI file PF70065/V. An MI5 official similarly observes in the files, 'Reggie has paraded his opinions [so] flamboyantly that his friends thought that he was consequently in danger of losing his job'. Manning was also kept under close watch by British security services, but they concluded that 'enquiries have failed to show that

she shares her husband's political creed, though she appears to condone it'. See also Ben McIntyre, 'The Bumbling British Hero who Was a Communist "Spy"', *Times* (3 March 2007), pp. 36–7. Smith's 'Notes towards an Autobiography' mentions that during his time in Romania he pursued 'undercover CP contacts', and again in Palestine 'party work, undercover'.

34. Francis King, *Yesterday Came Suddenly: An Autobiography* (London: Constable, 1993), p. 244; Olivia's remark is cited by Braybrooke, *Olivia Manning: A Life*, p. 75. Manning is variously reported as having engaged in espionage; see interview with Ruth Inglis which states that: '[W]hile her husband was working for the British Council in the Balkans, she did a shadowy stint for MI5, an autobiographical sequence left out of the new novel.' 'Who Is Olivia Manning?', *Observer Colour Supplement* (6 April 1969), pp. 24–7. More likely is the allusion in Dilys Powell's profile of Manning, which notes that, while in Jerusalem, 'she made a small contribution to wartime intelligence with some work on a secret report on conditions in the Dodecanese'; 'Observer in the Crowd', *Guardian* (7 March 1960), p. 6.

35. *Operation Autonomous: With S.O.E. in Wartime Rumania* (London: Chatto & Windus, 1989), p. 23. Ivor Porter was initially a British Council lecturer in Romania; he moved to the British Legation there and was subsequently recruited into the Special Operations Executive.

36. Isobel English traces Manning's gradual move, politically, from a youthful Shavian Fabianism towards a right-wing perspective, in her introduction to *The Wind Changes*, p. xv.

37. 'Olivia Manning: A Female Voice as Critique of Utopian Socialism', *Gender Studies: Revista de Studii de Gen a Centrului de Studii Feministe al Universitatii de Vest, Timişoara*, vol. 1, no. 4 (2005), p. 140.

38. *Twentieth-Century Epic Novels* (Newark: University of Delaware Press, 2005), p. 96.

39. *The Sum of Things*, *BT*, p. 514. Steinberg suggests that the significance of Guy cutting the text of *Troilus and Cressida* reflects his reductionist views of epic and, therefore, of empire itself (*Twentieth-Century Epic Novels*, p. 116).

40. *Colonial Strangers*, p. 6.

41. 'Olivia Manning and her Masculine Outfit', in Marina MacKay and Lyndsey Stonebridge (eds), *British Fiction after Modernism: The Novel at Mid-Century* (Basingstoke: Palgrave Macmillan, 2007), p. 151.

42. See Birkett's essay 'The Spectacle of Europe: Politics, P.E.N. and Prose Fiction: The Work of Storm Jameson in the Inter-War Years', in Angela Kershaw and Angela Kimyongur (eds), *Women in Europe between the Wars: Politics, Culture and Society* (Aldershot: Ashgate, 2007).
43. 'In Europe', 1942, in *Collected Poems* (London: Faber, 1960).
44. Cited in Braybrooke, *Olivia Manning: A Life*, p. 113.
45. Betty Miller's daughter Sarah Miller recalls that the family, having moved to St John's Wood in July 1945, had frequent literary visitors to the house in this period, including their neighbours Olivia Manning and Reggie Smith, Stevie Smith, Inez Holden and Naomi Lewis. See her 'Introduction' to Miller's 1945 novel *On the Side of the Angels* (London: Virago, 1985), p. xv. On Phyllis Bottome and other British women writers on this subject, see Judy Suh, *Fascism and Anti-Fascism in Twentieth-Century British Fiction* (Basingstoke: Palgrave Macmillan, 2009).
46. MacNeice, 'Refugees', in *Collected Poems* (London: Faber, 2007), pp. 197–8, originally published in *Plant and Phantom* (London: Faber, 1941); see also *The Strings Are False*, p. 199. For a critical analysis of the *Unconditional Surrender* episode (and Waugh's misreading of the Yugoslavian situation), see Alan Munton, *English Fiction of the Second World War* (London: Faber, 1989), pp. 87–93.
47. Stevie Smith, *Over the Frontier* (London: Virago, 1989), p. 158; Virginia Woolf, *Between the Acts* (London: Penguin, 1992), p. 74.
48. *British Women Writers of World War Two: Battlegrounds of their Own* (London: Macmillan, 1998), p. 234.
49. The history of the Jerusalem Forum is traced in more detail in Chapter Five. John Connell was the pseudonym of John Henry Robertson, working in pro-British propaganda in the Middle East while the Smiths were in Jerusalem. See his autobiographical account of this period in *The House by Herod's Gate* (London: Sampson, Low & Marston, n.d.).
50. Interview with Kay Dick, *Friends and Friendship*, p. 31.
51. 'Books I Have Read', in Frederic Raphael (ed.), *Bookmarks* (London: Cape, 1975), p. 119; *Palestine Post* (4 May 1945), p. 7.
52. 'Books I Have Read', p. 122. 'My journey out of literary darkness reads like one of those post-Wellsian novels much written in the '30s: lower middle-class hero, unlettered but aspirant, comes upon a copy of *John O'London's Weekly* and never looks back', Manning commented in this piece, p. 116.

53. 'Books I Have Read', p. 116; Braybrooke, *Olivia Manning: A Life*, p. 34n. Manning was born on 2 March 1908 but frequently pretended to be younger than she was. Vesna Goldsworthy traces the dates of birth (between 1908 and 1918) variously provided for the writer, sometimes by herself, and the implications of this for the character of Harriet in the trilogies; see her 'Olivia Manning's "Bucharest": Reality and Imagination in the *Balkan Trilogy*', unpublished MA thesis (University of London, 1992), pp. 5–6, and 17.
54. 'Notes on the Future of the Novel', *Times Literary Supplement* (15 August 1958). Manning continues: 'This seemed to me proved by the fact that experimental writers like Joyce and Richardson have had so little influence. Each produced a sterile monster, seldom read.' Reggie Smith, too, came to express doubts about the modernists: in a public lecture delivered in Jerusalem in 1943 he touched on the 'excessive obscurity through private symbols and a private homemade-and-always-under-repair philosophy' which marred even his hero, Lawrence. R.D. Smith, 'English Writers and the Moral Crisis', *British Council Winter Lecture Series* (1943–4), p. 14. My thanks to Gerry Harrison for the original text of this lecture.
55. *Palestine Post* (23 November 1945), p. 7.
56. *Palestine Post* (28 November 1947), p. 7.
57. Introduction, in Kristin Bluemel (ed), *Intermodernism: Literary Culture in Mid-Twentieth-Century Britain* (Edinburgh: Edinburgh University Press, 2009), p. 3. Bluemel includes Manning in her appendix of intermodernist writers. See also Bluemel's opening observations in *George Orwell and the Radical Eccentrics*, p. 2. Manning's somewhat heterodox literary community, in this respect, is well exemplified by an issue of *The New Savoy*, in which one of her stories appeared in 1946; the other contributors included Arthur Koestler, George Orwell, Stevie Smith and Anthony Powell.
58. *Abroad: British Literary Travelling between the Wars* (Oxford: Oxford University Press, 1980), p. 11.
59. *Palestine Post* (4 July 1947), p. 7.
60. *Palestine Post* (9 May 1947), p. 7; Manning subsequently reviewed Waugh's *Work Suspended* from a similar perspective: *Palestine Post* (22 July 1949), p. 4.
61. Cited by Hilary Spurling in *Ivy: The Life of Ivy Compton-Burnett* (London: R. Cohen, 1995), p. 531.

62. See Geoffrey Household's account of involvement in the wartime plot to sabotage the Ploeşti oilfields in Romania (and subsequently his military work in Greece, North Africa and Palestine), in his autobiography *Against the Wind* (London: Michael Joseph, 1958).
63. *Palestine Post* (8 November 1946), p. 7.
64. Pamela Frankau was Manning's stablemate at Heinemann; see John St John, *William Heinemann*, p. 342. Useful studies of the wartime fiction phenomenon include Holger Klein, *The Second World War in Fiction* (London: Macmillan, 1984), Alan Munton, *English Fiction of the Second World War* (London: Faber, 1989), and Mark Rawlinson, *British Writing of the Second World War* (Oxford: Clarendon, 2000). On the women writers discussed here, see Gill Plain, *Women's Fiction of the Second World War*, and Jenny Hartley, *Millions Like Us*.
65. See Victoria Stewart, *Narratives of Memory: British Writing of the 1940s* (Basingstoke: Palgrave Macmillan, 2006), pp. 132–6. For a more conventional view of writers struggling to produce material in the adverse conditions of the war, see Robert Hewison, *Under Siege: Literary Life in London, 1939–1945* (London: Methuen, 1988).
66. *Romancing: The Life and Work of Henry Green* (London: Faber, 2000), p. 193.
67. Manning's comment was made in relation to novelist Jocelyn Brooke (discussed further below), who had served abroad in the Medical Corps during the war. See her article '"An Enemy in the Mind": Jocelyn Brooke: The Man and His Work', *Times Literary Supplement* (8 May 1969), p. 492.
68. *Palestine Post* (23 November 1945), p. 7.
69. Typescript with author's emendations, Olivia Manning Collection, HRC.
70. 'Holy Fire' was rejected by Dick (who as editor used the name Edward Lane); Manning later managed to place it with Harpers, 'who seem to pay extraordinarily well' (OM to Kay Dick, n.d. 1946, McFarlin).
71. Interview with Kay Dick, *Friends and Friendship*, p. 31. In the same exchange Manning added ruefully, 'I wish my friends would write longer novels. But the modern novel, which tends to be subtle rather than profound, entertaining rather than instructive, unmoral and reflective of our chaos, is too disturbing a companion for the long, despondent hours of night', pp. 123–4.
72. One exception, in terms of delayed output, was Edith Pargeter, whose *Eighth Champion of Christendom* trilogy (1945–7) was also published by

Heinemann, following quickly on the heels of her autobiographical wartime service novel *She Goes to War* (1942).

73. *Narratives of Memory*, p. 132.

74. Burgess, whom Manning knew well, praised her fiction on several occasions; he discusses the trilogies in *The Novel Now: A Student's Guide to Contemporary Fiction* (London: Faber, 1971); see also Braybrooke, *Olivia Manning: A Life*, p. 182.

75. Interview with Kay Dick, *Friends and Friendship*, p. 113; Braybrooke, *Olivia Manning: A Life*, p. 182.

76. *Palestine Post* (22 July 1949), p. 4. Manning details Brooke's response and their subsequent plans to exchange novels in the future, in '"An Enemy in the Mind"', pp. 492–3.

77. OM to Jocelyn Brooke, 1 May 1955, HRC; OM to Jocelyn Brooke, 1 June 1961, HRC; OM to Jocelyn Brooke, 18 July 1961, HRC; OM to Jocelyn Brooke, 6 May 1965, HRC. Anthony Powell was probably a closer model for the *Levant* sequence; Manning's letters to her fellow author in the early 1970s praise the achievement of his *Dance to the Music of Time* sequence in tandem with mentioning the progress of what would become the *Levant Trilogy*: 'How magnificent the work is as it draws to its conclusion, both in conception & execution', she wrote. 'When you write the last word you will feel as Gibbon did at the end of *Decline and Fall* – that you have completed a work that will make you immortal', OM to Anthony Powell, 24 October 1973. (I am grateful to Gerry Harrison for this reference.)

78. '"An Enemy in the Mind"', p. 493.

79. *A History of the Second World War* (London: Purnell, in collaboration with the Imperial War Museum, 1966–9, general editor Basil Liddell Hart, series editor Barrie Pitt). Manning's contributions were 'Rumanian *Coup D'État*', vol. 1, pp. 337–9; 'The Greeks at War', vol. 1, pp. 356–9; 'The Great Flap', vol. 2, n.p. Davin's 'The Flight from Athens' appeared in vol. 2, pp. 492–3. John Connell (J.H. Robertson), Reggie Smith's colleague at the Palestine Broadcasting Corporation and founder of the Jerusalem Forum, published a renowned biography of Wavell after the war; his account of the desert campaign in this journal appeared posthumously following his sudden death, shortly after finishing the piece, in October 1965.

80. On Crane and Tolstoy as sources, see Braybrooke, *Olivia Manning: A Life*, pp. 157, 114. Manning's papers include issues of a journal series, *The War Papers* (relating mainly to Rommel, the North African Campaign generally

and Alamein in particular), and several reproduction issues of wartime newspapers, McFarlin (Series 2, Box 1).

81. 'Olivia Manning and her Masculine Outfit', p. 153.

82. Stevie Smith's *The Holiday* was almost entirely based on versions of her friends, including George Orwell, the partial basis for Basil, and a disgruntled Inez Holden, who featured as Lopez: see chapter one of Kristin Bluemel's *George Orwell and the Radical Eccentrics*. Manning's real-life referents will be discussed in more detail throughout this study; see also attributions by Vesna Goldsworthy, 'Olivia Manning's "Bucharest"', and Artemis Cooper, *Cairo in the War, 1939–1945* (London: Hamish Hamilton, 1989).

83. Ivor Porter recalls Hugh Seton-Watson (son of historian and Balkan specialist Richard Seton-Watson) in *Operation Autonomous*, p. 18. On Dobson, see Frances Donaldson, *The British Council: The First Fifty Years* (London: Cape, 1984), p. 90, and on Dundas, see Artemis Cooper, *Cairo in the War*, pp. 158–9, and Braybrooke, *Olivia Manning: A Life*, p. 109.

84. In Derek Mahon, 'Never a Day without a Line' (BBC, 1981).

85. See Frances Donaldson, *The British Council*, pp. 89, 97.

86. On various interactions with Patmore, discussed later in this study, see Braybrooke, *Olivia Manning: A Life*. Paul Willets suggests Maclaren-Ross to have been the model for Yakimov, *Fear and Loathing in Fitzrovia*, p. 328. Maclaren-Ross was used as a character source by Anthony Powell, a point mentioned by Manning – who knew Ross through Reggie – in a letter to Powell, 18 March 1971 (courtesy of Gerry Harrison).

87. Leigh Fermor did not overlap significantly with the Smiths either in Romania or Greece, but their contact increased after the war, partly through sharing mutual publication platforms such as *Encounter*. For details of Gwynne's life and work for the embassy in Cairo, see Artemis Cooper, *Writing at the Kitchen Table: The Authorized Biography of Elizabeth David* (London: Penguin, 2000), and Lisa Chaney, *Elizabeth David: A Biography* (London: Macmillan, 1998).

88. *Palestine Post* (4 July 1947), p. 7: Manning notes the potential amusement of the book for those who recognised themselves as characters, but suggested that it was otherwise 'half-digested'. She reviewed the book (again negatively) for *Our Time* (July 1947); see Keith Ovenden, *A Fighting Withdrawal*, p. 223.

89. Braybrooke, *Olivia Manning: A Life*, p. 153; see also Francis King, *Yesterday Came Suddenly*, p. 239.
90. Braybrooke, *Olivia Manning: A Life*, p. 346. See also the report of the case in *The Times*: 'However, last summer, after Panther had published a paperback edition of the novel, Mr Barbu Călinescu, the late Prime Minister's son, drew the publisher's attention to the fact that both he and his mother and certain other relations survived the massacre. "It was my error, made completely in good faith" said Miss Manning, who is married to Mr R.D. Smith, a BBC Drama Producer', *Times* (3 February 1968), p. 8.
91. *The Sum of Things*, *LT*, p. 516.
92. *The Sum of Things*, *LT*, pp. 533–4. Artemis Cooper reports that in fact Haggard's breakdown and suicide were the result of a failed love affair with an Egyptian woman (*Cairo in the War*, p. 160).
93. Davin's position is outlined by Keith Ovenden, *A Fighting Withdrawal*, p. 159; on Durrell's response, see Ian MacNiven, *Lawrence Durrell*, pp. 241–2. Leigh Fermor's reaction is cited by Sue Summers, 'Portrait of the Artist as a Truly Awful Wife'; Artemis Cooper, who also details the incident, suggests Manning's use of it was her 'subtle revenge' for being ignored in Cairo by the Smarts, who ran an influential literary salon at their home (*Cairo in the War*, pp. 157–8). For further reactions to the case, see Braybrooke, *Olivia Manning: A Life*, pp. 123–4. The incident suggests, yet again, the isolation of the Smiths from a close expatriate group in Cairo, and an exclusion confirmed by Denis Hills, who wrote that, following their evacuation to Egypt, 'Reggie Smith and Olivia were for a time without jobs, and accused the British Council of neglecting them. They had only themselves to blame. Reggie was still spouting a woolly Communism which made him into a joke figure. Olivia was diffident and rude'; *Tyrants and Mountains: A Reckless Life* (London: John Murray, 1992), p. 80.
94. Jed Esty, *A Shrinking Island: Modernism and National Culture in England* (Princeton, NJ: Princeton University Press, 2004), p. 9.
95. See her *Colonial Strangers*, to which the present study is indebted.
96. Manning gives her own descriptions of these in 'Books I Have Read', p. 119.
97. In a review of books on wartime Egypt Manning picked out for attention 'that extraordinary man' Orde Wingate, the distinguished British military commander whose breakdown and suicide attempt in Cairo, in 1941, became a notorious public event; *Palestine Post* (29 July 1949), p. 6.
98. *The Novel Now*, p. 95.

99. *Twentieth-Century Epic Novels*, p. 91.
100. Introduction, *Northanger Abbey*, p. 18.
101. As detailed in *The Great Fortune*, *BT*, p. 267.
102. 'Either the autobiography serves to create the illusion of a unified self out of the fragments of identity, or the text reveals, in its fissures, its doublings and its incompleteness, the fragmentation of the subject and its lack of self-confidence.' Laura Marcus, *Autobiographical Discourses: Saving the Subject* (Manchester: Manchester University Press, 1994), p. 218. See also Victoria Stewart's useful discussion of women's war autobiographies and textualisation, in *Women's Autobiography: War and Trauma* (Basingstoke: Palgrave Macmillan, 2003), pp. 20–2.
103. The two writers had come into contact occasionally: in 1937, Jameson provided a *Sunday Times* 'puff' for the paperback cover of *The Wind Changes* and had featured alongside Manning in an issue of *Modern Reading*. See also Braybrooke, *Olivia Manning: A Life*, p. 60.
104. *Friends and Heroes*, *BT*, p. 703. In *The Doves of Venus*, poverty-stricken Ellie Parsons is similarly emaciated and collapses with hunger. For criticism in this area, see, for example, Petra Rau's introduction to her edited *Conflict, Nationhood and Corporeality in Modern Literature* (Basingstoke: Palgrave Macmillan, 2010).
105. *The Sum of Things*, *LT*, p. 386. Harriet's deteriorated physical condition reflects Manning's health during the same period. In July 1945 Reggie Smith had written to the Chief Secretary in Jerusalem requesting official leave from his post as Director of Broadcasting at the Palestine Broadcasting Service in order to accompany his wife to Port Said, where she was due to board ship for the UK. Smith describes her 'reduced' physical condition as a result of amoebic dysentery and a nervous breakdown following a miscarriage the previous year. (Reference courtesy of Gerry Harrison.)
106. OM to Francis King in 1965; cited in John St John, *Heinemann*, p. 246.

Chapter Two: The *Balkan Trilogy*: Romania and the far end of Europe

1. *Athene Palace, Bucharest: Hitler's New Order Comes to Romania* (London: Constable, 1943), p. 25. Manning's descriptions of the hotel bar of the Athénée Palace in Bucharest, home to the corps of foreign press, the remnants of old aristocratic Romania and, as her story progresses, the newly arrived officers of the Nazi regime, contributed to the hotel's still-legendary status in European history. One of her likely material sources for Romanian

material generally was the highly evocative and historically detailed account of the year 1939/40 in the Romanian capital, written by the American-born journalist Rosa Waldeck, one of the few women correspondents in the field (and very possibly the model for the 'woman' spotted among the press corps by Yakimov in *The Great Fortune*).

2. *Roumanian Journey* (1938; Oxford: Oxford University Press, 1992), p. 1. The spelling of the country's name varies, depending on Latin or Slavic orientations, from the modern 'Romania', Sitwell using the French-derived form and Manning using the pre-communist form of 'Rumania'. Vesna Goldsworthy, to whose work I am much indebted throughout this chapter, notes astutely that the Romanians paid Sitwell a subsidy of £500 for this account, which may help explain its exuberance: see her 'Olivia Manning's "Bucharest": Reality and Imagination in *The Balkan Trilogy*', p. 35; *Roumanian Journey*, introduction, p. iii. Patrick Leigh Fermor had passed through the country during his 1933/4 walk across Europe (and was in Moldavia during the first year of the war) but did not publish his recollections of the country until 1986, in the second volume of his travel narrative *Between the Woods and the Water: On Foot to Constantinople: From the Middle Danube to the Iron Gates* (London: John Murray, 1986).

3. See Tom Gallagher, *Outcast Europe: The Balkans from the Ottomans to Milosevic, 1789–1989* (London: Routledge, 2001), for a detailed political history of Romania, and particularly his comments on the country's separate identity from the Balkan region generally (pp. vi–ix); on the same subject and the complex derivation of the term 'balkanisation' in colonial and diplomatic history, see Maria Todorova, *Imagining the Balkans* (New York and Oxford: Oxford University Press, 1997), pp. 21–30, and Vesna Goldsworthy, *Inventing Ruritania: The Imperialism of the Imagination* (New Haven and London: Yale University Press, 1998), pp. 3–9.

4. See Goldsworthy, *Inventing Ruritania*, p. 189.

5. Hugh Seton-Watson was sent to Romania by the Foreign Office, effectively on a surveillance and propaganda mission (the first hinted at in Manning's references to David Boyd's mysterious bird-watching trips to the Danube Delta, the second in the character's lengthy speeches in favour of Soviet control of Eastern Europe [*BT*, p. 569]). His friendship with diplomat Ivor Porter appears to have been the basis for Guy Pringle's relationship with David Boyd in the Bucharest novels: Porter recalls, 'I used to sit outside cafés with Hugh Seton-Watson, who had been sent out to the Balkans on a

roving mission, discussing how best to bring about King Carol's downfall and, in our youthful way, criticizing the British Government for not backing Maniu openly against him' (*Operation Autonomous*, p. 18). See also Denis Hills, who recalls Seton-Watson, dressed in 'Russian fur hat and mittens', in the company of the British Council staff (*Tyrants and Mountains*, p. 65).

6. 'The Tragedy of the Struma', *Observer* (1 March 1970), p. 8.
7. *Operation Autonomous*, p. 23. Porter was posted to Romania as a British Council lecturer, holding a post at Bucharest University in 1938 (Manning gave his job to the fictional Guy Pringle, he explains in this autobiographical account, p. 22), but he transferred shortly afterwards to the British Legation, where he remained until it withdrew from diplomatic operations – Romania having ceded to Germany – in February 1941. Recruited into the Special Operations Executive, he returned to Romania in 1943 to participate in a resistance plot, also detailed in his memoir of the period.
8. *Tyrants and Mountains*, p. 65.
9. *British Women Writers of World War Two*, p. 233.
10. See *BT*, pp. 261–72, for relevant scenes. The dovetailing of stage-play and historical reality is carefully structured in the novel, with the fall of Troy in *Troilus and Cressida* paralleling the fall of Paris, at the time of its performance, to the Nazis. (This is a deliberate deviation by Manning; in fact the play produced by Reggie Smith and performed at Bucharest's National Theatre was *Othello*. Denis Hills recalls Smith in the title role, together with the fact that Olivia, though she helped with make-up, 'refused to act' in the play; *Tyrants and Mountains*, p. 67.)
11. See *BT*, pp. 181–3. Commander Sheppy, a 'white-haired, dark-skinned little crow of a man' (*BT*, p. 127), complete with an eye-patch and false hand, may owe more than a little to Waugh's Ritchie Hook in *Sword of Honour*. Ivor Porter gives some details of the various actual plots conceived during the war to blow up access routes to the Ploeşti oilfields north of Bucharest (and thereby restrict valuable oil supplies to Germany), suggesting that in most cases such sabotage operations were doomed to failure: 'These were on the whole unsuccessful and rather typical of our predilection for amateur status in the early stages of the war. The first plan was to block the Iron Gates – the narrow Danube channel, with its bypass canal, through which all river craft going to Germany had to pass' (*Operation Autonomous*, p. 42). See also Geoffrey Household's accounts of similar sabotage attempts in his autobiography *Against the Wind*, pp. 107–8.

12. Though she does allude to certain American treatments, including Saul Bellow's Romania-set novel *The Dean's December* (1982), Goldsworthy's main focus in her extensive scholarship on the subject is a British literary and filmic tradition: '[T]he Balkan worlds of popular imagination are peopled by British creations', she argues in her introduction to *Inventing Ruritania*, p. x. More significantly, one might look at Geoffrey Household's stories of an exotic pre-war Romania such as 'Sabres in the Sand', from his collection *The Europe that Was* (Newton Abbot and London: David & Charles, 1979).
13. See, in particular, Larry Wolff, *Inventing Eastern Europe: The Map of Civilization on the Mind of the Enlightenment* (Stanford: Stanford University Press, 1994), and several contributors to Andrew Hammond (ed.), *The Balkans and the West: Constructing the European Other, 1945–2003* (Aldershot: Ashgate, 2004).
14. Goldsworthy, *Inventing Ruritania*, p. 2; Hammond, *The Balkans and the West*, p. xiv. This treatment of Romania, as poised between West and East, a gateway to the Orient and therefore contaminated by it, is characteristic of almost all travelogues of the wartime period: note, for example, Ivor Porter's description of arriving in the country on the Orient Express: 'In a side street, stuck behind an ox cart, I had my first whiff of the Orient – a mixture of raw sheepskin, rough wool, herbs, sun-baked manure. This was Wallachia, a gateway to the East through which Romanians would always look westwards' (*Operation Autonomous*, p. 2).
15. 'The Red Threat: Cold War Rhetoric and the British Novel', in *The Balkans and the West*, p. 46.
16. *Corridors of Mirrors: The Spirit of Europe in Contemporary British and Romanian Fiction* (New York: University of America Press, 2000), p. 42. Other relevant discussions by Romanian critics include Oana Godeanu, 'The Construction of Exoticism in Olivia Manning's *Balkan Trilogy*: An Imagogical Approach', *British and American Studies/Revista de Studii Britanice şi Americane*, 11 (2005), pp. 199–210; Carmen Andraş, 'Romania and its Images in British Travel Writing: In Between Peripherality and Cultural Interface', *TRANS: Internet-Zeitschrift fur Kulturwissenschaften*, 14 (April 2003); Eugenia Gavriliu, 'Gender Influences in the Construction of Romania in the *Balkan Trilogy*', in Rita Monticelli (ed.), *Travel Writing and the Female Imaginary* (Bologna: University of Bologna Press, 2001).

17. *Inventing Ruritania*, p. 11; see also pp. 184–98 for Goldsworthy's discussion of the *Balkan Trilogy*.
18. *Guests at a Marriage*, a 166-page typescript with author's corrections, is with the Olivia Manning papers in the Harry Ransom Collection, University of Texas; see Braybrooke, *Olivia Manning: A Life*, for further comments on its relationship to the *Balkan Trilogy*.
19. Derek Patmore, *Invitation to Roumania* (London: Macmillan, 1939). Perhaps this connection and the indulgent tenor of Patmore's recollections reinforce the claim that he provided a model for Yakimov, as discussed in Chapter One.
20. 'Rumanian *Coup d'État*', in Basil Liddell Hart (ed.), *History of the Second World War*, vol. 1, pp. 337–9. For various other literary treatments of the train journey into Romania, see Goldsworthy, 'Olivia Manning's "Bucharest"', pp. 29–30.
21. Goldsworthy discusses Stoker's use of Transylvania in *Inventing Ruritania*, pp. 73–87.
22. Ivor Porter refers to the same feature of the city in *Operation Autonomous*, pp. 3–4.
23. *A History of the Roumanians: From Roman Times to the Completion of Unity* (Cambridge: Cambridge University Press, 1934). Seton-Watson worked in British intelligence and propaganda during the war; his work on the Balkans is discussed briefly by Tom Gallagher in *Outcast Europe: The Balkans, 1789–1989* (London: Routledge, 2001).
24. OM to Jocelyn Brooke, 12 June 1961, HRC.
25. See, in particular, their editorial 'Introduction' to *Gothic Modernisms* (Basingstoke: Palgrave Macmillan, 2001), p. 3.
26. See Jan B. Gordon, 'Charlotte Bronte's Alternative "European Community"', in Suzanne Fendler and Ruth Wittlinger (eds), *The Idea of Europe in Literature* (London: Macmillan, 1999); reading the Brontës in this light, Gordon suggests that Europe operates as a 'geography of interruption', in which Gothic fiction finds 'a congenial topography . . . where distinctions of gender and genre, and those enforced by political boundaries, were less fixed and, consequently, disguise and substitutions created an economy of potentially perpetual dissimulation' (p. 5).
27. Hammond refers to this as a form of 'discursive collaboration', through which the subject and object are not always antagonistic in the production of images, *The Balkans and the West*, p. xvi.

28. Manning's earthquake takes place in high summer of 1940. Ivor Porter recalls quakes of that year as happening in October and November; these, it was rumoured, were really the result of explosions at Ploieşti detonated by exiled British engineers (*Operation Autonomous*, p. 60). In *Friends and Heroes*, Dobbie Dobson tells Harriet, now in Greece, that their apartment block has been destroyed by this later tremor.
29. Codreanu's body was not in fact reburied until 1941, after Manning had left the country, but she noted the event in her 1970 article on the *Struma* and it was also detailed by various writers, including Rosa Waldeck and Ivor Porter: the latter recalls that '[F]rom their pension on the Calea Victoriei Denis and Iona Wright watched the reburial of Codreanu and the other thirteen "heroes"' (*Operation Autonomous*, p. 47). See also a reading of Manning's use of this event by Ernest H. Latham, 'Privind de la fereastra: Olivia Manning in Romania', *Journal of the American-Romanian Academy of Arts and Sciences*, 20 (1995), pp. 92–112.
30. 'Rumanian *Coup D'État*', in Basil Liddell Hart (ed.), *History of the Second World War*, vol. 1, pp. 337–9.
31. Galpin is possibly based on David Walker, the *Daily Mirror* correspondent in Romania, who, according to Ivor Porter, 'though a serious political observer, never missed a good body-in-the-bath story' (*Operation Autonomous*, p. 2).
32. The story is reworked in *The Spoilt City* when Yakimov, deputising for the journalist Galpin, is sent to cover the fleeing of the Romanians from the Transylvanian town of Cluj and takes the opportunity to visit an old acquaintance, the German Gauleiter Freddy von Flugel. Manning gives her own account of the trip in 'Rumanian *Coup D'État*', where she describes her attempt to interview the peasant party leader Maniu and her return to a Bucharest in the first throes of revolution.
33. 'In a Winter Landscape', first published in *The Windmill* in 1945 and subsequently in the collection *A Romantic Hero and Other Stories* (London: Heinemann, 1967). The story was originally dedicated to Prince Antoine Bibesco, and dated 'Cairo, 1941'.
34. Hannah Arendt, *Eichmann in Jerusalem: A Report on the Banality of Evil* (London: Faber, 1963), pp. 190–1. See also Raul Hilbert, *The Destruction of the European Jews* (Chicago, 1961) for further reports (pre-dating Manning's composition of the trilogy) on this issue.

35. ‘The Tragedy of the *Struma*’, p. 8. She also records, though as hearsay, an earlier pogrom in the northern city of Jassy (Iasi) in which some 8,000 male Jews were slaughtered (a reference to this is also made briefly by Evelyn Waugh, in his 1938 novel *Scoop*). Her version of events coincides with Arendt’s account of the country’s extremist anti-Jewish policy: by 1942, Arendt claims, some 300,000 Jews were killed within the country by Romanians themselves (*Eichmann in Jerusalem*, pp. 192–3).
36. Ivor Porter recalls, ‘[A]s the shadow of war lengthened, Romanians, many of them Jews, flocked to the Institute to learn or brush up on their English’ (*Operation Autonomous*, p. 23).
37. *British Women Writers*, p. 237.
38. *British Women Writers*, p234.
39. Manning reviewed the July 1945 issue of *Horizon*, which contained journalist Alan Moorehead’s description of his visit to Belsen after its liberation by the British, *Palestine Post* (17 August 1945), p. 7. Harriet experiences similar emotions when, later in the novel, she manages to attend the trial of Sasha’s father, Emmanuel Drucker, now a broken, limping casualty, ‘an elderly stooping skeleton’, after three months in a Romanian prison cell (*BT*, p. 417).
40. *Against the Wind*, p. 106.

Chapter Three: From Athens to Alexandria: The contexts of *Personal Landscape*

1. ‘Last Civilian Ship’, first published in *The Windmill*, vol.1 no. 2 (1945), pp. 117–19.
2. OM to Jocelyn Brooke, 13 September 1964, HRC.
3. David Roessel discusses Woolf’s visit to Athens in 1906 and her subsequent short story ‘A Dialogue on Mount Pentelicus’, in which the author suggests that ‘Germans are tourists and Frenchmen are tourists but Englishmen are Greeks’: *In Byron’s Shadow: Modern Greece in the English and American Imagination* (Oxford: Oxford University Press, 2002), p. 162.
4. *Inventing Ruritania*, p. 195. In fact Manning had already spent time in Athens: she and her husband travelled to the Greek capital from Romania in the spring of 1940 to witness the celebration of Greek Easter, as she mentions in ‘Last Civilian Ship’, p. 117.
5. See Chapter Nine, in particular, of Roessel’s *In Byron’s Shadow* and, on the Durrell–Miller Greek liaison, Edmund Keeley, *Inventing Paradise: The Greek Journey, 1937–1947* (New York: Farrar, Straus & Giroux, 1999).

6. *Collected Poems*, p. 346. When he took up his posting, MacNeice was keen to counter Reggie Smith's despondency about Greece under its post-war regime; writing to E.R. Dodds in May 1950 he wrote, 'I am v. glad I came out here, for all Reggie's efforts to stop me. He & the boys are really talking through their hats. Of course there is injustice done (with some pretty nasty frills) but there is not complete suffocation as in Reggie's pet places due north of us' (*Letters of Louis MacNeice*, p. 527).
7. For further information on Durrell's time in Athens, see Ian MacNiven, *Lawrence Durrell*, pp. 218–22.
8. 'An Anatomy of Exile', *Personal Landscape: An Anthology of Exile* (London: Editions Poetry/Nicholson & Watson, 1945), p. 13. Fedden's colleague Bernard Spencer was preparing material at the time for the first volume of his *Aegean Islands*, a *paean* to his idyllic if temporary homeland, eventually published after the end of the war in 1946.
9. As recounted in his *Balkan Correspondent* (New York: Harper, 1941).
10. *Images of Greece* (London: Country Life, 1944); *Greek Horizons* (Athens: The Icaros Publishing Company, 1946), vol. 1, no. 1.
11. See Frances Donaldson, *The British Council*, p. 89, on this sequence of appointments and Anglo-Greek academic connections; Burn, later author of *The Pelican History of Greece* (1965), features in George Thaniel's account of the period in *Seferis and Friends* (Stratford, Ontario: Mercury, 1994).
12. There are echoes perhaps of Patrick Leigh Fermor here, and his effective 'disappearance' into the Greek mountains, disguised as a shepherd, as part of S.O.E. undercover operations with the Resistance in Crete. Leigh Fermor was already well known in Greek circles by the late 1930s; he later published his memoirs of the country in *Mani: Travels in the Southern Peleponnese*, in 1958, and *Roumeli*, in 1962.
13. See Braybrooke, *Olivia Manning: A Life*, p. 95, and also Patrick Leigh Fermor's writing on Ghikas, *Encounter* (February 1957).
14. *Inventing Ruritania*, p. 196. 'Evzoni' were Greek light infantry: 'fustanella' their traditional military skirt.
15. For a full account of life immediately before and during the Nazi occupation see Mark Mazower, *Inside Hitler's Greece: The Experience of Occupation, 1941–1944* (New Haven: Yale University Press, 2001).
16. Manning's references to the initial German bombing raids on the city follow closely the actual events of the period, including the explosion at Piraeus on 6 April 1941, when the Luftwaffe blew up a munitions ship berthed in

the harbour. Compare the description given in Roald Dahl's account of his experiences as a Royal Air Force fighter pilot stationed over Greece, in *Going Solo* (London: Cape, 1986).

17. It is possible Callard is loosely based on the Honourable Edward Gathorne-Hardy, also in Athens at the time with the British Council, described by Artemis Cooper as 'delightfully camp' and by Roger Bowen as one of the lecturers who caused so much concern to the British Council hierarchy; '*Many Histories Deep*': *The Personal Landscape Poets in Egypt* (London: Associated University Presses, 1995), pp. 43–4. Callard had initially been befriended in Athens by Durrell and Henry Miller; see Ian MacNiven, *Lawrence Durrell*, p. 219.

18. Lawrence Durrell, letter to Anne Ridler, June 1940, in Alan G. Thomas (ed.), *Spirit of Place; Letters and Essays on Travel* (London: Faber, 1971), p. 65. Elsewhere, however, Durrell mentions that the Legation is in a poor state: 'For the last month I have been working for the Legation here as a sort of private Godfrey Winn, checking on opinion. Now a new man has arrived from England and sacked the whole of a very efficient and necessary department . . . good English departmentalism has triumphed over those of us who knew Greece and Greek, and liked both. His Majesty's Press Attaché rules the roost. The same inert supine attitude as the last war; the same idiotic complacence and over-confidence' (letter to Anne Ridler, October 1939, *Spirit of Place*, p. 62). See Frances Donaldson, *The British Council*, pp. 88–90, on attitudes to the organisation generally in Greece, including its propaganda role in the Balkans.

19. See Roger Bowen, '*Many Histories Deep*', pp. 40–1.

20. Cited in Donaldson, *The British Council*, p. 95.

21. See Donaldson, *The British Council*, pp. 95–7.

22. Published in *The Windmill*, vol. 1, no. 2 (1945), pp. 117–19. Manning also describes the voyage in her 'Poets in Exile' article for *Horizon* (as discussed further below). Seferis gave an account of the same journey in his diary; see Roderick Beaton, *George Seferis: Waiting for the Angel* (New Haven and London: Yale University Press, 2003), p. 195.

23. *In Byron's Shadow*, Chapter Eight.

24. See David Roessel, *In Byron's Shadow*, pp. 218–21. Durrell wrote of Smyrna that 'it is more than the injustice, the cruelty, the madness of the whole episode which sticks in the mind of the modern Greek. It is also a sense of a lost richness, a lost peace of mind . . . It has become a memory which he

touches from time to time, like a man fingering a cicatrice.' Preface to *Aeolia*, by Ilia Venezis (trans. E.D. Scott-Kilvert), pp. v–vi, cited in Richard Pine, 'War, Agón and the Greek Literary Imagination', in Eve Patten and Richard Pine (eds), *Literatures of War* (Newcastle: Cambridge Scholars Publishing, 2008), p. 84.

25. Published in *Personal Landscape: An Anthology of Exile*, p. 21. On the poet's background, see Roderick Beaton's biography *George Seferis: Waiting for the Angel* (New Haven and London: Yale University Press, 2003).
26. 'Poets in Exile', *Horizon*, vol. 10 (October 1944), p. 275.
27. 'Anatomy of Exile', *Personal Landscape: An Anthology of Exile*, p. 15 (the translation referred to is Papadimitriou's own).
28. 'Three Recitatives from *Anatolia*', in *Personal Landscape: An Anthology of Exile*, pp. 92–4. These were originally published between 1942 and 1945 in individual issues of the journal. See Roger Bowen, '*Many Histories Deep*', p. 211, n. 3.
29. Manning collaborated with Reggie Smith in a translation of Papadimitriou's 'The Christian Soldier, in memory of G. Sarandaris', *The Windmill*, vol. 1, no. 2 (1945), pp. 126–8.
30. 'Poets in Exile', p. 273. Manning kept in touch with Papadimitriou for some time, mentioning that she has heard from her in a letter to Edward Lane (Kay Dick), 16 November 1944, McFarlin (Series 1).
31. *Many Histories Deep*, p. 49. Bowen also notes here Papadimitriou's influence on Manning and Durrell's dedication of his own recitative, 'In Europe', to the Greek poet, in 1942.
32. 'Poets in Exile', p. 275. See also Manning's recollections of the poetry circle in this period in 'Cairo: Back from the Blue', *Sunday Times Colour Supplement* (17 September 1967), pp. 49–55.
33. The context of poetry publishing in wartime Middle East is dealt with at length by Roger Bowen, *Many Histories Deep*, and Jonathan Bolton, *Personal Landscapes: British Poets in Egypt during the Second World War* (London: Macmillan, 1997). See also Ian MacNiven on the pacifist leanings of the *Personal Landscape* group, in *Lawrence Durrell*, p. 247.
34. Jonathan Bolton, *Personal Landscapes*, Prologue, pp. xiv–xv; Richard Pine, *Lawrence Durrell: The Mindscape* (Basingstoke: Macmillan, 1994), p. 254.
35. Epilogue to *Prospero's Cell: A Guide to the Landscape and Manners of Corcyra* (London: Faber, 1975). Manning and Reggie lived in the flat with

Liddell, after Durrell had left, briefly in October 1941 (Braybrooke, *Olivia Manning: A Life*, p. 104).

36. On Durrell's use of the city, see, in particular, Richard Pine, *Lawrence Durrell: The Mindscape*, and also Michael Diboll, *Lawrence Durrell's* Alexandria Quartet *and its Egyptian Contexts* (New York: Edwin Mellen, 2004). Despite their overlap in wartime scenery and community, Durrell and Manning have rarely been compared as writers; see, however, Nancy Lewis, 'Lawrence Durrell and Olivia Manning: Egypt, War and Displacement', *Deus Loci* (NS4 1995–6), pp. 97–104.

37. E.M. Forster, *Alexandria: A History and Guide* (London: Michael Haaf, 1982), p. x. The legacy is discussed in detail by Jane Pinchin, *Alexandria Still: Forster, Durrell and Cavafy* (Princeton, NJ: Princeton University Press, 1977), and Edmund Keeley, *Cavafy's Alexandria: Study of a Myth in Progress* (Princeton, NJ: Princeton University Press, 1996).

38. 'Anatomy of Exile', *Personal Landscape: An Anthology of Exile*, p. 14.

39. *Personal Landscapes*, p. 32.

40. *Personal Landscapes*, p. 44.

41. 'Cairo in those Days', unpublished typescript, Olivia Manning collection, HRC, p. 5.

42. George Fraser's response to Manning is cited by Artemis Cooper, *Cairo in the War* (London: Hamish Hamilton, 1989), p. 155; Lawrence Durrell's comment features in a letter to Meary Tambimittu (editor of *Poetry London*), cited in Braybrooke, *Olivia Manning: A Life*, p. 113. See also Ian MacNiven, *Lawrence Durrell*, p. 242, on Durrell's dislike of Manning's 'sharp, critical manner'.

43. *A Stranger and Afraid*, pp. 124–5. Fraser includes one of Reggie's attempts at a war poem, 'beginning, incredibly, "H. copped it at Sidi Rezegh. . ."', as evidence of his friend's clumsiness with the form (p. 125).

44. On Bullen in Egypt, see Roger Bowen, '*Many Histories Deep*', pp. 55–7. Richard Pine queries the idea of Durrell as a basis for Castlebar, suggesting that, despite the circumstantial parallels, the 'likeness is hard to see'; *Lawrence Durrell: The Mindscape*, p. 38.

45. '*Many Histories Deep*', p. 48.

46. Ibid., p. 49.

47. The quotations are taken from the text reprinted in *Personal Landscape: An Anthology of Exile*, pp. 69–70.

48. For these details, see Ian MacNiven, *Lawrence Durrell*, p. 250. Fedden's contributions, 'Where Shall John Go? – Egypt', ran in *Horizon*, vol. 11 (1945).
49. In her review of Connolly's *The Condemned Playground*, in *Palestine Post* (8 February 1946), p. 7. Braybrooke gives some background to the *Horizon* article in the diplomatic bag; *Olivia Manning: A Life*, p. 108.
50. 'Poets in Exile', pp. 270–9.
51. Cited in Bowen, '*Many Histories Deep*', p. 63.
52. Cited in Braybrooke, *Olivia Manning: A Life*, p. 113.
53. '*Many Histories Deep*', p. 64. See the highly adverse review of the *Personal Landscape* anthology by 'Cleric', *Palestine Post* (21 September 1945), p. 7, complaining of Fedden's 'querulous and guilty apologia' with which the book opens, and listing Tiller and Durrell as also belonging to the 'spoilt boy' category; of Durrell: 'Certainly much of his verse, with its implicit longing both for personal protection from the world's buffets and for his stepfatherland of Greece, is only a highflown, sometimes rhythmical expression of a psychological state for which Freud had a name.' Tiller, meanwhile, is as 'sterile as any hothouse plant'.
54. 'Poets in Exile', pp. 275, 279.

Chapter Four: Egypt, the desert war and the *Levant Trilogy*

1. *The House by Herod's Gate*, p. 3.
2. Robert Liddell's *Unreal City*, set mainly in Cavafy's Alexandria, was published in 1952; Newby's *Picnic at Sakkara*, from his Egypt trilogy, and Enright's *The Academic Year*, based on his experiences as a university lecturer in Egypt, in 1955.
3. Of Pennethorne Hughes' book on the infamous Cairo hotel and its environs Manning wrote: 'To the English, cooped up in England during the years of bombs, overwork and daily uncertainty, the thought of escape to the Middle East suggested delights that were undreamt of at home. It is a good thing that someone is telling the truth. Yet the truth was even grimmer than most people realized. They groaned through the Cairo summer when the heat beat down, and the heat beat up, whilst the noise mounted to a scream, the smells to a nausea, the flies in swarms, and even the soldiers in the desert said they could not stand Cairo for more than a few days.' *Palestine Post* (29 July 1949), p. 6. Manning reviewed Davin's book in *Palestine Post* (4 July 1947), p. 7, and also in *Our Time* (July 1947).

4. For further details of wartime Cairo and the various writers, academics and diplomatic figures at large during the time of Manning's sojourn there, see Trevor Mostyn, *Egypt's Belle Époque: Cairo, 1869–1952* (London: Quartet, 1989), and Artemis Cooper, *Cairo in the War*.
5. Fedden's commissioned pieces on Egypt, among the insightful contemporary reports on the political state of the country towards the end of the war, ran in *Horizon*'s 'Where Shall John Go?' series, vol. 11, nos 61–2 (January/February 1945).
6. *The Remarkable Expedition: The Story of Stanley's Rescue of Emin Pasha from Equatorial Africa* (London: Weidenfeld & Nicolson, 1985), pp. 1–2, 11 (originally published by Heinemann, 1947).
7. Diboll's discussion of the Coptic plot in *Mountolive* expands on Nessim's vision of an Alexandrine, cosmopolitan and Mediterranean Egypt under threat, as he explains to Clea: 'You know, we all know, that our days are numbered since the French and the British have lost control of the Middle East. We, the foreign communities, with all we have built up, are being gradually engulfed by the Arab tide, the Moslem tide. Some of us are trying to work against it; Armenians, Copts, Jews and Greeks here in Egypt, while others elsewhere are organizing themselves'; cited in his *Lawrence Durrell's* Alexandria Quartet *and its Egyptian Contexts*, p. 128.
8. *The Remarkable Expedition*, p. 13.
9. Commenting on this episode of 'tentative sympathy' in *The Sum of Things*, the journalist Martin Woollacott has drawn out the novel's relevance to a contemporary process of Western intervention in the Middle East: 'Manning was too clear-eyed a chronicler to suggest that the life of the Europeans caught up in the swirl of war in the Middle East touched in more than a superficial way on that of even educated Arabs. Uncertain relations between individuals reflected conflicting national purposes. The Europeans had their purposes and the Arabs had theirs and they were not often the same. At the end of the war waged by the Europeans, "peace, precarious peace, came down upon the world and the survivors could go home". For the Arabs, however, conflict continued, and the familiar, necessary and sometimes demeaning task of constantly weighing western policies to see what combination of opportunities and dangers they might represent, went on after the war just as it had done during and before it.' *Guardian* (11 October 2002).
10. 'Cairo Memories', *Encounter*, vol. 62, no. 5 (May 1984), p. 78.

11. *Egypt's Belle-Époque*, p. 133.
12. The war inevitably put an end to Egypt's place on Western tourist itineraries, the 'grand tour' tradition started by Thomas Cook in the 1860s from his office in the grounds of Shepheard's Hotel and drawing generations of English travellers to the sites of the pyramids, the Valley of the Kings and, after its opening in 1869, the Suez Canal; see the accounts in Robin Fedden's *Egypt, Land of the Valley* (1977; London: Michael Haag, 1986).
13. Fitzroy MacLean, *Eastern Approaches* (London: Cape 1949), p. 390; Freya Stark, *Dust in the Lion's Paw: Autobiography, 1939–46* (1961) (London: Arrow, 1990), p. 56.
14. *British Writing of the Second World War*, p. 114.
15. Cairo experienced several episodes of panic, individually referred to phlegmatically by Cecil Beaton and other observers as 'the flap', when civilians struggled to evacuate the city, in *Near East* (London: Batsford, 1943).
16. *A Stranger and Afraid*, p. 122.
17. Editorial introduction to Keith Douglas, *Alamein to Zem Zem* (London: Faber, 1966), p. 12. Elizabeth David's biographer Lisa Chaney describes the troops arriving for recreation in Cairo as one of the city's most poignant features: 'Those fortunates who survived returned to the cities for respite, with pay in their pockets and a desperate will to enjoy themselves if it was the last thing they did before returning to the desert and a good chance of maiming or death.' *Elizabeth David: A Biography* (London: Pan, 1991), p. 161.
18. *Take These Men* (1955; London: Constable, 1985), pp. 171–2. Cyril Joly served as an officer in the 7th Armoured Division of the Desert Rats.
19. See *LT*, p. 270. Various strategy details from Montgomery's account, including descriptions of dummy-pipelines and lorries, the digging of slit-trenches for the infantry, and of the commander's personal message read to all ranks on the evening before the charge at El Alamein on 23 October, appear in Manning's version of the campaign. Her title for the second volume of the trilogy, meanwhile, though taken from Shakespeare's *Macbeth*, clearly echoes the text of this speech. See Field-Marshal the Viscount Montgomery of Alamein, *El Alamein to the River Sangro* (1948; London: Barrie Jenkins, 1973), the most relevant volume of memoirs.
20. *Near East*, p. 57.

21. In Kay Dick's *The Shelf*, reference is made to Sophie's brother having died at Alamein, but in fact Manning's brother Oliver was lost in his plane off the Dorset coast; see Braybrooke, *Olivia Manning: A Life*, pp. 104–5.
22. *Alamein to Zem Zem*, p. 16. For a stylistic analysis of Douglas's text in this respect, see Adam Piette, *Imagination at War*, Chapter One.
23. Doubtless she had read, in 1941, *Horizon*'s discussion of the future of war writing, in an article pleading that creative writers be recognised, like journalists, as a reserved occupation in wartime. Signed by figures from inside and outside the forces, including Cyril Connolly, Arthur Koestler, Alun Lewis, George Orwell and Stephen Spender. The suggestion was that a 'cultural front' must be recognised, and writers used in same way as the visual artists employed so effectively during the First World War. See Arthur Calder-Marshall et al., 'Why Not War Writers? A Manifesto', *Horizon*, vol. 4, no. 22 (October 1941), pp. 236–9. The debate reflected an awareness, too, that this war demanded a new kind of prose, sturdy and pragmatic, and quite different to the poetry that characterised its predecessor. Despite her attention to poetry through *Personal Landscape* and the efforts of *Salamander* and *Oasis*, Manning's own *Artist Among the Missing*, from 1949, also implied that the artist as a fragile and poetic sensibility would not survive the sheer psychological battering of this conflict.
24. *Sword of Honour* (London: Penguin, 1999), p. 144.
25. In *Near East*, Beaton writes of the healthiness of desert existence: 'Life here is primeval. It is simple with the simplicity of the animals: yet it seems that from this simplicity springs a new contentment. In the desert the men are contented, they become "sand happy"' (p. 40).
26. There are various sources for the role played by women's auxiliary corps in Egypt. One of the closest in terms of reference to Manning's depiction of Mortimer and Philips is the account given by Anita Leslie, a niece of Churchill, from Castle Leslie, County Monaghan, in Ireland, who served in the Mechanised Transport Corps. Leslie's various duties included driving on the desert front and overland from Cairo to Jerusalem; see her memoir *Train to Nowhere* (London: Hutchinson, 1948), republished as *A Story Half Told: A Wartime Autobiography* (London: Hutchinson, 1983), in which she also celebrates the figure of Lady Hester Stanhope, 'that embittered, brilliant Englishwoman who nursed her grievances and memories and dreams to death in the wild beauty of the Lebanon' (p. 39).

Chapter Five: 'John Bull's Other Ireland': Manning's Palestine fiction

1. The poet Louis Lawler is cited by Braybrooke, *Olivia Manning: A Life*, p. 121 (though the year is likely to have been early 1945). Koestler almost certainly met Manning through Gershon Agronsky, proprietor and editor of the *Palestine Post*, who threw a party for the celebrated writer on his arrival in Jerusalem in order to introduce him to various Jewish political leaders, British diplomats and local intellectuals. On Koestler's Jerusalem connections, including details of his 1945 visit, see David Cesarani, *Arthur Koestler: The Homeless Mind* (London: Vintage, 1999), pp. 235–8. (Cesarani also notes that during Koestler's sojourn he had 'affairs with a number of women', p. 240.) The *Palestine Post* reported on Koestler's departure for London after six months in Jerusalem on 8 August 1945.
2. *Thieves in the Night: Chronicle of an Experiment* (London: Macmillan, 1946); *Promise and Fulfilment: Palestine, 1917–1949* (1949; London: Macmillan, 1983), p. 128.
3. On Koestler's Zionism, see Cesarani, *The Homeless Mind*, p. 248. Reggie Smith's critique, 'Detours and Oases: A Note on Arthur Koestler', *Orion* (Autumn 1945), pp. 55–61 – a response to Koestler's article 'The Intelligentsia' (which had appeared in *Horizon* in March 1944) – had been commissioned by the then editors of *Orion*, Cecil Day Lewis and Rosamond Lehmann. The *Palestine Post* drew its readers' attention to the piece (and its pre-empting of George Orwell's similarly negative treatment of the writer in the *Times Literary Supplement*) as follows: 'Many Palestinians will be interested to read R.D. Smith (ex P.B.S.) on Arthur Koestler, a visitor to Jerusalem last winter. Mr Smith wrote the article eighteen months ago and during the period it awaited publication in the "Orion" offices, the "Times Literary Supplement" started a separate debunking of Mr Koestler's somewhat inflated reputation' (22 March 1946), p. 4.
4. *Tyrants and Mountains*, p. 111.
5. *Palestine Post* (26 July 1945), p. 4.
6. *The House by Herod's Gate*, p. 174; the British Council lecture series is advertised in the *Palestine Post* (19 January 1945), p. 4.
7. *The House by Herod's Gate*, p. 175. The *Forum* was noted in the *Palestine Post* in a report on various local agencies working towards integration: 'It appears that the "Jerusalem Forum" also aims at fostering understanding between the various communities, while the British Council hopes that an appreciation of Britain on the part of Arabs and Jews will lead to both

peoples forging closer mutual ties', but the writer also noted the lack of connection to representatives of Palestinian communities in both organisations: *Palestine Post* (10 December 1942), p. 4. Activities staged by the *Forum* included a visit by Ifor Evans, Professor of Language and Literature at the University of London, *Palestine Post* (26 January 1943), p. 2, and a debate, 'Music serves no higher purpose than the titillation of emotion', at which the mover was Reggie Smith. The motion was defeated, *Palestine Post* (20 August 1942), p. 3.

8. A *Palestine Post* editorial of June 1948 berated Koestler for criticising the government's campaign against the Irgun; this was followed by a front-page article attacking him for his pro-Irgun stance (see Cesarani, *The Homeless Mind*, pp. 248–9). On the history of the *Palestine Post*, Erwin Frenkel, *The Press and Politics in Israel: The Jerusalem Post from 1932 to the Present* (Westport: Greenwood Press, 1994), and the archives databased by the Historical Jewish Press initiative (with the assistance of Tel Aviv University and the Jewish National and University Library) at http://jpress.tau.ac.il. (It is likely that Reggie Smith also wrote frequently for the paper but under a pseudonym.)
9. See Walter Allen, *As I Walked Down New Grub Street*, p. 146.
10. On the political history of this period, see Michael J. Cohen, *Palestine: Retreat from the Mandate – the Making of British Policy, 1936–1945* (London: Paul Elek, 1978); also, Naomi Shepherd's useful account, *Ploughing Sand: British Rule in Palestine, 1917—1948* (London: John Murray, 1999).
11. For a full account of civilian life in Jerusalem, see A.J. Sherman, *Mandate Days: British Lives in Palestine, 1918–1948* (London: Thames & Hudson, 1983). Political attitudes within both communities are also covered by Tom Segev, *One Palestine, Complete: Jews and Arabs under the British Mandate* (London: Abacus, 2002).
12. On long-established traditions of British Arabism, see A.J. Sherman, *Mandate Days*, pp. 25–8, and Kathryn Tidrick, *Heart Beguiling Araby: English Romance and Arabia* (Cambridge: Cambridge University Press, 1981).
13. Further details of British political positions are discussed by Cohen, *Palestine*, Chapter Three, and Bernard Wasserstein, *Britain and the Jews of Europe, 1939–1945* (2nd ed; London: Leicester University Press, 1999), Chapter One.

14. *The House by Herod's Gate*, p. 69. Several British Cabinet members were also disquieted by the broader transitions of Zionism in the period from the placid and gentlemanly diplomacy of old-school leader Chaim Weizmann to the pragmatic and forceful dynamism of his successors emerging in the war years, including future leader David Ben Gurion: see Cohen, *Palestine: Retreat from the Mandate*, Chapter Ten.
15. Braybrooke records details of Manning's exchange with an Arab colleague at the Public Information Office in Jerusalem (where she worked temporarily), whom she accused of secretly learning German; *Olivia Manning: A Life*, p. 115.
16. Manning's account of Lynd's trip to Petra is closely based on her own visit: she visited the site in the spring of 1943, armed with Lanchester Harding's *Guide to Petra*, and wrote a prose poem about the experience: Braybrooke, *Olivia Manning: A Life*, p. 114.
17. *Colonial Strangers*, p. 34.
18. *Mandate Days*, p. 12.
19. See A.J. Sherman, *Mandate Days*, p. 239, for a full account of the newspaper's reaction.
20. 'The Ship of Death', section vii. From *The Complete Poems of D.H. Lawrence* (London: Wordsworth, 1994), p. 605.
21. There are several accounts of the episode and the losses at sea which preceded it: see Bernard Wasserstein, *Britain and the Jews of Europe*, pp. 128–45, and Douglas Frantz and Catherine Collins, *Death on the Black Sea: The Untold Story of the 'Struma' and World War II's Holocaust at Sea* (New York: HarperCollins/Ecco, 2003).
22. See Wasserstein, *Britain and the Jews of Europe*, pp. 141–3, on policy changes in the wake of the disaster.
23. On the reaction within Palestine, see A.J. Sherman, *Mandate Days*, pp. 156–7.
24. 'The Tragedy of the *Struma*', *Observer* (1 March 1970), p. 8. Manning had drawn attention to the event while still in Palestine; in a review of a volume of new short stories, edited by Reginald Moore in 1945, she commented on the account written by her contemporary in the Middle East, Alex Comfort: 'Particularly interesting to Jewish readers in Palestine is Alex Comfort's "The Ship", which deals with the rescue of an infant from the ill-fated "Struma". Mr Comfort gets his facts wrong – the "Struma" did not lie in Haifa harbour and the Haifa atmosphere is obviously not painted from

experience, but the story is touching and deeply felt'; *Palestine Post* (23 November 1945), p. 7. At one stage Graham Greene had also planned to write about the treacherous sea voyage taken by Romanian Jews from Constanta to Palestine, in a series provisionally entitled 'Refugee Ship'; see his letter to Nancy Pearn, 15 July 1939, in Richard Greene (ed.), *Graham Green: A Life in Letters* (London: Abacus, 2007), p. 98.

25. Manning's review of Tabori's novel appears in the *Palestine Post* (4 July 1947), p. 7.
26. *Colonial Strangers*, p. 20.
27. *Palestine Post* (28 November 1947), p. 7.
28. As noted in Chapter One, this character was taken to be a version of Manning's erstwhile landlady in Jerusalem, Clarissa Graves, sister of the poet Robert; see Braybrooke, *Olivia Manning: A Life*, p. 153.
29. *Colonial Strangers*, p. 26.
30. Manning herself experienced a miscarriage while in Jerusalem; for medical reasons she was obliged to carry the baby, which died in her womb at seven months, to full term. See Braybrooke, *Olivia Manning: A Life*, p. 119.
31. Cited in *A Stranger and Afraid*, pp. 119–20.
32. *Palestine Post* (23 September 1949), p. 7. The review is appreciative of Orwell's attempt at the subject of totalitarianism but also complains of his sentimentality in the novel.
33. *Nineteen Eighty-Four* (Harmondsworth: Penguin, 1981), p. 11.
34. 'The Invisible Sources of *Nineteen-Eighty-Four*', *Journal of Popular Culture*, vol. 26 (Summer 1992), p. 99.
35. Of Hanley Manning wrote, 'Hanley is an accomplished novelist with a long-standing reputation as a writer of rather depressing books about seamen and the sea'; *Palestine Post* (17 August 1945), p. 7. Koestler, *Thieves in the Night*, p. 59.
36. In 'The Children', the image of the figurehead of the ship is similarly described: 'the long, anguished face of the wooden Eurydice sinking back into the underworld, never to return again. The long, wooden hands were raised with all the long, round, pointed fingers separate' (*Growing Up*, p. 34). Manning's memoir article 'The Irish Coast and Portsmouth' appeared in the *Palestine Post* (2 June 1944), p. 5.
37. *Times Literary Supplement* (10 December 1951), p. 641.

Conclusion

1. Review of *Growing Up*, in *The Tatler and Bystander* (26 May 1948), pp. 246–7.
2. Manning's comments to Kay Dick in the early 1970s reflect her awareness of the post-war acceleration of ageing: of both personal and professional status, she observed that 'I think middle age is a very, very painful time, because one grows up seeing oneself as the centre of the universe. One is the young generation, the coming, the brilliant, new, with the future before you; then suddenly, at a certain age, which I'd say is thirty-five or so, you find that a whole new generation is taking your place' (Kay Dick, *Friends and Friendship*, p. 36).
3. MI5 files for the year include several references to Reggie's continuing relationship with various Romanian political figures, *British National Archives* KV/2/2533.
4. See *Olivia Manning: A Life*, p. 128, for details of some of these.
5. The remark is made by Roy Foster, 'Friendly Disdain', a review of *Olivia Manning: A Life*, by Neville and June Braybrooke, *Financial Times* (15 April 2005).
6. See comments to this effect by Hugh Herbert, 'Forest Worlds' (interview with OM), *Guardian* (2 April 1974), p. 12.
7. Manning almost certainly read Lawrence Durrell's elegant descriptions of Cyprus, where he served as a government administrator during the 1950s, in his 1957 book *Bitter Lemons*, and this too may have provided inspiration.
8. See Braybrooke, *Olivia Manning: A Life*, p. 213.
9. For reports on the fate of the British and Italian film crew, *Guardian* (5 June 1971), p. 2, and (7 June 1971), p. 4.
10. OM to Kay Dick, 10 July 1971, McFarlin.
11. See Braybrooke, *Olivia Manning: A Life*, p. 215, and the interview with Herbert, 'Forest Worlds', on this period of Manning's creative life.
12. See 'Notes towards an Autobiography'. Reggie remained in this post till 1978, when he became Professor of Anglo-Irish Literature at the New University of Ulster, Coleraine.
13. Letter courtesy of Gerry Harrison; see also Braybrooke, *Olivia Manning: A Life*, p. 120.
14. Ambrose was based on a real figure: in conversation on this 'major Manning character' Manning explained to interviewer Hugh Herbert that he 'was based on a literary journalist – now dead – who was the most brilliant man

of his year at university but somehow never quite lived up to his promise' ('Forest Worlds', p. 12). The concept of an empire disintegrating in the hands of inferior 'middle men' is a standard conceit of the fiction of the period, and an idea sketched more than once in the course of the *Levant Trilogy*; in *The Sum of Things*, for example, diplomat Dobbie Dobson laments in his exchange with Guy Pringle the handing over of colonial affairs from local governors to an increasingly inept Colonial Office in London: 'Guy considered it: "You mean, individuality became answerable to the machine?" "Excellently put," Dobson scribbled on an envelope: "We no longer have great men like Bentinck, the Wellesleys, Henry Laurence, James Kirk: men who developed their initiative by exercising it. Now the service is dependent on a pack of non-entities. You agree?"' (*LT*, p. 512).

15. On the prize, see Braybrooke, *Olivia Manning: A Life*, pp. 265–7: see also Lavinia Greacen's record of Farrell 'devouring' Olivia Manning, among other writers, in 1966, in *J.G.Farrell: The Making of a Writer*, p. 214.

16. In Farrell's novel, 'The Palm Court proved to be a vast, shadowy cavern in which dusty white chairs stood in silent, empty groups, just visible here and there amid the gloomy foliage. For the palms had completely run riot, shooting out of their wooden tubs (some of which had cracked open to trickle little cones of black soil on to the tiled floor) towards the distant murky skylight, hammering and interweaving themselves against the greenish glass that glowed sullenly overhead. Here and there between the tables beds of oozing mould supported banana and rubber plants, hairy ferns, elephant grass and creepers that dangled from above like emerald intestines'; *Troubles* (London: Phoenix, 1993), p. 20. It is hard not to see echoes of Farrell's Palm House in Manning's short story 'The Banana House', published in December 1970 in the *Sunday Times Magazine*; in the tale, an impoverished solicitor's clerk in London has an erotic dream set in the Great Conservatory at Kew: 'He looked up at the sun-bright roof and saw, at the top, fitted like a mop into the central bubble, a palm with trusses of green nuts. Beside it were the spears of the giant bamboo and a rubber tree that let down a waterfall of leaves like monstrous oak leaves. . . . And there was a banana flower on a ridged stem, hanging purple and dejected like, yes, Bert knew exactly what it was like and he began to titter. There were other flowers: hibiscus flowers, a purple Banhinia (he saw the label clearly), a yellow flower from Japan with throat so deep and brown, a bee would be lost in it. These were strange enough, but stranger were the flowers of the

dwarf palms, red and pink, rising from the ground on their own heavy trunks, so strange they were unnerving.'

17. In the intervening time it seems likely that Manning became pregnant again and either suffered a miscarriage or underwent a termination of some kind; British Intelligence records a phone conversation on 30 October 1950 between Manning and a friend in which the former was reported as saying that 'she was going to have a baby. Reggie did not want her to have it – it meant too much responsibility and the Party meant more than anything else to him' (*British National Archives* KV/2/2533).
18. On Manning's fears about over-population, which dovetail with several ideas in *The Rain Forest*, see her remarks to Kay Dick, in *Friends and Friendship*, p. 39.
19. *British Women Writers*, p. 240.
20. 'Ladies without Escort', published in *Penguin Modern Stories*, vol. 12 (1972).

Bibliography

Works by Olivia Manning

Novels

The Wind Changes (1937; London: Virago, 1988).

Artist Among the Missing (1949; London: Heinemann, 1975).

School for Love (1951; Harmondsworth: Penguin, 1982).

A Different Face (1953; London: Heinemann, 1975).

The Doves of Venus (1955; London: Virago, 1984).

The Great Fortune (1960); *The Spoilt City* (1962); *Friends and Heroes* (1965); published as the *Balkan Trilogy* (1987; London: Mandarin, 1990).

The Play Room (1969; London: Virago, 1984); published in the US as *The Camperlea Girls* (1969).

The Rain Forest (1974; Harmondsworth: Penguin, 1977).

The Danger Tree (1977); *The Battle Lost and Won* (1978); *The Sum of Things* (1980); published as the *Levant Trilogy* (Harmondsworth: Penguin, 1982).

Short-story collections

Growing Up (London: Heinemann, 1948).

A Romantic Hero and Other Stories (London: Heinemann, 1967).

Original sources for various uncollected and collected short stories are cited in the notes; individual short stories appeared in several serial publications including Penguin's *Modern Short Stories*, Macmillan's *Winter's Tales*, *Modern Reading*, *The New Savoy*, *New Stories*, *Vogue*, *Encounter*, *Harper's Bazaar*, *Sunday Times Magazine*.

Miscellaneous books

The Dreaming Shore (London: Evans Bros, 1950).

The Remarkable Expedition: The Story of Stanley's Rescue of Emin Pasha from Equatorial Africa (1947; London: Weidenfeld & Nicolson, 1985).

My Husband Cartwright (London: Heinemann, 1956).

Extraordinary Cats (London: Michael Joseph, 1967).

Romanian Short Stories, intro. by Olivia Manning (Oxford: Oxford University Press, 1971).

Northanger Abbey by Jane Austen, intro. by Olivia Manning (London: Pan, 1979).

Journalism and articles

'Last Civilian Ship', *The Windmill*, vol. 1, no. 2 (1945), pp. 117–19.

'Poets in Exile', *Horizon*, vol. 10 (October 1944), pp. 270–9.

'Middle East Letter', in Reginald Moore (ed.), *Modern Reading*, no. 9 (1944).

'Rumanian *Coup d'État*', 'The Greeks at War', 'The Great Flap', in Basil Liddell Hart (ed.), *A History of the Second World War* (London: Purnell, 1966–9), vol. 1, pp. 337–9; vol. 1, pp. 356–9; vol. 2, n.p.

'Notes on the Future of the Novel', *Times Literary Supplement* (15 August 1958).

'Pleasure in Reading', *Times* (9 November 1961).

'Speaking of Writing', *Times* (30 January 1964).

'Cairo: Back from the Blue', *Sunday Times Colour Supplement* (17 September 1967), pp. 49–55.

'"An Enemy in the Mind", Jocelyn Brooke: The Man and His Work', *Times Literary Supplement* (8 May 1969).

'The Tragedy of the Struma', *Observer* (1 March 1970), pp. 8–17.

'Olivia Manning on the Perils of the Female Writer', *Spectator* (7 December 1974), pp. 734–5.

'Books I Have Read', in Frederic Raphael (ed.), *Bookmarks* (London: Cape, 1975).

'Voyages around My Father', *Times* (24 May 1975), p. 6.

'The Thirteenth Apostle has a Great Deal to Answer for', *Times* (24 December 1975), p. 5.

Review articles in the *Palestine Post* as cited in the notes, accessed at http://jpress.tau.ac.il.

Correspondence and private papers

Olivia Manning Collection, McFarlin Special Collections, University of Tulsa.

Olivia Manning Papers, Harry Ransom Research Center, University of Texas.

Olivia Manning MSS (1965 correspondence with various writers on the campaign to honour William Gerhardi), Manuscripts, Lilly Library, University of Indiana.

British National Archives, Cat. Ref. KV/2/2533; MI file PF70065/V.

General sources

Allen, Walter, *As I Walked Down New Grub Street: Memories of a Writing Life* (London: Heinemann, 1981).

—, *Tradition and Dream: A Critical Survey of British and American Fiction from the 1920s to the Present Day* (Harmondsworth: Penguin, 1965).

Andraş, Carmen, 'Romania and its Images in British Travel Writing: In Between Peripherality and Cultural Interface', *TRANS: Internet-Zeitschrift fur Kulturwissenschaften*, no. 14 (April 2003).

Arendt, Hannah, *Eichmann in Jerusalem: A Report on the Banality of Evil* (London: Penguin, 1976).

Barbera, Jack, *Stevie: A Biography of Stevie Smith* (London: Heinemann, 1985).

Beaton, Cecil, *Near East* (London: Batsford, 1943).

Beaton, Roderick, *George Seferis: Waiting for the Angel: a Biography* (New Haven and London: Yale University Press, 2003).

Bellow, Saul, *The Dean's December* (Harmondsworth: Penguin, 1982).

Bluemel, Kristin, *George Orwell and the Radical Eccentrics: Intermodernism in Literary London* (Basingstoke: Palgrave Macmillan, 2004).

— (ed.), *Intermodernism: Literary Culture in Mid Twentieth-Century Britain* (Edinburgh: Edinburgh University Press, 2009).

Bolton, Jonathan, *Personal Landscapes: British Poets in Egypt during the Second World War* (London: Macmillan, 1997).

Bowen, Elizabeth, 'Growing Up', a review, *The Tatler and Bystander* (26 May 1948), pp. 246–7.

—, '*Artist Among the Missing*', a review, *The Tatler and Bystander* (13 April 1949), pp. 60–8.

Bowen, Roger, '*Many Histories Deep*': *The Personal Landscape Poets in Egypt* (London: Associated University Presses, 1995).

Brannigan, John, *Orwell to the Present: Literature in England, 1945–2000* (2003).

Braybrooke, Neville and June (with Francis King), *Olivia Manning: A Life* (London: Chatto & Windus, 2004).

Brinzeau, Pia, *Corridors of Mirrors: The Spirit of Europe in Contemporary British and Romanian Fiction* (New York: University of America Press, 2000).

Brooke, Jocelyn, *The Orchid Trilogy* (London: Penguin, 1981).

Burgess, Anthony, *The Novel Now: A Student's Guide to Contemporary Fiction* (London: Faber, 1971).

Calder-Marshall, Arthur, et al., 'Why not War Writers? A Manifesto', *Horizon*, vol. 4, no. 22 (October, 1941), pp. 236–9.

Cesarani, David, *Arthur Koestler: The Homeless Mind* (London: Vintage, 1999).

—, and Paul A. Levine (eds), *Bystanders to the Holocaust: A Re-evaluation* (London: Frank Cass, 2002).

Chaney, Lisa, *Elizabeth David: A Biography* (London: Macmillan, 1998).

Cohen, Michael J., *Palestine: Retreat from the Mandate – the Making of British Policy, 1936–1945* (London: Thames & Hudson, 1983).

Connell, John, *The House by Herod's Gate* (London: Sampson, Low & Marston, n.d.).

Cooper, Artemis, *Cairo in the War* (London: Hamish Hamilton, 1989).

—, *Writing at the Kitchen Table: The Authorized Biography of Elizabeth David* (London: Penguin, 2000).

Dahl, Roald, *Going Solo* (London: Cape, 1986).

Davin, Anna, 'R.D. Smith', *History Workshop Journal*, no. 21 (Spring 1986), pp. 227–8.

Davin, Dan, *For the Rest of Our Lives* (London: Nicholson & Watson, 1947).

Diboll, Michael, *Lawrence Durrell's* Alexandria Quartet *and its Egyptian Contexts* (New York: Edwin Mellen, 2004).

Dick, Kay, *Friends and Friendship: Conversations and Reflections* (London: Sidgwick & Jackson, 1974).

—, *The Shelf* (London: Hamish Hamilton, 1984).

Donaldson, Frances, *The British Council: The First Fifty Years* (London: Cape, 1984).

Douglas, Keith (writing as Peter Cameron), *Alamein to Zem Zem*, intro. by Lawrence Durrell (London: Faber, 1966).

Durrell, Lawrence, *Bitter Lemons of Cyprus* (London: Faber, 1959).

—, *The Alexandria Quartet* (London: Faber, 1962).

—, *White Eagles over Serbia* (London: Faber, 1957).

—, *Spirit of Place: Letters and Essays on Travel by Lawrence Durrell*, ed. Alan G. Thomas (London: Faber, 1971).

—, *The Avignon Quintet* (London: Faber, 1992).

—, *Prospero's Cell: A Guide to the Landscape and Manners of Corcyra* (London: Faber, 1975).

Esty, Jed, *A Shrinking Island: Modernism and National Culture in England* (Princeton, NJ: Princeton University Press, 2004).

Farrell, J.G. *Troubles* (London: Phoenix, 1993).

Fedden, Robin et al., *Personal Landscape: An Anthology of Exile* (London: Editions Poetry/Nicholson & Watson, 1945).

—, 'An Anatomy of Exile', in Robin Fedden et al., *Personal Landscape: An Anthology of Exile* (London: Editions Poetry/Nicholson & Watson, 1945).

—, *Egypt: Land of the Valley* (London: Michael Haag, 1986).

Fendler, Suzanne, and Ruth Wittlinger (eds), *The Idea of Europe in Literature* (London: Macmillan, 1999).

Fermor, Patrick Leigh, *Between the Woods and the Water: On Foot to Constantinople: From the Middle Danube to the Iron Gates* (London: John Murray, 1986).

Forster, E.M., *Alexandria: A History and Guide*, intro. by Lawrence Durrell (London: Michael Haag, 1982).

Foster, Roy, 'Friendly Disdain – a review of *Olivia Manning: A Life*, by Neville and June Braybrooke', *Financial Times* (15 April 2005).

Frankau, Pamela, *The Willow Cabin* (London: Virago, 1989).

Frantz, Douglas, and Catherine Collins, *Death on the Black Sea: The Untold Story of the* Struma *and World War II's Holocaust at Sea* (New York: HarperCollins/Ecco, 2003).

Fraser, George, *A Stranger and Afraid: The Autobiography of an Intellectual* (Manchester: Carcanet, 1983).

Frenkel, Erwen, *The Press and Politics in Israel: The Jerusalem Post from 1932 to the Present* (Westport: Greenwood Press, 1994).

Fussell, Paul, *Abroad: British Literary Travelling between the Wars* (Oxford: Oxford University Press, 1980).

—, *Wartime: Understanding and Behaviour in the Second World War* (Oxford: Oxford University Press, 1989).

Gallagher, Tom, *Outcast Europe: The Balkans from the Ottomans to Milosevic, 1789–1989* (London: Routledge, 2001).

Gavriliu, Eugenia, 'Gender Influences in the Construction of Romania in the *Balkan Trilogy*', in Rita Monticelli (ed.), *Travel Writing and the Female Imaginary* (Bologna: University of Bologna Press, 2001).

Gilmore, Leigh, *Autobiographics: A Feminist Theory of Women's Self-Representation* (Ithaca: Cornell University Press, 1994).

Godeanu, Oana, 'The Construction of Exoticism in Olivia Manning's *Balkan Trilogy*: An Imagogical Approach', *British and American Studies/Revista de Studii Britanice şi Americane,* vol. 11 (2005), pp. 199–210.

Goldsworthy, Vesna, 'Olivia Manning's "Bucharest": Reality and Imagination in the *Balkan Trilogy*', unpublished MA thesis, University of London (1992).

—, *Inventing Ruritania: The Imperialism of the Imagination* (New Haven and London: Yale University Press, 1998).

Gordon, Jan B., 'Charlotte Bronte's Alternative "European Community"', in Suzanne Fendler and Ruth Wittlinger (eds), *The Idea of Europe in Literature* (London: Macmillan, 1999).

Greacen, Lavinia, *J.G.Farrell: The Making of a Writer* (London: Bloomsbury, 1999).

—, (ed.), *J.G. Farrell in his Own Words: Selected Letters and Diaries* (Cork: Cork University Press, 2009).

Greene, Richard (ed.), *Graham Green: A Life in Letters* (London: Abacus, 2007).

Hammond, Andrew, '"The Red Threat": Cold War Rhetoric and the British Novel', in Andrew Hammond (ed.), *The Balkans and the West: Constructing the European Other, 1945–2003* (London: Ashgate, 2004).

Hartley, Jenny, *Millions Like Us: British Women's Fiction of the Second World War* (London: Virago, 1997).

Herbert, Hugh, 'Forest Worlds', an interview with Olivia Manning, *Guardian* (2 April 1974), p. 12.

Hewison, Robert, *Under Siege: Literary Life in London, 1939–1945* (London: Methuen, 1988).

Hills, Denis, *Tyrants and Mountains: A Reckless Life* (London: John Murray, 1992).

Household, Geoffrey, *Against the Wind* (London: Michael Joseph, 1958).

—, *The Europe that Was* (London: David & Charles, 1979).

Humble, Nicola, *The Feminine Middlebrow Novel, 1920s–1950s* (Oxford: Oxford University Press, 2001).

Inglis, Ruth, 'Observer in the Crowd', *Guardian* (7 March 1960), p. 6.

Joly, Cyril, *Take these Men* (London: Constable, 1985).

Keeley, Edmund, *Cavafy's Alexandria: Study of a Myth in Progress* (Princeton, NJ: Princeton University Press, 1996).

—, *Inventing Paradise: The Greek Journey, 1937–1947* (New York: Farrar, Straus & Giroux, 1999).

Kershaw, Angela, and Angela Kimyongur (eds), *Women in Europe between the Wars: Politics, Culture and Society* (Aldershot: Ashgate, 2007).

King, Francis, *Yesterday Came Suddenly: An Autobiography* (London: Constable, 1993).

Klein, Holger (ed.), *The Second World War in Fiction* (London: Macmillan, 1984).

Koestler, Arthur, *Thieves in the Night: Chronicle of an Experiment* (London: Macmillan, 1946).

—, *Promise and Fulfilment: Palestine, 1917–1949* (London: Macmillan, 1983).

Lassner, Phyllis, *British Women Writers of World War Two: Battlegrounds of Their Own* (London: Macmillan, 1998).

—, *Colonial Strangers: Women Writing the End of the British Empire* (New Brunswick: Rutgers University Press, 2004).

Latham, Ernest H., 'Privind de la fereastra: Olivia Manning in Romania', *Journal of the American-Romanian Academy of Arts and Sciences*, vol. 20 (1995), pp. 92–112.

Lawrence, D.H., *Complete Poems*, ed. David Ellis (London: Wordsworth Editions, 1994).

Leslie, Anita, *Train to Nowhere* (London: Hutchinson, 1948).

—, *A Story Half Told: A Wartime Autobiography* (London: Hutchinson, 1983).

Lewis, Nancy, 'Lawrence Durrell and Olivia Manning: Egypt, War and Displacement', *Deus Loci* (1995–6), pp. 97–104.

Liddell, Robert, *Unreal City* (London: Cape, 1952).

Light, Alison, *Forever England: Femininity, Literature and Conservatism between the Wars* (London: Routledge, 1991).

Lilley, George, *Anthony Powell: A Bibliography* (Winchester: St Paul's, 1993).

Lowry, Malcolm, *Under the Volcano* (London: Penguin, 2000).

Mackay, Marina, *Modernism and World War Two* (Cambridge: Cambridge University Press, 2007).

—, and Lyndsey Stonebridge (eds), *British Fiction after Modernism: The Novel at Mid-Century* (Basingstoke: Palgrave Macmillan, 2007).

MacLean, Fitzroy, *Eastern Approaches* (London: Cape, 1949).

MacNeice, Louis, 'Landscape and Legend', a review of *The Dreaming Shore* by Olivia Manning, *Observer* (17 September 1950).

—, *The Strings Are False: An Unfinished Autobiography* (London: Faber, 1965).

—, *Collected Poems*, ed. Peter McDonald (London: Faber, 2007).

—, *Letters of Louis MacNeice*, edited and selected by Jonathan Allison (London: Faber, 2010).

MacNiven, Ian, *Lawrence Durrell: A Biography* (London: Faber, 1998).

Mahon, Derek (writer and presenter), '*Never a Day without a Line*', BBC radio broadcast, 23 July 1981, BBC Ref. 42607 (1).

Marcus, Laura, *Autobiographical Discourses: Saving the Subject* (Manchester: Manchester University Press, 1994).

Mazower, Mark, *Hitler's Greece: The Experience of Occupation, 1941–1944* (New Haven: Yale University Press, 2001).

McIntyre, Ben, 'The Bumbling British Hero who Was a Communist "Spy"', *Times* (3 March 2007), pp. 36–7.

McLoughlin, Kate (ed.), *The Cambridge Companion to War Writing* (Cambridge: Cambridge University Press, 2009).

Miller, Betty, *Farewell Leicester Square* (London: Persephone, 2000).

Miller, Kristine, *British Literature of the Blitz: Fighting the People's War* (Basingstoke: Palgrave Macmillan, 2009).

Montgomery of Alamein, Field-Marshal, *El Alamein to the River Sangro* (London: Barrie & Jenkins, 1973).

Mooney, Harry J., 'Olivia Manning: Witness to History', in Thomas F. Staley (ed.), *Twentieth-Century Women Novelists* (London: Macmillan, 1982).

Morris, Robert K., *Continuance and Change: The Contemporary British Novel Sequence* (Carbondale: Southern Illinois University Press, 1972).

Mostyn, Trevor, *Egypt's Belle Époque: Cairo, 1869–1952* (London: Quartet, 1989).

Munton, Alan, *English Fiction of the Second World War* (London: Faber, 1989).

Orwell, George, *Nineteen Eighty-Four* (Harmondsworth: Penguin, 1981).

Ovendon, Keith, *A Fighting Withdrawal: The Life of Dan Davin, Writer, Soldier, Publisher* (Oxford: Oxford University Press, 1996).

Papadimitriou, Elie, 'Three Recitatives from Anatolia', in Robin Fedden et al., *Personal Landscape: An Anthology of Exile* (London: Editions Poetry/Nicholson & Watson, 1945).

Patmore, Derek, *Invitation to Roumania* (London: Macmillan, 1939).

—, *Balkan Correspondent* (New York: Harper, 1941).

—, *Images of Greece* (London: Country Life, 1940).

—, (ed.), *Greek Horizons* (Athens: The Icaros Publishing Company, 1946), vol. 1, no. 1.

—, *Private History: An Autobiography* (London: Cape, 1960).

Patten, Eve, 'Olivia Manning: Imperial Refugee', in Nicholas Allen and Eve Patten (eds), *That Island Never Found* (Dublin: Four Courts Press, 2007).

—, and Richard Pine (eds), *Literatures of War* (Newcastle: Cambridge Scholars Publishing, 2008).

Peterson, Robert C., 'Lesser Breeds without the Law: Olivia Manning's *Balkan Trilogy*', Tennessee Philological Association Conference (20–22 February 1986), unpublished paper courtesy of the author.

Piette, Alan, *Imagination at War: British Fiction and Poetry, 1939–1945* (London: Macmillan Papermac, 1995).

Pinchin, Jane, *Alexandria Still: Forster, Durrell and Cavafy* (Princeton, NJ: Princeton University Press, 1977).

Pine, Richard, *Lawrence Durrell: The Mindscape* (Basingstoke: Macmillan, 1994).

—, 'War, Agón and the Greek Literary Imagination', in Eve Patten and Richard Pine (eds), *Literatures of War* (Newcastle: Cambridge Scholars Publishing, 2008).

Plain, Gill, *Women's Fiction of the Second World War* (Edinburgh: Edinburgh University Press, 1996).

Porter, Ivor, *Operation Autonomous: With S.O.E. in Wartime Rumania* (London: Chatto & Windus, 1989).

Rau, Petra, *Conflict, Nationhood and Corporeality in Modern Literature* (Basingstoke: Palgrave Macmillan, 2010).

Rawlinson, Mark, *British Writing of the Second World War* (Oxford: Clarendon, 2000).

Roessel, David, *In Byron's Shadow: Modern Greece in the English and American Imagination* (Oxford: Oxford University Press, 2002).

Rose, Jonathan, 'The Invisible Sources of Nineteen Eighty-Four', *Journal of Popular Culture*, vol. 26 (Summer 1992).

St John, John, *William Heinemann: A Century of Publishing, 1890–1990* (London: Heinemann, 1990).

Salmon, Mary, 'Towards a Critical Biography of Olivia Manning', unpublished PhD thesis, University College, Dublin (1985).

—, 'Nowhere to Belong: The Fiction of Olivia Manning', *Linenhall Review*, vol. 3, no. 3 (Autumn, 1986), pp. 11–13.

Scanlan, Margaret, *Traces of Another Time: History and Politics in Postwar British Fiction* (Princeton, NJ: Princeton University Press, 1990).

Sebastian, Mihail, *Journal, 1935–1944*, trans. Patrick Camiller (London: Heinemann, 2001).

Segev, Tom, *One Palestine, Complete: Jews and Arabs under the British Mandate* (London: Abacus, 2002).

Seton-Watson, Robert, *A History of the Roumanians, from Roman Times to the Completion of Unity* (Cambridge: Cambridge University Press, 1934).

Shepherd, Naomi, *Ploughing Sand: British Rule in Palestine, 1917–1948* (London: John Murray, 1999)

Sherman, A.J., *Mandate Days: British Lives in Palestine, 1918–1948* (London: Thames & Hudson, 1983).

Sitwell, Sacheverell, *Roumanian Journey*, intro. by Patrick Leigh Fermor (Oxford: Oxford University Press, 1992).

Smith, Andrew, and Jeff Wallace (eds), *Gothic Modernisms* (Basingstoke: Palgrave Macmillan, 2001).

Smith, R.D., 'English Writers and the Moral Crisis', *British Council Winter Lecture Series* (1943–4).

—, 'Detours and Oases: A Note on Arthur Koestler', *Orion* (Autumn 1945), pp. 55–61.

—, 'Notes towards an Autobiography' (private collection, R.D. Smith estate).

Smith, Sidonie, *Twentieth-Century Women's Travel Writing* (Minneapolis: University of Minnesota Press, 2001).

—, and Julia Watson (eds), *Women, Autobiography, Theory: A Reader* (Madison: University of Wisconsin, 1998).

Smith, Stevie, *Novel on Yellow Paper* (London: Virago, 1980).

—, *Over the Frontier* (London: Virago, 1980).

—, *The Holiday* (London: Virago, 1993).

—, *Mother, What Is a Man?* (London: Cape, 1942).

Spalding, Frances, *Stevie Smith: A Critical Biography* (London: Faber, 1988).

Spurling, Hilary, *Ivy: The Life of Ivy Compton-Burnett* (London: R. Cohen, 1995).

Stallworthy, John, *Louis MacNeice* (London: Faber, 1996).

Stark, Freya, *Dust in the Lion's Paw: Autobiography, 1939–46* (London: Arrow, 1990).

Steinberg, Theodore L., *Twentieth-Century Epic Novels* (Newark: University of Delaware Press, 2005).

Stevens, Auriol, 'Olivia Manning and her Novel', *Guardian* (13 March 1969).

Stewart, Victoria, *Women's Autobiography: War and Trauma* (Basingstoke: Palgrave Macmillan, 2003).

—, *Narratives of Memory: British Writing of the 1940s* (Basingtoke: Palgrave Macmillan, 2006).

Stonebridge, Lyndsey, *The Writing of Anxiety: Imagining Wartime in Mid-Century British Culture* (Basingstoke: Palgrave Macmillan, 2007).

Suh, Judy, *Fascism and Anti-Fascism in Twentieth-Century British Fiction* (Basingstoke: Palgrave Macmillan, 2009).

Summers, Sue, 'Portrait of the Artist as a Truly Awful Wife', *Daily Mail* (9 November 1987).

Tidrick, Kathryn, *Heart Beguiling Araby: English Romance and Arabia* (Cambridge: Cambridge University Press, 1981).

Todorova, Maria, *Imagining the Balkans* (Oxford: Oxford University Press, 1997).

Tomkinson, Fiona, 'Olivia Manning: A Female Voice as Critique of Utopian Socialism', *Gender Studies: Revista de Studii de Gen a Centrului de Studii Feministe al Universitati de Vest, Timişoara*, vol. 1, no. 4 (2005), pp. 138–46.

Treglown, Jeremy, *Romancing: The Life and Work of Henry Green* (London: Faber, 2000).

—, 'Olivia Manning and her Masculine Outfit', in Marina Mackay and Lyndsey Stonebridge (eds), *British Fiction after Modernism: The British Novel at Mid-Century* (Basingstoke: Palgrave Macmillan, 2007).

Wahba, Magdi, 'Cairo Memories', *Encounter*, vol. 62, no. 5 (May 1984).

Waldeck, R.G., *Athene Palace: Bucharest – Hitler's New Order Comes to Romania* (London: Constable, 1943).

Waller, John, and Erik de Mauny (eds), *Middle East Anthology* (London: Drummond, 1946).

Wasserstein, Bernard, *Britain and the Jews of Europe, 1939–1945* (Oxford: Oxford University Press, 1988; 2nd ed. London: Leicester University Press in association with the Institute for Jewish Policy Research, 1999).

Waugh, Evelyn, *Put out More Flags* (London: Penguin, 2000).

—, *Scott-King's Modern Europe/Work Suspended* (Harmondsworth: Penguin, 1951).

—, *Scoop* (London: Penguin, 2003).

—, *The Sword of Honour Trilogy* (London: Penguin, 1999).

Willets, Paul, *Fear and Loathing in Fitzrovia: The Bizarre Life of Writer, Author and Soho Dandy Julian Maclaren-Ross* (Stockport: Dewi Lewis, 2003).

Wolff, Larry, *Inventing Eastern Europe: The Map of Civilization on the Mind of the Enlightenment* (Stanford: Stanford University Press, 1994).

Index